Innovative Cities

Innovative Cities

Edited by James Simmie

London and New York

First published 2001
by Spon Press
11 New Fetter Lane, London EC4P 4EE

Simultaneously published in the USA and Canada
by Spon Press
29 West 35th Street, New York, NY 10001

Spon Press is an imprint of the Taylor & Francis Group

Typeset in 10 on 12½pt Sabon by Wearset, Boldon, Tyne and Wear
Printed and bound in Great Britain by Biddles Ltd, Guildford and King's Lynn

British Library Cataloguing in Publication Data
A catalogue record for this book is available from the British Library

Library of Congress Cataloging in Publication Data
Innovative cities/edited by James Simmie.
    p. cm.
    Includes bibliographical references and index.
    1. Cities and towns – Europe – Case studies. 2. Urban economics – Case studies.
3. Amsterdam (Netherlands) 4. London (England) 5. Milan (Italy) 6. Paris (France)
7. Stuttgart (Germany) I. Simmie, James.

    HT131.I42 2001
    307.76′094–dc21

                                                                    00-069609

    ISBN 0 415 23184 1 (hbk)
    ISBN 0 415 23404 2 (pbk)

To Linda, Imogen and Hamish

Contents

Contents

Notes on contributors

Roberta Capello is Associate Professor of Economics and Regional Economics at the University of Molise, and at the Politecnico of Milan. She has a PhD in Economics. She was National Secretary of the Italian Section of the Regional Science Association International (1995–98) and now Member of the Board and Treasurer of the European Regional Science Association (ERSA). She is the author of many publications concerning innovation and local development.

Jeanine Cohen is a geographer working in the Institute of Geography, University of Paris I, the Sorbonne. She is a researcher at the Centre National de la Recherche Scientifique (CNRS) laboratory for Social Dynamics and Space Resetting (LADYSS). Her main research interests are the socio-spatial division of labour, local development and innovation. She has completed several cooperative Franco-British research projects in these areas. These have been most notably published as Jeanine Cohen, Douglas Hart and James Simmie (eds) (1977), *Recherche et développement regional, Travaux franco-britanniques*, University of Paris I, Publications de la Sorbonne.

Elisabeth Decoster is a researcher at the Centre TMU (Théorie des mutations urbaines) which is a department of the CNRS laboratory 'Cities'. She works mainly on innovation dynamics, and on the relations between science and industry and local governance.

Jan G. Lambooy is Professor (since 1969) of Regional and Urban Economics, University of Amsterdam and University of Utrecht. He has published on urban and regional economic development, dual labour markets, real estate, innovation, evolutionary and institutional economics and is a member of various national committees on economic and regional issues.

Walter J. J. Manshanden graduated from the University of Amsterdam in 1988. His major was economic geography. From 1989 to 1995 he worked as a researcher for the Economic-Geographic Institute of the University of Amsterdam, focusing on the role of business services in regional-economic growth. In 1995 he was appointed researcher at the Foundation for Economic Research of the University of Amsterdam. The title of his doctoral dissertation (1996) was 'Business Services and Regional-Economic Development: the Economies of Proximity'. At present, as a quantitative regional-economic researcher he works on the annual Amsterdam Economic Prospects, impact analyses of the sea harbour in the Amsterdam Region, the prospects of the building industry in the Netherlands and the economic structure and history of neighbourhoods in Amsterdam.

James Sennett is a full-time research associate at Oxford Brookes University working in the field of innovation and regional economic development. He has a background in economics and planning and completed his PhD on the subject of innovation and the spatial dimension of sources of information in the small firm community. He was research assistant on the ESRC study of innovation in the five European cities at University College London before moving to Oxford Brookes in the summer of 1999.

James Simmie since 1999 has been Professor of Innovation and Urban Competitiveness at Oxford Brookes University. He is the Director of the ESRC project on which this book is based. Recent research includes studies of innovation in the London region, particularly Hertfordshire, and analyses of the ecology of specialised economic clusters in and around the City of London. He previously worked at University College London and Reading University. He is the author of several books and papers on the subject of innovation and its relationship to the geography and competitiveness of cities.

Simone Strambach since 1993 has been working as a researcher and teacher at the University of Stuttgart in Economic and Social Geography. She studied geography, sociology and business economics at the University of Mannheim. After graduation in geography (diploma) she was member of a Graduate College for Social Science at the University of Cologne installed by Max-Planck Institute for Society Research, Research Institute for Sociology and Institute for Applied Social Research. In this framework she prepared her doctoral thesis. Her research field is in the professional knowledge economy, especially focusing on the role of knowledge-intensive business services in technological and socio-economic change in Germany and EU countries. She has published a book on knowledge-intensive business services and interorganisational networks and several articles in this field. Her major research areas are national and regional innovation systems, and regional policy development.

Muriel Tabariés is a researcher at the Centre MATISSE (Modélisation appliquée, Transformations Institutionnelles, Stratégies Socio-Economiques – Centre de recherche sur l'Industrie, la Finance, l'Espace et les Services) connected with the CNRS and the Paris I-Panthéon-Sorbonne University. She works mainly on the problems of innovation diffusion and the relations between science and industry, on innovative milieux and on social polarisation in the case of a metropolitan region.

Peter Wood is Head of the Department of Geography at University College London. His long-term interests are in manufacturing change and regional development, but his focus in recent years has been on the service sector, especially the growth of producer and business services. His research projects supported by the ESRC and the European Commission have included investigations into business service growth in England and Scotland; the regional conditions influencing their foreign market development; their role in providing clients with technical and managerial expertise and its regional implications; and the impacts of consultancy use on client innovation.

Acknowledgements

This book is the result of collaboration between five research teams based in the UK, Amsterdam, Milan, Paris and Stuttgart. A number of very congenial colleagues have worked on the project for around three years. In particular, I should like to thank Peter Wood, James Sennett and Doug Hart in the UK, Walter Manshanden in Amsterdam, Roberta Capello in Milan, Jeanine Cohen in Paris and last, but by no means least, Simone Strambach in Stuttgart. A number of other colleagues also worked on the research and are listed with thanks in the appropriate chapters.

Finance for the research was provided as part of the ESRC research programme on Cities: Competitiveness and Cohesion. Grant L 130251051 provided funding for three years. This European work was developed to provide some empirical background to a more detailed study of innovation in the London Metropolitan region. The results of this subsequent work are being published in due course.

Introduction

James Simmie

Background

The origins of this book lie in the Economic and Social Research Council (ESRC) research programme on 'Cities: Competitiveness and Cohesion'. For some years prior to this programme, most of the authors had been working together in various contexts. The focus of much of this work was on international comparisons of innovation and attempts to encourage high-technology industries to continue or develop in particular places. Considerable amounts of information had been built up, over the years, particularly with respect to those city regions in which the universities of the researchers were located. The new ESRC programme provided an opportunity to develop a more systematic analysis of this rich collection of local insights and to conduct some original empirical research, based on the ideas developed in this exercise.

The first objective of the research was to compare and contrast the contributions made by the urban assets of a sample of European cities that, in the past, had proved to be among the most innovative in Europe. The aim was therefore to focus on those elements external to firms that made significant contributions to specific innovations developed within them.

A second objective of this first stage of the work was to provide an international context within which to conduct more detailed empirical studies of innovation and competitiveness in the London Region. The aim was to show how innovation in this region could be understood in terms of the particular history of the area, its special place in the United Kingdom's urban hierarchy, and its international trading connections.

For the purposes of this research, innovation is defined as 'new commodities, new technologies, new sources of supply and new types of organisation' (Schumpeter, 1942). Since Schumpeter's day innovation has moved to the heart of economic policy-making. As a result, definitions of the concept have multiplied. Among those that capture the way in which it is understood today is that of the European Commission's Directorate XIII which is responsible for Science and Technology. It defines innovation as:

The commercially successful exploitation of new technologies, ideas or methods through the introduction of new products or processes, or through the improvement of existing ones. Innovation is a result of an interactive learning process that involves often several actors from inside and outside the companies.

(EC DG XIII and XVI, 1996, p. 54)

In order to operationalise the research objectives local research teams were brought together led by Walter Manshanden in Amsterdam, James Simmie in London, Roberta Capello in Milan, Jeanine Cohen in Paris, and Simone Strambach in Stuttgart. Each team was asked to combine two main requirements. The first was to express freely, on the basis of their accumulated local knowledge, the main reasons why the conditions in their respective cities provided environments that were conducive to innovation among their local firms. The second was to conduct some directly comparable research on this question so that empirical comparisons and contrasts could be made between them.

Structure

The results of these analyses have led to the structure of the book. It is divided into eight chapters. These include this introduction which outlines the arguments of the book, the methods used to conduct the comparative analyses, and the reasons that emerged from these analyses for the particular order in which we deal with the separate cities. Chapter 1 summarises and evaluates the main arguments that have been advanced to explain the links between geography and innovation. Chapters 2–6 present our research findings for the individual cities. A final chapter draws out the conclusions that we are able to reach.

In Chapter 1 we argue that early attempts to explain the links between innovation and cities were based on a combination of early Schumpeterian thought and the traditional agglomeration theory of Marshall (1919) and Scitovsky (1963) by Hoover (1948), Vernon (1966) and Perroux (1955) to form the basis of product life-cycle and growth pole theory. These theories formed the conventional wisdom of how to explain the relationships between innovation and space up to the 1970s.

Two alternative explanations to this original work emerged during the 1970s and 1980s. The first of these was inspired by the work of Piore and Sabel (1984). The two main critiques, inspired by their arguments, were the new industrial districts thesis of Becattini (1990), along with the concept of innovative milieu developed by the GREMI (Aydalot, 1986), and institutional analyses also drawing on the work of Coase (1937) and Williamson (1975). Both argued the need for smaller innovative firms to concentrate in local production systems in order to accommodate continuous change and minimise networking and transaction costs.

More recently, later Schumpeterian ideas have been combined with new trade theory in order to provide some explanation of why innovation is particularly concentrated in world cities and other large metropolitan international trading nodes. This work recognises that in order to be commercially successful, innovations need to be internationally competitive and to be traded successfully around the globe. Markets, competitiveness and trade are therefore important requirements for successful innovation.

Inspiration for this work has been provided by Porter (1990) who has argued for the benefits of local competition in stimulating more world-class company performance. Krugman (1991) has also developed the idea that comparative advantages have been lost by most first world economies to lower wage regions. This means that they are now more dependent on absolute advantages that are often based on their innovative capabilities.

It has also been argued that, contrary to some theories' belief in the formation of new industrial districts and regions, urban hierarchies, and those among them that are especially innovative, have been extremely persistent over many decades. The more innovative among them tend to be at or near the top of their national urban systems. Some other large metropolitan areas, high in their national urban systems, are also noted for their innovative capacities.

Various elements of these arguments are then used to analyse the contributions made to innovation by the environments and urban assets of Stuttgart in Chapter 2, Milan 3, Amsterdam 4, Paris 5, and London 6. The reasons for this order are, first, their relative positions in their respective national hierarchies. Stuttgart and Milan are medium-sized regional capitals while Amsterdam, Paris and London are medium to large national capital cities. These positions give rise to a spectrum of differences that include both the significance of size *per se* and the kinds of economic and political power that are associated with the numbers and rank of their firms and decision-making institutions. We shall be arguing later that size still matters in terms of the richness and variety of factors external to firms that they may draw on to facilitate innovation.

Second, the institutional arrangements external to firms that contribute to their innovations also constitute a spectrum of differences. These start with the organised German system in Stuttgart where the *Land* (regional) government established a long-term strategy to encourage innovation. This is backed up by formal institutional arrangements that typically bridge the divide between the academic knowledge base and its practical uses in local companies. That of Milan follows the organised Stuttgart system. External innovation supports in this city are characterised by a combination of informal innovative milieu networks, mostly among smaller firms, and city size advantages enjoyed by mostly larger companies.

The innovation environment in Amsterdam is characterised by two main features that distinguish it from Stuttgart and Milan. These are, first, that, being such a comparatively small country, individual cities in the Netherlands tend to form part of a national spatial division of innovation. While high-tech manufacturing innovation is spatially concentrated in the south-west around Eindhoven, Amsterdam performs an essentially capital city service function for the rest of the Dutch economy. The manufacturing innovation found there is often linked to the knowledge and information needs of a capital city. The second important distinguishing feature of innovation in the Amsterdam Region is its high level of external national and international linkages and collaborations. It is more of an international trading system than the first two cities.

Paris provides both a bigger and a more mixed innovation environment than Amsterdam. Long-term central and regional strategic planning has influenced both the location of government-funded research and development (R&D) and the crucial regional and international transport and communications infrastructure. Central decisions concerning the location of facilities such as civil nuclear research and universities has led to a large concentration of R&D activities in and around the city. The Plateau of Saclay to the immediate south of Paris has become a major location for such activities. The planned regional and international transport and communications system is, along with Amsterdam, one of the best in Europe. This facilitates international knowledge exchanges that are crucial to innovation.

Finally, we examine London. This is both the largest capital city region and the most market-driven. Over the years there has been little overt coordination between those responsible for science policy, infrastructure provision and land use planning. Despite this, the London Region is by far and away the most significant market-driven concentration of innovative activities in the United Kingdom. In this, like Amsterdam, it has been helped by its long-term history of international trade. Many of the linkages between innovative companies and their environments are with collaborators and customers abroad. These are a prime source of world best practice for the companies located in the London region.

These different characteristics of the five cities are explored in greater depth in the individual city chapters. One feature that will become apparent during these analyses is that no one single explanation fits the circumstances found in all the cities. This is one important reason why the theoretical debates and controversies surrounding the reasons why there is a geography of innovation that are based on particular case studies tend to come to markedly different conclusions.

Methods

The methods employed to analyse innovation in the five cities were, first, to ask the teams to produce distillations of their local knowledge on the

4

development and characteristics of their respective cities. This was combined with a focus on those aspects that appeared, to the local teams, to have been significant in the development, over the years, of environments that were conducive to innovation among firms located in their respective cities. The reason for adopting this approach was that we believe that the specific historical development of cities plays an important part in the development of their particular innovation environments and the persistence of their innovative success over long periods of time.

Second, samples of innovative firms were drawn from two sources in the five cities. The first source was the lists of firms that had won the common European award for Basic Research for Industrial Technologies for Europe (BRITE). This was a European award for innovation provided under the Brite-EuRam III programme. It provided support to industry for pre-competitive collaborative research in materials, design and manufacturing technologies. The aims of the programme were to stimulate technological innovation through the incorporation of new technologies and scientific and technological collaboration. A total of 113 completed projects in separate firms across the five cities were identified from these lists. The leaders of these projects within the firms were approached to be interviewed by telephone. Some seventy-nine responded positively to these requests. This provided an overall successful response rate of 70 per cent.

These numbers were augmented from local databases of firms in order to acquire interviews with larger numbers of smaller firms. There were few of these in the BRITE sample. In all the cities except Amsterdam it proved possible to find local sample frames of innovative firms. These varied between twenty-two in Milan to thirty-seven in Stuttgart. The response rate of successful interviews varies between 100 per cent in Milan to 48 per cent in London. Amsterdam provided a unique problem in that a large sample frame of all firms held by the local Chamber of Commerce had to be interrogated to find a small number of innovative firms. This meant that a total sample frame of 213 firms of all types yielded successful interviews with only twenty innovative firms. This represented a response rate of only 9 per cent of the total.

As a result of the specific difficulties with the Amsterdam sample frame, a total of 431 firms were approached across all five cities. Of these, 160 innovative firms were successfully interviewed. The total numbers interviewed in each city were Amsterdam 26, London 35, Milan 33, Paris 33 and Stuttgart 33. This represents an overall response rate of 37 per cent.

The individual numbers for each city are small. The analyses based on them should therefore be regarded as suggestive and illustrative. Nevertheless, they provide a consistent picture of the similarities and differences across the five cities. The total sample numbers also provide a reasonable baseline with which to compare the data for the individual cities.

Taken together, the results reported here for the five cities therefore represent a combination of local historical and contemporary knowledge and original empirical work. The survey results are also interpreted by the local research teams. In this way, some of the richness of the detailed experience possessed by these teams is conveyed in their individual chapters.

Conclusion

The final chapter draws together and interprets the arguments and results presented in the earlier chapters. We conclude first that the relative innovativeness of our case study cities strongly reflects the experiences of their national innovation systems combined with their position in their respective urban systems. The stronger the national innovation performance and the higher they are in their national urban hierarchies, the more their local environments facilitate innovation within the firms located there.

Second, long-term historical developments are important in explaining the contemporary positions of our case study cities. Their capacity to deal with changing circumstances and to re-invent themselves over centuries is one of the keys to their relative success in the twenty-first century. The growing rather than declining roles of large firms are important drivers of change. Corporate strategies have important urban and regional dimensions. These may now be changing to favour smaller rather than larger cities. It remains to be seen how this affects the innovation environment in the former.

Third, some cities possess knowledge assets that allow them to reach beyond the capacity of the national innovation and urban systems within which they are embedded. This arises from the development of their global role. Within our sample this condition most strikingly applies to Paris and London. One of the most important findings of this research is the significance of international linkages with customers as a key driving force behind innovation. Those cities that facilitate time proximity to the international markets for world-leading innovations are those that tend to be most competitive and successful.

Two major kinds of urban assets form the basis of this success. The most important is highly qualified and knowledgeable labour. These are the people who devise the innovations, have the knowledge to scan and transcode the world's best practice in their specialised fields. They tend to 'stick' to their original city regions and therefore make up one of their key urban assets. The second important urban asset is fixed infrastructure and telecommunications. These make a significant difference to the abilities of innovators to meet easily within their regions. More importantly, they also determine how easy it is to access international contacts, customers and those with leading edge knowledge and experience.

References

Aydalot, P. (ed.) (1986) *Milieux innovateurs en Europe*, Paris, GREMI.

Becattini, G. (1990) 'The Marshallian industrial district as a socio-economic notion', in F. Pyke, G. Becattini and W. Sengenberger (eds), *Industrial Districts and Inter-firm Co-operation in Italy*, Geneva, International Institute for Labour Statistics, pp. 37–56.

Coase, R.H. (1937) 'The nature of the firm', *Economica* NS 4, 386–405.

European Commission (1996) Dgs XIII and XVI *RITTS and RIS Guidebook: Regional Actions for Innovation*, Brussels, European Commission.

Hoover, E.M. (1948) *The Location of Economic Activity*, New York, McGraw-Hill.

Krugman, P. (1991) *Geography and Trade*, Cambridge, MA, MIT Press.

Marshall, A. (1919) *Industry and Trade*, London, Macmillan.

Perroux, F. (1955) 'Note sur la notion de "pôle de croissance"', *Economie Appliquée*, Jan.–June, 307–20.

Piore, M.J. and Sabel, C.F. (1984) *The Second Industrial Divide: Possibilities for Prosperity*, New York, Basic Books.

Porter, M.E. (1990) *The Competitive Advantage of Nations*, The Free Press.

Schumpeter, J.A. (1942) *Capitalism, Socialism and Democracy*, New York, McGraw-Hill.

Scitovsky, T. (1963) 'Two concepts of external economies', reprinted in A.N. Agarwala and S.P. Singh (eds), *The Economics of Underdevelopment*, Oxford, Oxford University Press, pp. 295–308.

Vernon, R. (1966) 'International investment and international trade in the product cycle', *Quarterly Journal of Economics*, vol. 80, pp. 190–207.

Williamson, O.E. (1975) *Markets and Hierarchies*, New York, Free Press.

CHAPTER 1

Innovation and Agglomeration Theory

1 Innovation and Agglomeration Theory

James Simmie

Introduction

This chapter examines the answers to two main questions. These are 'Why and when does innovation take place?' and 'Why is it concentrated in some places rather than others?' Answers to the first of these will be sought in Schumpeterian evolutionary economic theory. The rudiments of this rich vein will be outlined to provide an explanatory background that will be used to evaluate alternative answers to the second question. Explanations of the geography of innovation, which forms one of the central concerns of this book, will be summarised and evaluated. Elements of these different explanations will then be combined to form theoretical analyses of why innovation is especially concentrated in the five European cities studied here.

The chapter is divided into three main sections. The first section outlines the original Schumpeterian arguments explaining innovation. This focuses on the Schumpeter I model. This argues that exogenous inventions are sought out by entrepreneurs, brought into their small companies and turned into commercial innovations. Swarms of these emerge around the depression and recovery periods of long waves of economic change. This process is pushed along by new technological inventions.

This formed the basis of early attempts to explain the spatial concentration of innovations. It was combined with the traditional agglomeration theory of Marshall (1919) and Scitovsky (1963) by Hoover (1948), Vernon (1966) and Perroux (1950) to form the basis of product life-cycle and growth pole theory. These theories formed the conventional wisdom of how to explain the relationships between innovation and space up to the 1970s.

The second section evaluates the two main alternatives to these original arguments that emerged during the 1970s and 1980s. The first of these was inspired by the work of Piore and Sabel (1984). They argued that

11

there was a sea change taking place in firm structures and relationships. The key features of this were the breakdown of vertically integrated corporations and the adoption of flexible specialisation among the resulting networks of smaller firms. The two main critiques, inspired by these arguments, of the traditional innovation agglomeration theories were the new industrial districts thesis of Becattini (1990), along with the concept of innovative milieu developed by the GREMI, and institutional analyses also drawing on the work of Coase (1937) and Williamson (1975). Both argued the need for smaller innovative firms to concentrate in local production systems in order to accommodate continuous change and minimise networking and transaction costs.

The first of these critiques relies on the assumptions that firms are in general deverticalising and that the resulting congeries of smaller firms must group together in order to work as close-knit production networks. In reality many successful firms are increasing their degrees of vertical integration through growth, mergers and acquisitions. They are also not so much concerned with local production systems as international markets. So far, only a few unique examples of new industrial districts have been identified empirically.

The closely related concept of an innovative milieu, while offering descriptions of several local productions areas well known for their exceptional rates of innovation, does not provide much by way of explanation of why they exist. It is essentially a descriptive concept. It also lapses into tautology when describing causal sequences in the emergence of milieux.

The second major alternative to traditional evolutionary economics explanations why innovations tend to be concentrated in particular spaces is institutional analysis. This is inspired by the work of Coase (1937) and Williamson (1975). They argue that there is a third alternative to neo-classical economics assumptions about the structure and relationships between firms. While the neo-classical position is that firms are either organised into large-scale hierarchies or separate entities related by market transactions, institutionalists argue that they may also be organised into networks.

The Californian School has used this assumption to argue that networked production systems group together in order to minimise transaction costs (Scott, 1990) or to maximise the benefits of untraded interdependencies (Storper, 1994a). In both cases there is a focus on local production systems to the relative exclusion of the significance of international markets. Some of the empirical examples used are also confined to older, design and craft-based industries, such as the Parisian high fashion industry and smaller firms, such as the Emilia-Romagna ceramic tile industry. These are not representative of the dominant high-technology corporations who are the major players of the new knowledge-based international economy.

The third section goes on to evaluate modern evolutionary theory and to combine it with new trade theory in order to provide some explanation of why innovation is particularly concentrated in world cities and other large metropolitan international trading nodes. This starts with the Schumpeter II model. This recognises the growing significance of large corporations and the systematic R&D carried out within them.

Following Schumpeter, Nelson and Winter (1982) and Dosi *et al.* (1988) have developed the modern version of evolutionary economic theory. Collectively, they emphasise the significance for innovation of uncertainty, selection and path dependency confronting firms both in terms of the difficulties facing them and the circumstances in which they must operate for most of the time.

Within this theoretical framework a number of analysts have pointed to individual phenomena that cause particular areas to become centres of innovative production. These include the power of firms to acquire both public and private funding for their R&D which then may lead to innovations (Markusen, 1985b). The local cultures within which this power is exercised and the entrepreneurial attitudes of the actors located in particular places are also said to play a role in the relative innovativeness of those areas (Saxenian, 1994).

Innovation is also argued to be a crucial element in the developing knowledge economy. National systems of innovation have been identified (Lundvall, 1992). These are reflected in how good local innovation systems are at acquiring and using new economic knowledge. Their relative capabilities in doing this are an important selection mechanism sorting the more from the less innovative cities.

Knowledge workers are crucial to the availability and use of new economic knowledge. Such workers are in high demand in advanced economies. Without them innovation cannot take place. It is therefore argued that the factors leading to the spatial concentration of such workers are also important in determining where innovation may take place.

There is a tendency in both traditional evolutionary theory and the more recent alternatives to focus on local production systems. However, in order to be commercially successful, innovations need to be internationally competitive and to be traded successfully around the globe. Markets, competitiveness and trade are therefore important requirements for successful innovation.

This was recognised by Vernon (1979) and Utterback (1988) in their updating of Vernon's (1966) original formulation of the product life-cycle theory. Subsequently, Porter (1990) has argued for the benefits of local competition in stimulating more world-class company performance. Krugman (1991) has also developed the idea that comparative advantages have been lost by most first world economies to lower wage regions. This means that they are now more dependent on absolute advantages that are often based on their innovative capabilities.

The ability to generate absolute trading advantages in high-tech and innovative activities is confined to a relatively small number of regions. These are often those that are the focus of international knowledge flows. They tend to be the international knowledge hubs of the global economy.

Contrary to some of the alternative theories' belief in the formation of new industrial districts and regions, urban hierarchies, and those among them that are especially innovative, have been extremely persistent over many decades. The more innovative among them tend to be at or near the top of their national urban systems.

Taken together, all these factors lead to systematic cumulative causation. Most of them favour world cities at the peak of their national urban hierarchies. Some other large metropolitan areas, high in their national urban systems, are also noted for their innovative capacities. All of them may be characterised as international knowledge trading hubs. They are among the first places to receive new knowledge from abroad, to recombine it into innovations, and to export them to international clients and customers.

Before proceeding to expand these analyses it is essential to define the main object of analysis in this book, i.e. innovation. Schumpeter provides one of the best, and most enduring early definitions. He defined innovation as a process of 'creative destruction'. He regarded it as the driving force of economic development. He defined innovation as including 'new commodities, new technologies, new sources of supply and new types of organisation'. This kind of 'quality competition', he argued, 'strikes not at the margins of the profits and the outputs of the existing firms, but at their foundations and their very lives' (Schumpeter, 1942).

Since then, innovation has moved to the heart of economic policymaking. As a result, definitions of the concept have multiplied. Among those that capture the way in which it is understood today is that of the European Commission's Directorate XIII which is responsible for Science and Technology. It defines innovation as:

the commercially successful exploitation of new technologies, ideas or methods through the introduction of new products or processes, or through the improvement of existing ones. Innovation is a result of an interactive learning process that involves often several actors from inside and outside the companies.

(EC DG XIII and XVI, 1996, p. 54)

Innovation is now monitored on a Europe-wide basis by the Community Innovation Survey and in the UK by such organisations as 3M and NatWest who have been producing an annual 'Innovation Trends Survey' for the last ten years. They say that:

Innovation occurs when a new or changed product is introduced to the market, or when a new or changed process is used in commercial production. The innovation process is the combination of activities (such as design, research, market investigation, process development, organisational restructuring, employee development and so on) which are necessary to develop and support an innovative product or production process.

(1999 3M–NatWest Innovation Trends Survey, 10th anniversary, p. 6)

Early theorists used to view innovation as a more or less linear process but this is no longer the case. There is now general agreement with the view that 'innovation is a complex interactive process involving multiple links between new science and technology, potential producers and consumers' (Rothwell, 1991). These multiple, interactive links also change over time according to industrial sector, the types of innovation involved and the timing of economic developments.

With these definitions in mind we shall now move on to outline the foundations of evolutionary theory and its application to understanding the geography of innovation.

The Beginnings of Evolutionary Economics

Schumpeter I

For many years Joseph Schumpeter was described as a 'footnote' in economic theory. It was generally believed that following Keynesian demand management policy governments could avoid any repetition of the deep depressions of the late 1920s and early 1930s. This belief was dented in the 1970s and was subjected to severe theoretical and practical shocks at the end of that decade and the early 1980s. The depression of the early 1980s, in particular, sparked a major revival of interest in neo-Schumpeterianism or evolutionary theory. The reasons for this are partly because of its focus on economic cycles and partly because it also opens up the 'black box' of the role of science and technology in economic growth and change.

Given the acknowledged importance of innovation as a main basis for competitiveness and economic growth, the first main questions examined in this chapter are, why does it take place and what are its causes? To trace the intellectual history of the main answers to these questions it is essential to summarise the main starting points for the debates and controversies in the work of Schumpeter himself. This is not a simple task because his analyses are both complex and change over time. Some economists such as Philips (1971) have distinguished 'two Schumpeters' and their accompanying theoretical differences. The first is the young pre-First World War economist who stressed the role of the entrepreneur and the small innovative enterprise. The second is the older Schumpeter emphasising the role of the big, monopolistic firm and the bureaucratised process of technical change.

Exogenous Invention

The differences in these two approaches are sufficiently significant to constitute two models of original Schumpeterian thought. In the first model Schumpeter examines how micro-economic factors can account for the causes of long waves in the economy (Davelaar, 1989; Marshall, 1987). The main focus of this model is inventions which are largely exogenous to existing firms and the creative entrepreneurs who take the risks involved in turning the inventions into commercial innovations (Freeman, 1982).

This view gives rise to the question of where firms that do not conduct much of their own research and development (R&D) acquire their new economic knowledge. One answer is that they spill over from third party firms or research institutions such as universities (Baptista, 1997). If this is the case, then this would provide a reason for small firms to locate in proximity to such sources of new knowledge.

Entrepreneurs

Entrepreneurs are said to play a crucial role in this explanation of innovation. They are the ones who recognise the importance of inventions when they see them. They are also the actors that bring together other resources necessary for the production and commercialisation of these new ideas.

Small Firms

In the Schumpeter I model entrepreneurs and small firms are the main engines of innovations and economic growth. This emphasis on small firms still persists today. This is despite the fact that in his second and later model, Schumpeter stressed the predominant role of large oligopolistic, bureaucratically organised firms in generating innovation. This was also associated with systematic R&D.

Swarming

In his early model Schumpeter's explanation of why the depression phases of long economic waves moved into recovery was that competition between innovative entrepreneurs was responsible for the clustering or 'swarming' of basic innovations at the beginning of the recovery period. He argued that this creates a 'band wagon' effect leading to an upswing as it becomes clear that the basic innovations can generate large profits. As these initial new industries mature, profits are driven down by competition. As a result, this leads to attempts to save costs and switches to process innovations which generate increases in the capital intensity of industries and stagnation in employment growth.

According to this view, temporal bursts of innovation are likely to occur before and during the recovery phases of major economic cycles. These will be led by entrepreneurs in mainly small firms importing externally produced inventions and combining them to produce commercially successful innovations. This process should therefore be marked by, among other phenomena, relatively high small firm birth rates. Such temporal swarming could also lead to spatial clustering.

Mensch, one of the most renowned neo-Schumpeterians, writing in the 1970s, set out to demonstrate empirically that this was indeed the case. His initial argument was that 'as the recessionary wave deepens, more radical basic innovations increase in frequency via an accelerator mechanism which reduces the time lag between scientific inventions and their application in technical innovations' (Marshall, 1987).

Freeman, Soete and Clark (1982) take issue with the argument that swarms of innovations cluster around the nadir of long waves. In their study they do not find a strong relation between innovation clusters and economic crises. Furthermore, they stress the diffusion of innovations and their ability to form a technology system. They argue that the diffusion process is important because a series of further innovations are generated as swarms of imitators move in to invest in a new technology, attracted by the exceptionally high profits. They regard the mutual relations between innovations, firms and the political and socio-institutional forces as conditions for an optimal diffusion process and thus for economic growth (Davelaar, 1989).

Technology Push

The view that entrepreneurs take up externally devised inventions and convert them into commercial innovations gave rise to one of the theoretical controversies started by Schumpeter. This was whether innovation was pushed by the supply of technology or pulled by consumer demand. Schumpeter himself was a clear proponent of the technology push thesis. However, during the 1960s and 1970s demand-led theories of innovation were fashionable and made a considerable impact on policy-makers. An empirical survey of over 500 innovations undertaken by Myers and Marquis (1969) appeared to justify the demand-pull approach. Schmookler (1966) examined patent statistics and investments and came to the conclusion that changes in demand appeared to precede patent cycles.

These demand-pull theories were strongly criticised in the 1970s. Mowery and Rosenberg (1979), for example, in their review of 'Market Demand and Innovation' argued that the empirical studies of innovation which were often cited in support of demand pull did not justify these conclusions and that the authors themselves repudiated this interpretation (Langrish et al., 1972; Freeman, 1974). These either/or judgements are harsh in view of the general agreement that innovation is an interactive and not a linear process. It is therefore argued here that innovation is partially caused by both technology push and demand pull. In the empirical chapters that follow, innovation is shown to be much more like an international systems and networking activity as defined by Rothwell (1994).

Schumpeter's Legacy

In contrast to neo-classical economics, the legacy of Schumpeter's key theoretical insights provides different concerns and starting points for economic analyses. In the first place it stresses the argument that capitalism is a fluctuating evolutionary process driven by technical and organisational innovation. Second, it emphasises the uncertainty and instability confronting firms in contrast with the perfect knowledge assumed in neo-classical theory. Third, it recognises that social institutions play a role in innovation and came to stress the particularly important role of large, oligopolistic firms.

Schumpeter's main legacy is that he has inspired serious consideration of four main ideas in economic theory. These are, first, that innovation is the main source of dynamism in capitalist economic development. Second, the importance of the historical perspective in understanding long-term economic change. Third, that it is essential to distinguish conceptually between invention, innovation and diffusion of innovations. Fourth, the importance of the links between organisational, managerial, social and technical innovations (Schumpeter, 1939, 1942).

Agglomeration Theory and Innovation
Marshall

As the preceding brief description of the beginnings of evolutionary economic theory shows, Schumpeter was not concerned with the spatial distribution of innovations. Similarly, traditional agglomeration theory was not concerned with innovation. It was based on neo-classical economics and conceptualised local economies as atomistic collections of competitors linked mainly through market relationships. It argued that the main reason why production is concentrated in a limited number of locations was because of internal economies of scale accruing to individual firms.

Alfred Marshall (1890) added to this view the argument that firms might also expand in a particular place because of the possibilities of using external economies. These could include pools of common factors of production such as land, labour, capital, energy, sewage systems and transportation. The larger the pools of these common factors are and the greater degrees of specialisation they permit, the greater will be the tendency to drive down factor prices or raise productivity. These possibilities provided the reasons why firms would choose to locate in some places rather than others.

Later on, Scitovsky (1963) added the idea that there might also be 'pecuniary external economies'. These were said to arise from the beneficial impacts of one firm's new investments on the possibilities for greater profitability among other local firms. These views remained the traditional neo-classical position on the reasons for agglomeration for some considerable time. Like neo-classical economics they treated innovation, science and technology as a taken-for-granted black box as far as both the internal and external economies of firms were concerned.

Perroux, Hoover and Vernon

During the 1950s this situation changed. Drawing on the work of Schumpeter I, dynamic theories of regional growth were developed in France by Perroux (1955) and in New York by Hoover and Vernon (1959) and Vernon (1966).

Perroux (1955) argued that dynamically growing and innovative firms and industries will grow at faster rates than those that are less so. These dynamic sectors will affect other industries through their backwards and forwards linkages. These will in turn affect relative prices and investors' expectations. These linkage and price effects will diffuse and multiply through complexes of linked industries and the places where they are located. In these ways innovative activity leads to agglomeration economies. With these arguments Perroux (1955) was the first to link Schumpeterian explanations of innovation to agglomeration.

Around this time Hoover and Vernon were working on the New York Metropolitan Region Study. As a result of this work they combined elements of the Schumpeter I model with information theory to produce a 'product life-cycle theory'. Vernon (1966) argued that, during the first innovative stage in a product's life-cycle, the inventors and firms of the Schumpeter I model are most likely to be found in large metropolitan agglomerations. The main reasons for this are that, unlike the traditional 'distance–transaction costs paradigm' based on the analysis of firms shipping well-defined standard goods between regular points in space, the introduction of new innovative products is highly dependent on communication and external economies.

During this first stage of the introduction of a new product, the design, the market and the inputs are still unstandardised. Initial production is therefore marked by:

- The need for flexibility with respect to the necessary inputs. This follows from the need to change inputs frequently during the initial innovative period.

19

- Lower sensitivity to input prices because of the low price elasticity of demand for new innovative products. Consequently, 'small cost differences count less in the calculations of the entrepreneur than they are likely to count later on' (Vernon, 1966).

- The entrepreneur's main concern is with the introduction of the new product to the market. This means that 'the need for swift and effective communication on the part of the producer with customers, suppliers, and even competitors is especially high at this stage' (ibid.).

The advantages accruing to high-technology regions in this model are that new ones are constantly replacing old products. This is argued to be a key feature of the self-sustaining strength of high-technology areas (Oakey, 1985). Innovative high-technology agglomerations are presumed not to suffer from standardisation or decline as the rapidly changing cycles of high-technology industries do not allow products to be standardised.

Subsequent studies of the agglomeration tendencies of the innovative phase of the product life-cycle model have mainly analysed 'location-specific factor cost efficiencies'. They have done this by defining unique locational factors, such as universities, airports, labour, venture capital and quality of life features, within specific areas, that are presumed to be required for innovative high technology development (Premus, 1982; Tichy, 1985; Markusen *et al.*, 1986; Malecki, 1987; Popp, 1987; Davelaar, 1989). The combination of all these factors is found most often in central metropolitan regions.

These studies also echo some of the earlier work on agglomeration theory by Hoover (1937, 1948). In this work he grouped the sources of agglomeration advantages into three categories. These were internal returns to scale, localisation economies, and urbanisation economies. To these we shall also add later globalisation economies to take account of the rapid development of the international economy since Hoover's time.

Following traditional neo-classical economic theory, Hoover's model of agglomeration presumes no form of co-operation between actors beyond what is in their individual interests in an atomised and competitive environment' (Gordon and McCann, 1998). The key variable is the size of the agglomeration. Greater size increases the chances of profitable local interactions through chance, the law of large numbers and natural selection of the businesses that can benefit from the multiple opportunities on offer. Given the critical factors of change and uncertainty that accompany innovation, one reason why the activity is so concentrated in large metropolitan core regions is the multiple opportunities for new combinations of inputs that exist in them. Urbanisation economies in particular appear to be important reasons for the disproportionate amounts of innovation found in some of the largest city regions.

This combination of the Schumpeter I model with growth pole, product life-cycle and agglomeration theory provided the dominant explanation of the decline of old industrial areas and the rise of new ones up until the late 1970s (Norton and Rees, 1979). By that time reactions were being developed which abandoned some of these key concepts somewhat prematurely. What was often ignored in these later theories was the continuing concentration of innovation in a few core metropolitan regions. These remain characterised by disproportionate shares of new and dynamic sectors, high rates of innovation and external economies resulting from their sheer size and consequential opportunities for new combinations of inputs. We shall return to the continuing salience of these issues later in the chapter.

New Industrial Geographies

Second Industrial Divide: Piore and Sabel

Economic shocks such as the oil price rise in the early 1970s and turbulence such as the first global depression of the early 1980s led to renewed interest in economic change. There was also a widespread feeling that a watershed had been reached in the capitalist economies. This was variously conceptualised as the coming of the 'fifth Kondratieff wave' (Hall, 1981; Perez, 1985; Freeman, 1986), the transition to a 'postFordist' era (Leborgne and Lipietz, 1988), and 'flexible accumulation' (Scott and Storper, 1986; Harvey, 1987). The most influential of these in terms of new agglomeration theory was, however, the notion of a 'second industrial divide' expounded by Piore and Sabel (1984) at MIT. Their work inspired the spatial analyses of both 'new industrial districts' and the 'institutional' analysis of networked economies.

Piore and Sabel took issue with a key element of Vernon's (1966) product life-cycle model. They argued that the inevitable transition to 'maturity' of standardised products was being undermined by the growing heterogeneity and uncertainty of market demand. Shortening product life-cycles, petroleum price shocks and volatile exchange rates were cited as contributing to this heterogeneity and uncertainty. They argued that, under pressure from consumers demanding more specialised and differentiated goods, which mass production systems typically cannot supply, the response of some firms is the development of flexible specialisation.

Flexible specialisation is a strategy of permanent innovation. Firms accommodate ceaseless change rather than try to control it. The strategy is based on vertical disintegration and flexible, multi-use equipment, skilled workers and the creation, through politics, of an industrial community that restricts the forms of competition to those favouring innovation. It is also argued that the spread of flexible specialisation amounts to a revival of craft forms of production that were marginalised during the first industrial divide which is usually referred to as the Industrial Revolution.

The flexible specialisation thesis argues that space matters. Apart from citing locally delimited examples of flexible specialisation in action, it also offers a theoretical explanation as to why firms might decide to cluster together in particular places. This is that the vertical disintegration of industry promotes spatial agglomeration as specialised producers achieve returns to scale through an external division of labour, locating in close proximity to reduce the cost of their unstandardised and unstable exchanges (Scott, 1988b).

Piore and Sabel argue that the spread of flexible specialisation represents such a major and pervasive change that it constitutes a shift of technological paradigm. They cite examples of the re-invigoration of craft-based industries in Italy, Germany and Japan in support of the pervasiveness of what they argue to be a new paradigm. Areas based on small, craft firms in places like Central and North-western Italy, Mondragon in the Basque Region of Spain (Stohr, 1986) and the high fashion areas of Paris (Storper, 1993) have been studied intensively to illustrate the main characteristics of flexible specialisation.

Few other examples have been identified empirically. It is also the case that the vertical disintegration of large and successful firms is far from being the current norm in such firms' behaviour. In the UK, for example, funds that track the top 100 companies and the all share index are having great difficulty keeping within their maximum permitted holdings in any individual company. This is because of the continued vertical integration of companies by continuing acquisitions and mergers. Flexible specialisation and the examples provided should therefore be regarded as special cases rather than a general and definitive shift of technological paradigm.

Before this conclusion could be reached on the basis of repeated empirical evidence, the thesis inspired two major schools of thought on why innovation is spatially concentrated. These are the new industrial district/innovative milieu and institutional analyses of networked economies.

New Industrial Districts: Becattini

The first of these theses linking economic change to explanations of why innovation has a spatial configuration was also partly inspired by the work of Alfred Marshall. He coined the phrase 'industrial district' in 1890. He subsequently developed the idea that:

The leadership in a special industry, which a district derives from an industrial atmosphere, such as that of Sheffield or Solingen, has shown more vitality than might have seemed probable in view of the incessant changes of technique. It is to be remembered that a man can generally pass easily from one machine to another, but that the manual handling of a material often requires a fine skill that is not easily acquired in the middle age: for that is characteristic of a special industrial atmosphere. Yet history shows that a strong centre of specialised industry often attracts much new shrewd energy to supplement that of native origin, and is thus able to expand and maintain its lead.

(Marshall, 1919, p. 287)

The idea was taken up and re-invigorated by Becattini (1989). Studies, originally inspired by the idea of flexible specialisation in fast-growing industries such as textiles, footwear, and ceramic tiles in the Third Italy, claimed to have rediscovered industrial districts in the areas specialising in these industries. It has also been argued that some high-tech industrial complexes in California operate as industrial districts (Saxenian, 1991; Scott, 1993).

One common thread exemplifying the practical activities of these different systems is the promotion and development of intensive networks. In most of the original examples these link local congeries of small firms, each highly specialised in a particular process or phase of production (Bianchi, 1986; Bellini, 1987). In later examples they are said to connect large firms and suppliers in regions and enable the introduction of flexible specialisation by facilitating subcontracting. In this way the networks reduce the manufacturing depth of larger companies. Such networks are said to foster smooth diffusion of innovation throughout the whole regional economy (Grabher, 1991).

The explanation offered in this work of why innovation is spatially concentrated is that companies adapt to change and the new pressures of demand by deverticalising into smaller but locally networked firms concentrated in specialised industrial districts. They need the advantages of local proximity in order to minimise the costs of their constant innovation and change. These advantages are similar to those identified as localisation economies within industries by Hoover (1937, 1948).

Genuine examples of these phenomena in new industrial districts are the exception rather than the rule. They do not extend much beyond those listed above as exemplifying flexible specialisation. Many of them are composed of firms in older craft, creative or design industries that never have been large. They have not therefore usually been subject to vertical disintegration. The main reason for them grouping together in districts usually seems to be their use of local networked forms of production. The generality of such local systems of production is in question and will be examined in more detail below.

Innovative Milieu: GREMI

A further development of the industrial district idea was proposed by the Groupement Européen des Milieux Innovateurs (GREMI). The exposition of the idea of innovative milieux can be found mainly in the writings of

Aydalot (1986), Aydalot and Keeble (1988), Camagni (1991), Maillat and Perrin (1992), and Maillat *et al.* (1990, 1993). Like Vernon (1966) the theory is especially concerned with the incubation phase of new innovations.

It is argued that one of the main problems of producing innovations, namely the uncertainties confronting firms, is reduced by the characteristics found in innovative milieux. Briefly, these include a set of collective and dynamic processes incorporating many actors within a given region that lead to networks of synergy-producing inter-relationships. Among the most significant of these are processes of co-operative learning that help to reduce the degree of uncertainty during changes in technological paradigms. This co-operative learning is brought about primarily through the mobility of employees, inter-relationships between regional suppliers and purchasers, and face-to-face contacts which are all facilitated by spatial proximity.

Lawson identifies four main uncertainty-reducing processes said to exist in innovative milieux. These are:

1 Collective information gathering and selection which takes place through informal discussions between firms;

2 Collective learning processes which, as has already been pointed out, take place mainly through the regional labour market and 'cafeteria' effects which contribute to the transcoding of new information;

3 Collective processes selecting decision routines which result from managerial mobility and co-operative decision-making through local associations;

4 Informal processes of decision co-ordination through interpersonal linkages, families, clubs and associations.

(1997, p. 15)

These collective uncertainty-reducing activities are said to benefit mainly small firms during the incubation period of their innovations. This view clearly develops some of the initial ideas of Schumpeter I and Vernon (1966). It also reiterates the importance attached to networks in the industrial district thesis. In this case, however, local networking is itself a learning mechanism. Within the milieu it aids innovation by building trust relationships between local collaborators. In addition, it is said to develop the skills needed to network not only within the milieu but also with the outside world as well. This is a critical addition to inward-looking and production-focused networks of industrial districts.

At first sight the innovative milieu thesis is highly persuasive. It is easy to accept the idea that co-operative economic activities dedicated to innovation are likely to assist small firms during the incubation periods of their innovations. As a result, it seems plausible that higher rates of innovation could be achieved in the spatial areas where such externality effects exist.

The main problem with the innovative milieu thesis is that it does not offer an explanation of why and how these highly desirable externalities arise in the first instance. Its attempts to rectify this lacuna often slip into tautological explanations in the form of innovative milieux assisting innovative firms and the presence of innovative firms creating innovative milieux.

Other problems with the concept include evidence such as that collected by Davelaar (1991) showing, in Holland at least, that there is no empirical evidence of any influence being exerted by regional product milieu on the innovative intensity of firms. Todtling (1990) also raises the issue of the lack of empirical evidence in support of the hypothesised benefits of milieux on innovation.

Thus there remain significant problems both in seeking to explain the existence of innovative milieux in the first instance and in showing that they actually foster or accelerate innovation where they already exist. For the present, the innovative milieu thesis does not explain why and how innovation is especially concentrated in some cities and not others.

Embeddedness

The concept of embeddedness is a key feature that distinguishes the analyses of both new industrial districts and innovative milieux from neo-classical agglomeration theory. The concept arose as a reaction to Polanyi's (1944) contention that economic action and behaviour had become separated or 'disembedded' from social relations with the development of industrial capitalism. This was disputed by Granovetter (1985). He and others argue that far from being a separate detached activity with its own independent forms of behaviour, economic activity is also a social phenomenon.

Among the social characteristics of economic activity are habits, conventions and norms of behaviour. These may be developed by the social interactions of actors 'embedded' within a regional context. The significance of the spatial context arises from the argument that one of the most important social relations is that of trust. This is built up through repeated personal contacts. These are likely to be facilitated by geographic proximity and hence the easier possibilities for multiple face-to-face contacts. Such regionally confined social interactions are part of the processes that build locally differentiated cultures. As a result, different regions come to be characterised by different collective ways of doing things and different socio-economic capacities (Jacobs, 1968).

One of the possibilities that arises from this argument is that, as a result of the different characteristics of embedded actors in different regions, innovation and technology systems may also be regionally specific (Storper, 1997). They may be characterised by localised technology learning (Feldman and Florida, 1994) which benefits from knowledge spill-overs which are facilitated by proximity and are also, therefore, region specific.

Socio-economic interactions like these are inherently difficult to research empirically. As a result, there is not much evidence one way or the other on the practical significance of embedding for linking different innovative performance to different regions. Intuitively it would seem plausible to hypothesise that distinctive regional cultural attributes could result from the long-term embeddedness and participation of local actors. However, the regions whose cultural distinctiveness is easiest to identify are often those more peripheral areas that are not usually also distinguished by their innovative performance. Conversely, those core metropolitan regions that are the locations for relatively high rates of innovation are some of the most open and culturally diverse. They are also particularly marked by their fast changing international interactions rather than their permanently embedded local ways of doing things.

Institutional Analyses: Coase and Williamson

Institutional analysis is a second line of criticism of neo-classical agglomeration economics. It draws inspiration from both the alternative institutional economic analysis and the flexible specialisation thesis. It emphasises the possible significance of networked economies and argues that re-agglomeration is a function of the need to minimise the transaction costs arising in such economies.

The institutional alternative to neo-classical economics is inspired by the work of Coase (1937, 1988) and Williamson (1975, 1985). Briefly, they argued that there is a third alternative to the neo-classical argument that economic relations are controlled either within the hierarchies of companies or by market relations between them. Williamson, in particular, argued that these economic relationships were being replaced by collaborative, networked forms of production. This result is very much like that predicted by Piore and Sabel (1984) as the product of the vertical disintegration of large companies.

Both schools of thought have therefore made a great deal of the spread and characteristics of networked production systems. The Californian School, led by Allen Scott (1988a, 1993), also argued that the development of such economic relationships was also leading to the re-agglomeration of production in order to minimise the transaction costs within these networked production systems.

Networks

Turning first to the notion of networks, this is not a new idea. It was developed by Perroux (1955) in his analysis of growth poles. He examined the use of supply links as part of the multiplier effects of dynamic sectors. Scott and Storper (1987) also argue that increases in demand generate possibilities for increased economies of scale that can be realised either by internal vertical integration or by external linkages with other firms through flexible, networked production complexes. Thus there are questions that need to be raised both about the 'newness' of networked systems of production and their relative importance as compared with continuing market and hierarchical systems.

Despite these caveats, there is a strong line of reasoning which currently suggests that restructuring in manufacturing industries in the advanced economies is generally moving in the direction of networked forms of production. This line of reasoning is so pervasive as to be labelled the new 'network paradigm' (Storper and Harrison, 1991; Amin and Thrift, 1992; Cooke and Morgan, 1993).

The hypothesised reasons for the increasing development of networks are as a response to the increasing uncertainty and instability of production and markets. These problems are met by increasing specialisation by increasing the division of labour. Elements of this can be achieved by disintegrating and externalising production into networked systems. But as Lovering (1990) points out, increasing uncertainty could lead to either rising or declining internal economies of scale. Some major innovative companies, such as Glaxo-Welcome, are meeting uncertainty by increasing their degree of vertical integration and maintaining their internal economies of scale that way.

There is also some debate about whether networks, where they do exist, primarily integrate innovative actors into global (Curran and Blackbourn, 1994) or local (Dicken *et al.*, 1994; Saxenian, 1994) networks. This gives rise to a major unresolved dispute about the geography of networks and whether they may be primarily inter- rather than intra-regional in nature. Studies in highly innovative core metropolitan regions such as London (Hart and Simmie, 1997; Simmie and Hart, 1999) and Paris (Decoster and Tabariés, 1986; Perrin, 1988) certainly indicate that local production networks do not play an important part in the production of innovations in those regions. Where this is the case, the arguments about how such networks lead to the re-agglomeration of production are seriously undermined.

As with the new industrial district thesis it would appear that the local network paradigm should be regarded as a relatively exceptional, minority case rather than a generally emerging or new form of production relationships. The minority of empirically verified cases where local networks have been shown to have made significant contributions to innovation and therefore related innovation to space are atypical. They only include a sub-sample of those areas that have been identified as new industrial districts. With the possible exception of California, they do not include the major metropolitan centres of innovation.

Transaction Costs

Finally, in this brief evaluation of the new industrial geographies, mention should be made of transaction cost analysis. Following the flexible special-isation thesis and the new network paradigm, Allen Scott (1985, 1986, 1988a, 1988b, 1989) proposed that transaction costs were the key causal mechanism in the re-agglomeration of industrial production. He argued that the economic process of vertical disintegration into extended and spe-cialised divisions of labour was leading to spatial pulls which encouraged smaller firms to concentrate in space. The explanation for this was that as firms proliferated and developed networked production systems the numbers of their critical linkages also multiplied. This was especially the case among smaller, innovative firms producing new, non-standard pro-ducts often on a small scale. The multiplying linkages in such a system imposed transaction costs on firms. Gathering in close proximity to each other was one way of minimising these transaction costs. It also produces the result of re-agglomeration.

This analysis was first applied to the women's clothing industry in Los Angeles. It was later extended to other forms of craft production, high technology, producer and financial services. Despite these empirical examples there is still considerable doubt about the general validity of the transaction cost thesis as an explanation of the agglomeration economics of innovative firms.

In the first place, as has been noted above, the vertical disintegration of innovative firms is by no means a general phenomenon. Without this pre-condition the theory can only apply mostly to new or pre-existing small firms. While they are important, they are by no means the main drivers of innovation. Second, firms of all types tend to guard crucial assets such as innovations and are not therefore likely to share them widely in local col-laborative networks. More general kinds of local linkages such as with banks and transport providers can be readily replaced in different loca-tions. In such circumstances transaction costs are not likely to be signific-ant enough to determine the locational behaviour of individual firms. Finally, during the development and early commercialisation of new inno-vations, cost considerations are not usually the most important entrepre-neurial considerations. Innovators expect to reap the monopoly profits of being first in the market. They are therefore not likely to make locational decisions primarily on the basis of the transaction costs of production.

Conclusion

The new industrial geographies have provided some interesting hypotheses to explain the reasons why new agglomeration economies may still affect the locational choices exercised by innovative firms. In general they appear to offer some insights into exceptional cases rather than generally applicable explanations.

The flexible specialisation thesis that has inspired elements of most of them is premised on the idea that there has been a general move towards vertical disintegration among large firms. In fact, among many successful innovative firms in both manufacturing and services the opposite is the case. Mergers and acquisitions are continuing to integrate firms into ever larger and fewer multinational corporations.

New industrial district theory relies partly on the notion of vertical disintegration for its explanation of why firms benefit from agglomeration economies by grouping together in local industrial networks. The cases that are cited in support of this thesis are atypical in two senses. First, the small firms found in them have not often been produced by processes of vertical disintegration. Second, they are often made up of older craft, design, or creative industries seeking to extend the life-cycles of relatively old product types. In general, there are strong similarities between this concept and the localisation economies of traditional agglomeration theory.

The innovative milieu concept focuses usefully on the incubation phase of innovations. It does not explain, however, which comes first, innovations or innovative milieux. Once in existence it does seem that the dynamic interactions between actors in an innovative milieu can encourage the continuation of further innovations. Nevertheless, how this virtuous circle is created remains much of a mystery. This makes it very difficult to understand the causal mechanisms that could turn a non-innovative area into an innovative milieu. In some respects the concept thus remains a dynamic counterpart to the descriptive notion of urbanisation economies.

Much is made in this literature of the argument that innovation is both an economic and a social process. In principle, this is surely correct. One of the concepts that has been used to grapple with this idea is that of embeddedness. While it is undoubtedly true that regional specific cultural and learning attributes may be identified, it is also often the case that those regions where these are easiest to see are among the least innovative. Conversely, the most innovative core regions are often marked by multiple and changing cultures. Embeddedness may therefore be more of a hindrance than a help to innovation.

A second important line of argument characterising the new industrial geography is institutional analysis. Two of the key explanatory concepts employed here are networks and transaction costs. It is argued that

29

networked forms of production are superseding those of hierarchies and markets. Within this paradigm local proximity of innovative firms is required to facilitate multiple and complex interactions. The empirical evidence supporting these contentions is mainly drawn from more rather than less peripheral regions. Among the most innovative core regions there is little evidence of local networking in the production of innovations. Instead, in these locations there is much more evidence of international networking between producers and their customers.

Transaction costs have also been used to explain the re-agglomeration of innovative firms in certain regions. Their weakness is first that they rely on the notions of vertical disintegration and consequential networking which have already been argued to be atypical. Second, innovative firms do not seem to be especially sensitive to production cost issues during the early stages of innovation. Local transaction costs are therefore unlikely to provide powerful reasons for the agglomeration of innovations.

Taken together, therefore, much of the new industrial geography seems to provide partial explanations supported by cases of limited generality. The main conclusion to be drawn from this is that there are, in fact, a number of different explanations that apply in different specific circumstances in different types of regions. In what follows we shall attempt to add further to this variety of explanations by focusing specifically on why innovation is so disproportionately concentrated in a limited number of core metropolitan regions. To do this we shall turn to modern evolutionary theory combined with new competition and trade theory.

Modern Evolutionary Theory

Schumpeter II: Oligopolies, Systematic R&D

The Schumpeter I model is still alive and well in the general concentration, in much of the contemporary literature, on innovation in small and medium-sized firms (SMEs). But as far back as the late 1940s the Schumpeter II model recognised the significance of endogenous research and development in large firms. The twentieth-century rise of industrial and public research and development (R&D) laboratories has bureaucratised innovation if not invention. These large R&D facilities can lead to more continuity of innovation behaviour based on the vehicle of larger firms (Todtling, 1991).

In the Schumpeter II model there is a strong positive feedback loop for successful innovation to increased R&D activities setting up a virtuous self-reinforcing circle leading to renewed impulses to increased market concentration (Freeman *et al.*, 1982). These possibilities are particularly interesting from two points of view that will be explored below. The first is that these impulses would seem to lead to greater vertical integration rather than disintegration among innovating firms. The second is the contribution that these impulses make to the establishment and persistence of R&D activities in particular cities.

Among those arguments concerned to explain innovation as a more continuous process of incremental change, the Schumpeter II model argues that large oligopolistic firms invest in R&D. This continuing investment in new ideas and their development produces a stream of innovations. The commercial success of these innovations stimulates the firms to continue investing in R&D. In this way a 'virtuous circle' of investment, innovation and increasing profits is established.

Modern Evolutionary Theory: Nelson and Winter, Dosi *et al.*

Schumpeter's ideas were taken up and developed in particular by Nelson and Winter (1982), and Dosi *et al.* (1988). Their work represents the basis of modern evolutionary theory. Their basic arguments may be summed up as follows:

1 Technical change is a fundamental force in shaping the patterns of transformation of the economy.

2 There are some mechanisms of dynamic adjustment, which are radically different in nature from those allocative mechanisms postulated by traditional theory.

3 These mechanisms have to do both with technical change and institutional change or the lack of it. As regards the former, we suggest it is both disequilibrating and a source of order for the directions of change and the dynamic adjustment processes as new technologies diffuse through the national and international economies . . .

4 The socio-institutional framework always influences and may sometimes facilitate and retard processes of technical and structural change, co-ordination and dynamic adjustment. Such acceleration and retardation effects relate not simply to market imperfections, but to the nature of the markets themselves, and to the behaviour of agents.

(Dosi *et al.*, 1988, p. 2)

As a result of these influential arguments, over the last two decades, innovation, understood as product, process and organisational innovation in the firm, as well as social and institutional innovation at the level of the industry, region and nation, has come to be considered as fundamental to competitive economic growth.

James Simmie

Large Oligopolies

As evolutionary theory has developed, so have arguments about the significance of the large corporations of the Schumpeter II model. Prominent among such writers are Froebel, Heinrichs and Kreye (1980), Henderson and Castells (1987) and Amin and Robins (1988). They argue that a global economy has developed which is dominated by large multinational corporations (MNCs). The decisions of these MNCs, on where they conduct such activities as R&D and production, determine to a large extent what economic activities agglomerate in particular places.

Contrary to Piore and Sabel (1984), there can be little doubt that capital is concentrating and centralising at the level of the international economy. The corporate vehicles for this concentration are the MNCs with control centralised in their respective headquarters that are often located in core metropolitan cities such as London, Amsterdam and Paris – three of the five European cities studied in this research.

There is plenty of data that confirms the significance of MNCs as major shapers of the world economy. Even by 1980, for example, only 350 of the largest of them controlled economic resources which were equivalent to more than a quarter of the combined Gross Domestic Products (GDPs) of all the developed and less developed countries put together. Somewhere between 25 per cent and 40 per cent of all world trade consists of purely internal transfers between the subsidiaries of MNCs (Sutcliffe, 1984). High technology firms are also some of the major players in the global economy. Characteristically they have low levels of forward linkages. This tends to confirm the findings of several researchers that high technology firms operate in global markets (Lyons, 1994).

The argument developed following these kinds of data is that localities, regions and even national territories are being reshaped according to the global economy and its main players, the MNCs. Following this formulation there is a spatial division of labour and a spatial division of innovation. The large enterprise is able to split its activities into units and to localise and disperse these units in the most favourable places in terms of work and industrial culture (Massey, 1984). Regions at the nodes of the global network are the focus of the international exchange of the latest ideas and also have a large autonomy to exploit them before they diffuse to other regions. The further they lie from this central node, the more regions are locked into the international division of labour and resemble the old Fordist branch centres (Amin and Robins, 1990).

It is argued, for example, that MNCs with their global networks have far more impact on the world economy than locally embedded firms. Therefore, to an MNC, flexibility is a matter of industrial organisation on a global rather than a local scale. As far as they are concerned, the issue is not how to increase local area autonomy but how to create more efficient

32

corporate integration. This makes industrial geography a series of maps of places with different roles in the international division of labour. As a result, local places experience different degrees of economic well-being and local production synergies (Amin and Robins, 1990; Amin, 1991; Praat, 1991).

Explanations of the relationships between innovation and core metropolitan regions must therefore incorporate both the activities of large and small companies. These must be linked to the key characteristics of innovation as identified by modern evolutionary theory.

Uncertainty, Selection and Path Dependency

The key concepts of contemporary evolutionary theory include variety, uncertainty, routines, path dependency, bounded rationality and selection (Lambooy and Boschma, 1998). These may take different forms in different environments and therefore lead to unpredictable results. Innovation is therefore characterised by elements of chaos as well as structured systems. To some extent this follows from two of the most important behavioural assumptions of evolutionary theory which are uncertainty and bounded rationality.

A part of the processes used by firms constrained by bounded rationality to overcome the uncertainties involved in innovation is locational decisions. For large firms this usually means establishing a spatial division of innovation combined with global scanning for new inventions. Both of these practices favour locating innovative R&D in core regions near decision-making and financing headquarters. Global scanning and the interchange of the latest international ideas also favour locating around international trading nodes with maximum connections to similar regions and firms around the world.

For SMEs co-operation, trust and collective learning are more important than they are for MNCs. This is because of the formers' own internal innovative limitations. They are also processes that may be used to overcome uncertainty. They are all processes that are built up by frequent personal interchanges. They are therefore facilitated by time proximity. This can lead to pulls towards geographic proximity. It can equally lead to pulls towards international hub airports which afford minimum time proximity to international linkages.

Two further concepts in evolutionary theory that bear upon the degrees of uncertainty confronting innovative firms are selection and path dependency. As far as selection is concerned, the local environment may act as a kind of selection mechanism. It may provide conditions that meet the new and changed requirements of innovation (Lambooy and Boschma, 1998). This was the case, for example, in the change from hot lead to electronic printing technologies in London. On the other hand, it may impede the

33

change to new industries as old ones decline. This was the case in many areas that used to be dependent on older heavy industries.

Evolutionary economics argues that the development, or indeed non-development, of technologies is path dependent. This is because they are the product of numerous interdependent choices. Over time these build up into technological trajectories. Depending on how significant these trajectories are, they may also lead to the establishment of whole new techno-economic paradigms. The rapid development of information and communication technologies in recent decades is one such example. Such technological trajectories are said to be path dependent primarily because, once under way, they are usually irreversible. It is currently inconceivable, for example, that we should give up such well-established technologies as motor cars or personal computers.

Path dependency is problematic both for continuing innovation and the regions in which they may take place. It can all too easily lead to lock-in (Henderson, 1986) of old ideas to exclusion of new ones. Paul Krugman (1994) has described this condition as the 'economics of QWERTY', referring to the inefficient but entrenched arrangement of the keys on keyboards. He goes on to argue that once a pattern of specialisation is established it tends to become 'locked in' because of the cumulative gains made by international trade. As a result, path dependency is also reflected in the patterns of specialisation and trade between countries.

The path dependency of major new innovations is therefore one reason why each new techno-economic paradigm is usually associated with a new region. Thus power looms were first associated with Lancashire, Bessemer converters with the Ruhr, automobiles with Detroit, and computers with Silicon Valley (Hall and Preston, 1988, p. 21). These regions did not have to break out of historical dependence on previous technological trajectories.

Evolutionary economists have argued that there are circumstances in which path-dependent innovative activities would be concentrated in some spaces. These are particularly where technological trajectories are especially open and based heavily on as-yet uncodifiable knowledge. Such circumstances generate the need for clear communication and understanding (Lundvall, 1990, 1992). This is facilitated by frequent face-to-face interchanges. These in turn are made easier by both time and geographic proximity. One result of these requirements is the agglomeration of innovative firms in particular regions.

Storper (1995) uses this reasoning as the basis for his analysis of the untraded interdependencies that bind innovative companies together in certain agglomerations. These untraded interdependencies include labour markets, conventions, common languages, and informal rules for developing, communicating and interpreting knowledge. In virtuous combinations these interdependencies and their associated spill-over effects permit the actors in some regions to travel along superior technological trajectories or do so more rapidly than those in other cities. As a result, they gain absolute advantages, as compared with comparative advantage, which shelters them from Ricardian competition.

This explanation suffers from much the same theoretical problem as that of innovative milieu. Once firms are established on superior technological trajectories, or are proceeding along them faster than those in other regions, it is clear why their cities would be more innovative than others. What is not clear, however, is how these virtuous circumstances are established in the first instance. If, as Lambooy and Boschma (1998) claim, innovative behaviour and adaptation to change are largely constrained by the boundaries of spatial matrices laid down in the past, how do some firms and regions break out of these constraints to become the minority of highly innovative city regions? In some ways the concept of path dependency provides a more plausible explanation of the lack of change and innovation than it does of the branching and break-out that are associated with new innovations.

Power and Oligopoly

One explanation that has emerged to explain how some cities both start and maintain their innovative economies is the notion of the oligopolistic power exercised by their firms. This idea was first mooted by Chinitz (1961). He studied the contrasts between New York and Pittsburgh. Both were large cities but the economic performance of New York was considerably better than that of Pittsburgh. Chinitz (1961) therefore argued that size alone was no guarantee of economic success. He suspected that differences between the dominant firms in the different cities were a key reason behind their differing economic performance. These dominant firms stimulated economic expansion not only in their own sectors but among leading firms in other associated sectors as well. The nature and type of the dominant firms in different cities are therefore argued to be key determinants of the ways in which those cities develop.

This explanation re-emerged in the 1980s. This time Galbraith's (1967) model of the large modern corporation capable of its own strategic planning was invoked by Storper (1985) and Markusen (1985a). They argued that large and powerful oligopolies have the power to short-circuit the maturation phase of innovation by relocating production to more profitable sites. Meanwhile they start producing their latest innovation in the usually metropolitan area where they conduct their R&D and launched their last innovation. That way, some areas remain the locations of continual waves of new innovations while others tend to receive their older counterparts some way through their product life-cycles.

As a result of these circumstances it may be argued, in line with

Schumpeter II, that innovation does not depend primarily on the continued re-seeding of new small firm start-ups because large firms can internalise the product life-cycle within themselves (Ferguson, 1988; Gilder, 1989; Florida and Kenney, 1990a; Saxenian, 1990). This also means that a principal source of the agglomeration of innovations is large oligopolies and the power that they wield.

A related argument is that of regional politics. Studies of the reasons behind the genesis of Silicon Valley (Markusen, 1985b; Markusen *et al.*, 1986; Markusen *et al.*, 1991) have shown the power of regional coalitions to secure high technology funding and resources. A major source of such funds has been the military industrial complex. Powerful oligopolies have been adept at extracting R&D funding from central governments for the development of military innovations of all types. This is clearly one mechanism that explains the initiation of certain kinds of innovations in some regions rather than others.

Knowledge

One of the major problems raised by Schumpeter was how firms innovate in conditions of uncertainty and imperfect knowledge and information. Information and knowledge are now recognised as key inputs to innovation. In so far as their generation and transference are related to space, they may also provide some explanation of the disproportionate concentrations of innovations in some regions rather than others.

First, it is essential to distinguish between information and knowledge. Information can be easily codified and has singular meanings and interpretations. Knowledge, particularly new knowledge, on the other hand, is often vague, difficult to codify and sometimes only recognised serendipitously. While codified information may be transmitted electronically around the world at little or no cost, the best way to exchange uncodified knowledge still appears to be by face-to-face contact. Von Hippel (1994), for example, has shown that what he calls 'sticky information' (what we would call knowledge) is best transmitted by face-to-face interaction involving frequent and repeated contacts. Knowledge rather than information is therefore seen as the more likely of the two to contribute to relationships between innovation and space.

The issue is addressed first by examining the ways in which firms learn about new knowledge (Lundvall, 1988, 1992). He addresses this phenomenon from the point of view of national systems of innovation. These are much more than a network of institutions supporting R&D. They involve inter-firm network relationships and especially user–producer linkages of all kinds (Andersen, 1992). Braczyk *et al.* (1998) have also argued that these processes also operate through specific regional innovation systems. These are composed of firms and research institutions that are geographically distinctive, interlinked organisations that support and conduct innovations.

In these local innovation systems it is argued that geographic proximity is important in facilitating the personal exchange of new knowledge between knowledge workers. Thus, for example, Saxenian (1990) studied local networks in Silicon Valley. She reached the conclusion that they were important in the exchange and sharing of knowledge between individuals and regional institutions such as universities, trade associations, business organisations, business consultancies, and venture capital firms. Local mechanisms such as meetings at trade shows, conferences, seminars and social activities contributed to the exchange of knowledge in the region.

It has also been argued that the propensity for innovative activity to cluster spatially will be strongest during the early stages of innovation when uncodified knowledge and experience are at their most important (see Audretsch (1998)).

There is also the argument that innovative firms will have difficulty in monopolising the new knowledge that they create. This will lead to knowledge spill-overs so that technological excellence comes in intellectual packages (Lundvall, 1990; Beije, 1992; Lundvall and Johnson, 1992). Glaeser *et al.* (1992) also argue that these are likely to take place in localities and hence provide advantages to innovative firms clustered in those places. Local knowledge spill-overs may be somewhat limited to one-way transfers. The reason for this, as Teece (1998) points out, is that most firms will not wish to share crucial assets with third parties because this could also lead to the sharing of profits. As a result, only firms with inadequate internal knowledge bases are likely to collaborate voluntarily in local knowledge pools.

A further important source of new knowledge that is largely ignored in these theories is the latest best practice or R&D from other advanced economies. In most cases international best practice or the latest technologies are not confined to a single region. International interchange between the most innovative regions is therefore an important source of new knowledge for them. In this instance, time rather than geographic proximity is the limiting factor for the essential face-to-face contacts. Time proximity is facilitated by geographic proximity to international hub airports.

Much new international information and knowledge is exchanged within the multinational manufacturing or service and consultancy companies. These will tend to have their knowledge-rich head offices and research sections located within the core metropolitan regions of their respective national urban hierarchies. International knowledge is also exchanged between firms of different sizes. The time proximity of these core regions facilitates long-distance knowledge spill-overs between them. These may then filter down their urban hierarchies taking more time to arrive there or decaying with distance from the core regions.

These international knowledge exchanges are one important mechanism which explains how some firms and regions are able to become innovative for the first time, to avoid becoming locked into path-dependent techno-logical trajectories and to maintain their innovative pre-eminence. Inter-national knowledge communicated by face-to-face flight dependent transport systems is a key input generating local innovation and avoiding lock-in.

Concentrations of Knowledge Workers

The most important local factor of production for knowledge-based inno-vative industries is highly educated and trained labour. The location of workers who can contribute to the production and commercialisation of new knowledge is critical to the agglomeration of innovative activities. Generally speaking, concentrations of such workers are limited to a few areas in the world (Audretsch, 1998). These are mostly core metropolitan regions and this is a further reason why they become and remain the main urban centres of innovation.

The limited number of labour markets that provide suitable pools of knowledge workers has a further effect on the location of innovations. Because such workers tend to 'stick' in their regional labour markets, this raises the propensity for innovative activities to cluster in the same region throughout all the phases of their life-cycles (Audretsch and Feldman, 1996). Thus both the current pace of innovation and the limited pools of knowledge workers tend to favour the regions where the innovations first start over most others through the duration of the product life-cycle.

The need for knowledge workers in the advanced economies is so great that it has shifted the demand for different kinds of labour. Bermen et al. (1997) have shown that in those advanced economies that belong to the Organisation for Economic Co-operation and Development (OECD), the demand for less skilled workers has fallen while the demand for more skilled knowledge workers has exploded. The strong demand for innova-tors gives such workers higher degrees of choice over where they want to live. Generally, the regions that possess agglomeration economies, high quality facilities and attractive environments are in a better position to attract and retain innovators and brainworkers (Lambooy and Boschma, 1998).

The advantages of core regions in attracting brainworkers are especially high in the European context where international labour mobility is still restricted by language barriers. The resulting choices open to brainworkers are therefore still pretty much restricted to those provided by their own national urban hierarchies. The most innovative cities therefore tend to be those at or around the top of those hierarchies. They enjoy the advantages of being able to attract and retain large pools of highly qualified labour.

Internal recruitment for these pools is also an important mechanism for transferring the exclusive knowledge present in those cities around to other firms and organisations located in them.

International Knowledge Flows: Vernon, Pred, Amin and Thrift

Vernon (1979) updated his previous product life-cycle model of the relationships between innovation and space to take account of the rapid internationalisation and globalisation of the world economy since the 1960s when he first introduced the concept. Reflecting the differences between Schumpeter I and II, he maintained that traces of his original product life-cycle model are still to be found among smaller firms initially tied to home sources of knowledge and markets.

Larger companies, however, now have both the resources and the incentives to scan the world for new ideas and knowledge. Vernon (1979) calls these 'global scanners'. Such companies may produce innovations anywhere in the world that they regard as suitable. However, where there are homogeneous demands for products such as petroleum and pharmaceuticals combined with large investments and high stakes, Vernon argues that the central core of innovative activities will be kept close to the companies' headquarters. As a result, something of the relationship between innovative product life-cycles and space still apply. Where this is the case, large world-ranked cities remain the most likely concentrations of innovation.

The agglomeration of innovation in world cities is also partly a function of their roles as the centres of international communication and interaction networks (Pred, 1966). He argued that regions at the centre of such networks have the highest probability of obtaining access to relevant information and adapting to change. This is because such networks transmit ideas, conceptual stimuli, information and bits of knowledge that are less available under conditions of relative geographic isolation.

Urban centres have a double advantage as the locations of innovation. Not only are they the crossroads for international knowledge exchanges but also they provide critical mass during the early stages of the innovation process (Amin and Thrift, 1992). Thus, within such centres social networks provide rapid reactions to new ideas and sometimes initial markets for them. The development of innovations can be more easily tracked in centres. Their agglomeration economies are particularly helpful in supporting the knowledge, communication and innovation systems necessary for maintaining absolute competitive advantages in global production centres (ibid.).

Amin and Thrift give the example of the City of London as an innovative centre in the global financial sector. The crucial knowledge and information concentration in the City is maintained in a number of different ways. First, it provides a base for much of the world's financial press. This operates from in or near the City. It provides much research and analysis for the sector (Kynaston, 1985; Driver and Gillespie, 1991). As a result, the City represents an important knowledge centre for world financial services.

Second, the City has an enormous throughflow of workers from other countries. It provides a focus for face-to-face meetings. Many of these take place in the global and regional headquarters located there. They represent the manifestation of the many global corporate networks focused on the City.

Finally, another characteristic of London that facilitates international knowledge flows is the number of foreign languages spoken there. One recent report, for example, shows that there are some 307 different languages spoken in London (Baker, 2000). As a result, when the European Bank for Reconstruction and Development set up in the City it needed 38 different language speakers. They could all be found within London (ibid.).

Maintenance of Urban Hierarchies as Nodes

The combined result of all the above factors is the persistent competitive and innovative success of cities at or near the peak of their national urban hierarchies. This phenomenon is the result of multiple and cumulative causation (Myrdal, 1957). But a corollary of the relative success of some cities is also the establishment of centre–periphery relations particularly within the more developed economies (Dicken and Lloyd, 1990; Krugman, 1995).

In their evaluation of neo-Marshallian nodes Amin and Thrift (1992) point out that most of the examples given in support of the concept do not include the major metropolitan areas such as London, Milan, Frankfurt and Paris. Nevertheless, these are all major centres of growth based on their attraction of finance, management, innovation, business services and infrastructure. Amin and Thrift conclude that these metropolitan areas will continue to be successful and that there is not likely to be much proliferation of new localised production complexes in more peripheral locations.

These hierarchical patterns have proved to be remarkably persistent over many decades. Thus, just as few urban areas are able to improve their positions in urban hierarchies, research has also shown that very few places have been able to develop new core high-technology agglomerations (Florida and Kenney, 1990b). Places like Silicon Valley are therefore unique exceptions to the general rule that central metropolitan regions are also the centres of most types of innovative activities. In general terms they are expected to be both the first producers and adopters of new products and services.

Freeman *et al.* (1982) describe the typical sectoral adoption pattern of specific high quality and broadly applicable new technologies in manufacturing. In general terms, the timing and rate of adoption of such technologies proceed from sectors linked to new trajectories to sectors linked to former trajectories. Because of their role in the development of new trajectories this pattern of adoption generally favours metropolitan areas.

This is confirmed in the influential work of Malecki and Varaiya (1986). According to them: 'Large urban areas are expected, ceteris paribus, to have higher rates of innovation, more rapid adoption of innovations, and higher proportions of skilled workers than smaller places, but technological change itself is not endogenous.' Further empirical confirmation of this general finding is provided by Martin *et al.* (1979), Thwaites (1982), and Camagni (1984).

There is, however, an important modification to this general principle that must be borne in mind when seeking to understand the role of metropolitan areas with respect to innovation. Research during the 1980s revealed that within metropolitan regions, innovation was less concentrated in their urban cores. Increasingly, the most favoured high-tech locations are suburban in character and outside the oldest parts of metropolitan areas (Scott, 1982; Aydalot, 1984; Storper, 1986). A spatial distinction therefore needs to made between metropolitan urban cores and their suburban rings. It is the characteristics of the latter that now seem to be most conducive to innovation.

Conclusion

Innovation is now seen as the major driving force behind competitive economic growth. It is an interactive and iterative rather than a linear process. It is more concentrated in some cities rather than others. As the driving force behind economic growth it also drives agglomeration economies. Once in existence, however, there are interactions between innovation and agglomeration economies. There are therefore some respects in which agglomeration economies also facilitate continual and future innovations.

There are a number of points at which one could break into this interactive process. In this study we have chosen to start with the requirements of the innovation process. From there we go on to examine how they could lead to agglomeration tendencies. After that we examine how, once in existence, both innovation and cities interact in both multiple and cumulative ways to facilitate innovation and maintain the primacy of the most innovative cities.

We have argued that innovation is conducted in different ways by the smaller firms of the Schumpeter I model and the larger firms of Schumpeter II. In the first model, entrepreneurs in small firms select external inventions, develop and commercialise them within the firms and produce innovations. This involves both temporal and spatial clustering. Swarms of innovations may arise around the beginning of recovery periods of new long-term economic cycles as entrepreneurs are attracted by new high profits. They may also cluster spatially near to third-party knowledge producers who are the sources of the inventions that they take up.

The original version of this model was very much a production-based view of innovation. It was argued that the main driving force behind innovation was technology push. This view tended to ignore the second half of the economic equation, namely the need for markets to realise profits and therefore the importance of demand pull. Our view is that to understand innovation we need to understand both the production of new technologies and the relationships between innovative firms and their clients and customers. While many of the new industrial geographies concentrate on production and production spaces, we argue that at least as much of the explanation of innovation and its spatial concentration is to be found in the relationships between firms and their customers. In this instance time proximity to demand is at least as significant as spatial proximity to production.

To some extent this view mirrors the differences between Porter (1990) and Krugman (1991). While Porter focuses on the attributes that lead to the establishment of competitive industrial production clusters, Krugman emphasises the importance of trade in producing external economies and agglomeration. Thus innovation may be seen as being driven by factors that are both endogenous and exogenous to the cities in which they are produced. In many respects external trading networks can be shown to be more significant than local production networks as far as innovation is concerned. In the first instance, innovative activity leads to agglomeration economies. This is because dynamic sectors grow themselves and affect other industries. Silicon Valley is the modern example of this process. In the space of a single generation a primarily agricultural economy has been transformed into the world's leading production cluster of new information technology. Alongside that economic development a collection of small towns has been transformed into a massive agglomeration that, at one time during the 1970s, was the fastest growing urban area in the United States.

Once in existence, agglomerations also interact with innovation in a supporting role. This role includes the accommodation of large pools of common factors that permit ever increasing degrees of specialisation. This may help by driving down factor prices or by raising productivity. The greater the size of agglomerations, the greater are the possibilities for profitable external economies. These include more opportunities to pick and mix new combinations of productive factors than are found in small urban areas. These conditions appear to be particularly helpful to the incubation period of new innovations.

The Schumpeter II model and modern evolutionary economics add a number of important dimensions to our understanding of innovation and its spatial ramifications. First, it draws attention to the important roles played by large oligopolies and their systematic R&D in the continuous development of innovations. Despite the attention given to smaller firms by both researchers and governments, large oligopolies remain the major generators of innovations. This is very much the result of their large expenditures on R&D.

Large corporations are in a position to overcome some of the key problems of innovation. The ways in which they accomplish this often have spatial implications. One such example is the way in which they tend to deal with the inherent problems of uncertainty and bounded rationality. This is tackled by developing a spatial division of labour and global scanning. The location of R&D in headquarters regions tends to make those regions the nodes of global information and communication networks. They become the global scanning hubs for world state-of-the-art knowledge. Again, this is aided by time proximity to similar organisations and customers in other global nodes. This is facilitated by infrastructures such as international hub airports which are also usually located in the same regions.

Innovation has a tendency to be path dependent. Once a new technological trajectory is established, firms usually continue up that trajectory even if it has obvious disadvantages such as the QWERTY keyboard configuration. This has dangers of lock-in and eventual economic decline. The larger core metropolitan cities are able to minimise this danger in two main ways. First, they seem to foster more open trajectories, particularly during their early stages when they are highly dependent on relatively uncodified knowledge. Second, at any one time, the more international cities tend to have more new trajectories and more possibilities for branching. This leaves them less susceptible to the effects of the collapse of any one old sector and more likely to contain new growing sectors than smaller and less international cities.

The power of oligopolies is also a factor influencing the concentration of innovation in particular cities. Two of the major markets for innovations are the 'life and death' industries. These are both, to a large extent, publicly funded either because they are established by governments or because governments are the main purchasers of their products and services. Large oligopolies have been particularly successful at securing defence contracts or selling pharmaceuticals to health services. In both cases these expenditures contribute to the growth of these industries in such regions as the South East of England.

One of the essential inputs to innovation is new knowledge. This is difficult to codify and is therefore best transferred by repeated and frequent face-to-face contacts. This leads to the argument that innovation is facilitated by geographic proximity among producers. This is said to be the case where they collaborate and share knowledge often in Porter-style clusters. Whether they choose to collaborate or not, it is also argued that it is difficult to monopolise new knowledge especially among smaller companies. This leads to knowledge spill-overs in knowledge-rich urban environments.

We argue, however, that most firms will be unwilling to share crucial economic knowledge with their local competitors. Sharing knowledge of their new innovations would most likely entail also sharing any eventual profits. Nevertheless, knowledge exchange is important to innovation but it is more likely to be with clients and customers than with other producers. In this respect we would support demand-pull theories concerning the generation of innovations.

Many customers for innovations are located in other advanced economies. They play a crucial role in the demand pull for innovation. They may set product design and performance criteria, test prototypes and contribute generally to innovation in the producer firm. Therefore, personal international knowledge exchanges are crucial in the development of innovations. This echoes the importance attached to international trade by Krugman. Again, time proximity to international clients and customers appears to be an important reason leading to the agglomeration of innovation in certain cities. This is represented by external interactions via hub airports located in the major world and international cities. The location of innovative firms within a maximum of about one hour from an international airport seems to be an important factor in an agglomeration economy.

Finally, innovation is dependent on high quality professional and technical labour. Therefore the cities that can provide pools of such labour are the favoured locations for innovative firms. High quality labour is one of the more 'sticky' local factors of production. Language barriers prevent its free mobility around Europe. The primary cities in each national economy therefore tend also to be the major national concentrations of such labour. This is also partly a matter of choice as far as such workers are concerned. Their generally higher incomes allow them to make significant choices about the kinds of housing, environments and localities that they are prepared to live in.

Altogether, we think that instead of focusing primarily on the relationships between the production of innovations and the localities in which they are produced, we should also consider the markets in which they are sold and the interactions between the customers there and the innovators. Some cities are much better equipped to make the connections between innovators and their markets than others. These are generally international cities with multiple interactions with similar cities in the global economy. All the cities included in this study follow this pattern at least to some degree.

References

Amin, A. (1991) 'Giant shapers and shakers of the world economy leave British hopes behind as wishful thinking', *The Guardian*, 7 January, p. 9.

Amin, A. and Robins, K. (1990) 'The re-emergence of regional economies? The mythical geography of flexible accumulation', *Environment and Planning D: Society and Space*, 8, 7–34.

Amin, A. and Thrift, N. (1992) 'Neo-Marshallian nodes in global networks', *International Journal of Urban and Regional Research*, 16, 4, 571–87.

Andersen, E.S. (1992) 'Approaching national systems of innovation from the production and linkage structure', in B. A. Lundvall (ed.) *National Systems of Innovation: Towards a Theory of Innovation and Interactive Learning*, London, Pinter.

Audretsch, D.B. (1998) 'Agglomeration and the location of innovative activity', *Oxford Review of Economic Policy*, 14, 2, 18–29.

Audretsch, D.B. and Feldman, M.P. (1996) 'Innovative clusters in the industry life cycle', *Review of Industrial Organization*, 11, 2, 253–73.

Aydalot, P. (1984) 'Reversals of spatial trends in French industry since 1974', in J.G. Lambooy (ed.) *New Spatial Dynamics and Economic Crisis*, Tampere, Finnpublishers, 41–62.

Aydalot, P. (ed.) (1986) *Milieux Innovateurs en Europe*, Paris, GREMI.

Aydalot, P. and Keeble, D. (eds) (1988) *High Technology Industry and Innovative Environments: The European Experience*, London, Routledge.

Baker, P. (2000) *Multilingual Capital*, London, Battlebridge Publications.

Baptista, R. (1997) 'An empirical study of innovation, entry and diffusion in industrial clusters', PhD dissertation, University of London, London Business School.

Becattini, G. (1990) 'The Marshallian industrial district as a socio-economic notion', in F. Pyke, G. Becattini and W. Sengenberger (eds) *Industrial Districts and Inter-firm Co-operation in Italy*, Geneva, International Institute for Labour Statistics, pp. 37–51.

Becattini, N. (1989) 'Sectors or districts: some remarks on the conceptual foundations of industrial economics', in E. Goodman and J. Bamford (eds) *Small Firms and Industrial Districts in Italy*, London, Routledge, pp. 123–35.

Beije, P. (1992) 'A network analysis of markets', *Journal of Economic Issues*, 26, 1, 87–114.

Bellini, N. (1987) 'Intermediaries and structural change in small firm areas: the Italian experience', paper presented at Ascona University, June.

Bermen, E., Bound, J. and Machin, S. (1997) *Implications of Skill-biased Technological Change: International Evidence*, Working Paper No. 6166, Cambridge, MA, National Bureau of Economic Research.

Bianchi, P. (1986) *Industrial Restructuring within an Italian Perspective*, Working Paper No. 2, Nomisma, September.

Braczyk, H.-J., Cooke, P. and Heindreich, M. (eds) (1998) *Regional Innovation Systems: The Role of Governance in a Globalized Economy*, London, UCL Press.

Camagni, R. (1984) 'Spatial diffusion of pervasive process innovation', paper presented at the 24th European Congress of the Regional Science Association, Milan, 28–31 August.

Camagni, R. (ed.) (1991) *Innovation Networks: Spatial Perspectives*, London, Belhaven-Pinter.

Chinitz, B. (1961) 'Contrasts in agglomeration: New York and Pittsburgh', *American Economic Review*, 51, 279–89.

Chinitz, B. (1964) 'City and suburb', in B. Chinitz (ed.) *City and Suburb: The Economics of Metropolitan Growth*, Englewood Cliffs, NJ, Prentice-Hall.

Coase, R.H. (1937) 'The nature of the firm', *Economica* NS 4, 386–405.

Coase, R.H. (1988) 'The nature of the firm: origin', *Journal of Law, Economics and Organisation* 4, 1, 3–47.

Cooke, P. (1986) *The Genesis of High Technology Complexes: Theoretical and Empirical Considerations*, Cardiff, University of Cardiff.

Cooke, P. and Morgan, K. (1993) 'The network paradigm: new departures in corporate and regional development', *Environment and Planning D*, 11, 543–64.

Curran, J. and Blackbourn, R.A. (1994) *Small Firms and Local Economic Networks: The Death of the Local Economy*, London, Routledge.

Davelaar, E.J. (1989) 'Incubation and innovation: a spatial perspective', PhD thesis, Free University of Amsterdam.

Davelaar, E.J. (1991) *Regional Economic Analysis of Innovation and Incubation*, Aldershot, Avebury.

Decoster, E. and Tabariés, M. (1986) 'L'innovation dans un pôle scientifique: le cas de la Cité Scientifique Ile de France Sud', in P. Aydalot (ed.) *Milieux Innovateurs en Europe*, Paris, GREMI, pp. 79–100.

Dicken, P. (1994) 'Global–local tensions: firms and states in the global space-economy', *Economic Geography*, 70, 2, 101–28.

Dicken, P. and Lloyd, P.E. (1990) *Location in Space: Theoretical Perspectives in Economic Geography*, New York.

Dosi, G., Freeman, C., Nelson, R., Silverberg, G. and Soete, L. (1988) *Technical Change and Economic Theory*, London, Pinter.

Driver, S. and Gillespie, A. (1991) *Spreading the Word? Communications Technologies and the Geography of Magazine Print Publishing*, Newcastle PICT Working Paper 1, University of Newcastle, Centre for Urban and Regional Development Studies.

European Commission Dgs XIII and XVI (1996) *RITTS and RIS Guidebook*, Regional Actions for Innovation, Brussels, EC.

Feldman, M.P. and Florida, R. (1994) 'The geographic sources of innovation: technological infrastructure and product innovation in the United States', *Annals of the Association of American Geographers*, 84, 2, 210–29.

Ferguson, M. (1988) 'From the people who brought you voodoo economics', *Harvard Business Review*, May–June, 55–62.

Florida, R. and Kenney, M. (1990a) 'High-technology restructuring in the USA and Japan', *Environment and Planning A*, 22, 233–52.

Florida, R. and Kenney, M. (1990b) *The Breakthrough Illusion: Corporate America's Failure to Move from Innovation to Mass Production*, New York, Basic Books.

Freeman, C. (1974) *The Economics of Industrial Innovation*, Harmondsworth, Penguin.

Freeman, C. (1986) 'The role of technical change in national economic development', in A. Amin and J. Goddard (eds) *Technological Change, Industrial Restructuring and Regional Development*, London, Allen and Unwin, pp. 100–14.

Freeman, C., Soete, L. and Clark, J. (1982) *Unemployment and Technical Innova-*

tion: A Study of Long Waves and Economic Development, London, Frances Pinter.

Froebel, F., Heinrichs, J. and Kreye, O. (1980) *The New International Division of Labour*, Cambridge, Cambridge University Press.

Galbraith, J.K. (1967) *The New Industrial State*, Boston, Houghton Mifflin.

Gilder, G. (1989) *The Law of the Microcosm*, New York, Simon and Schuster.

Glaeser, E., Kallal, H., Scheinkman, J. and Sheifer, A. (1992) 'Growth of cities', *Journal of Political Economy*, 100, 1126–52.

Gordon, I.R. and McCann, P. (1998) 'Industrial clusters, agglomeration and/or social networks?', paper presented at the Regional Science Association British and Irish Section conference, York.

Grabher, G. (1991) *The Embedded Firm: The Socio-Economics of Industrial Networks*, London, Routledge.

Granovetter, M. (1973) 'The strength of weak ties', *American Journal of Sociology*, 78, 1360–80.

Granovetter, M. (1985) 'Economic action and social structure: the problem of embeddedness', *American Journal of Sociology*, 91, 481–510.

Hall, P. (1981) 'The geography of the fifth Kondratieff cycle', *New Society*, 26, March, 535–7.

Hall, P. and Preston, P. (1988) *The Carrier Wave: New Information Technology and the Geography of Innovation 1846–2003*, London, Unwin Hyman.

Harrison, B. (1992) 'Industrial districts: old wine in new bottles?', *Regional Studies*, 26, 5, 469–83.

Hart, D. and Simmie, J.M. (1997) 'Innovation, competition and the structure of local production networks: initial findings from the Hertfordshire project', *Local Economy*, November, 235–46.

Harvey, D. (1987) 'Flexible accumulation through urbanization: reflections on "post-modernism" in the American City', *Antipode*, 19, 260–86.

Henderson, J. and Castells, M. (eds) (1987) *Global Restructuring and Territorial Development*, London, Sage.

Henderson, V. (1986) 'Efficiency of resource usage and city size', *Journal of Urban Economics*, 19, 1, 47–70.

Hoover, E.M. (1937) *Location Theory and the Shoe and Leather Industries*, Cambridge, MA, Harvard University Press.

Hoover, E.M. (1948) *The Location of Economic Activity*, New York, McGraw-Hill.

Hoover, E.M. and Vernon, R. (1959) *Anatomy of a Metropolis*, Cambridge, MA, Harvard University Press.

Isard, W. (1951) 'Location theory and trade theory: distance inputs and the space economy', *Quarterly Journal of Economics* 65, 181–98.

Jacobs, J. (1968) *The Economy of Cities*, London, Weidenfeld.

Krugman, P. (1991) *Geography and Trade*, Cambridge, MA, MIT Press.

Krugman, P. (1994) 'Competitiveness: a dangerous obsession', *Foreign Affairs*, March–April, 28–44.

Krugman, P. (1995) *Development, Economic Geography and Economic Theory*, Cambridge, MA, MIT Press.

Kynaston, D. (1985) *The Financial Times: A Centenary History*, London, Viking.

Lambooy, J.G. and Boschma R.A. (1998) 'Evolutionary economics and regional policy', paper presented to the 38th Congress of the European Regional Science Association, August, Vienna.

Langrish, J., Gibbons, M., Evans, P. and Jevons, F. (1972) *Wealth from Knowledge*, London, Macmillan.

Lawson, C. (1997) *Territorial Clustering and High-technology Innovation: From Industrial Districts to Innovative Milieux*, Working Paper 54, University of Cambridge, ESRC Centre for Business Research.

Leborgne, D. and Lipietz, A. (1988) 'New technologies, new modes of regulation: some spatial implications', *Environment and Planning D: Society and Space*, 6, 263–80.

Lovering, J. (1990) 'Fordism's unknown successor: a comment on Scott's theory of flexible accumulation and the re-emergence of regional economies', *International Journal of Urban and Regional Research*, 13, 159–74.

Lundvall, B.A. (1988) 'Innovation as an interactive process: from user–producer interaction to the national system of innovation', in G. Dosi, C. Freeman, R. Nelson, G. Silverberg and L. Soete (eds) *Technical Change and Economic Theory*, London, Pinter.

Lundvall, B.A. (1990) 'User–producer interactions and technological change', paper presented to the OECD-TEP Conference, Paris/La Villette, June.

Lundvall, B.A. (ed.) (1992) *National Systems of Innovation: Towards a Theory of Innovation and Interactive Learning*, London, Pinter.

Lundvall, B.A. and Johnson, B. (1992) 'The learning economy', paper presented to the European Association for Evolutionary Political Economy Conference, Paris, November.

Lyons, D. (1994) 'Agglomeration economies among high technology firms in advanced production areas: the case of Denver/Boulder', *Regional Studies*, 29, 3, 265–78.

Maillat, D., Crevoisier, O. and Lecoq, B. (1990) 'Innovation and territorial dynamism', paper for Flexible Specialisation in Europe Workshop, October, Zurich.

Maillat, D. and Perrin, J.C. (1992) *Enterprises innovantes et développement territorial*, Neuchatel, EDES.

Maillat, D., Quevit, M. and Senn, L. (eds) (1993) *Milieux innovateurs et réseaux d'innovation: un défi pour le développement régional*, Neuchatel, EDES.

Malecki, E. (1987) 'Hope or hyperbole: high tech and economic development', *Technology Review*, 90, 45–51.

Malecki, E.J. and Varaiya, P. (1986) 'Innovation and changes in regional structure', in P. Nijkamp (ed.) *Handbook of Regional and Urban Economics*, Amsterdam, North Holland, pp. 629–45.

Markussen, A.R. (1985a) *Profit Cycles, Oligopoly, and Regional Development*, Cambridge, MA, MIT Press.

Markussen, A.R. (1985b) *Regions, the Economics and Politics of Territory*, Totowa, NJ, Rowman and Altanheld.

Markussen, A. (1996) 'Sticky places in slippery space: a typology of industrial districts', *Economic Geography*, 72, 293–313.

Markussen, A.R., Campbell, C. and Deitrich, S. (1991) *The Rise of the Gunbelt*, New York, Basic Books.

Markusen, A., Hall, P. and Glasmier, A. (1986) *High-tech America: the What, How, Where and Why of the Sunrise Industries*, Boston, George Allen and Unwin.

Marshall, A. (1890) *Principles of Economics*, Basingstoke, Macmillan.

Marshall, A. (1919) *Industry and Trade*, London, Macmillan.

Marshall, A. (1925) *Principles of Economics*, London, Macmillan.

Marshall, M. (1987) *Long Waves of Regional Development*, London, Macmillan.

Martin, F., Swan, N., Banks, I., Barker, G. and Beaudry, R. (1979) *The Interregional Diffusion of Innovations in Canada*, Ottawa, Ministry of Supply and Services.

Martin, R. and Sunley, P. (1996) 'Paul Krugman's geographical economics and its implications for regional development theory: a critical assessment', *Economic Geography*, 72, 3, 259–92.

Massey, D. (1984) *Spatial Divisions of Labour*, London, Macmillan.

Mensch, G. (1979) *Stalemate in Technology: Innovations Overcome the Depression*, New York, Ballinger.

Mowery, D. and Rosenberg N. (1979) 'The influence of market demand upon innovation: a critical review of some recent empirical studies', *Research Policy*, 8, 102–53.

Myers, S. and Marquis, D.G. (1969) *Successful Industrial Innovation*, Washington, DC, National Science Foundation.

Myrdal, G. (1957) *Rich Lands and Poor*, New York, Harper.

Nelson, R. and Winter, S.G. (1982) *An Evolutionary Theory of Economic Changes*, Cambridge, MA, Harvard University Press.

Norton, R.D. and Rees, J. (1979) 'The product cycle and the spatial decentralisation of American manufacturing', *Regional Studies*, 13, 141–51.

Oakey, R. (1985) 'High technology industries and agglomeration economies', in P. Hall and A. Markussen (eds) *Silicon Landscapes*, Boston, Allen and Unwin, pp. 94–117.

Perez, C. (1985) 'Microelectronics, long waves and world structural change: new perspectives for developing countries', *World Development*, 13, 3, 441–63.

Perrin, J.C. (1988a) *Comment naissent les techniques?*, Paris, *Publisud*.

Perrin, J.C. (1988b) 'New technologies, local synergies and regional policies in Europe', in P. Aydalot and D. Keeble (eds) *High Technology Industry and Innovative Environments: The European Experience*, London, Routledge, pp. 139–62.

Perroux, F. (1950) 'Economic space: theory and applications', *Quarterly Journal of Economics*, 64, 89–104.

Perroux, F. (1955) 'Note sur la notion de "pôle de croissance"', *Economie Appliquée*, Jan.–June, 307–20.

Philips, A. (1971) *Technology and Market Structure*, Lexington, MA, Heath.

Piore, M.J. and Sabel, C.F. (1984) *The Second Industrial Divide: Possibilities for Prosperity*, New York, Basic Books.

Polanyi, K. (1944) *The Great Transformation*, New York, Holt and Rinehart.

Popp, K. (1987) 'Standortfaktoren und Standorte der Mikroelectronischen Industrie', *Geographie und Schule*, 49, 2–8.

Porter, M.E. (1990) *The Competitive Advantage of Nations*, New York, The Free Press.

Praat, A. (1991) 'The principles of networking', in M. Schmidt and E. Wever (eds) *Complexes, Formations and Networks*, Utrecht, Nijmegen.

Pred, A. (1966) *The Spatial Dynamics of Urban-industrial Growth 1800–1914: Interpretive and Theoretical Essays*, Cambridge, MA, MIT Press.

Pred, A. (1977) *City Systems in Advanced Economies: Past Growth, Present Processes and Future Development Options*, London, Hutchinson.

Premus, R. (1982) *Location of High Technology Firms and Regional*

Development, Joint Study Economic Committee, Washington, DC, US Congress.

Rothwell, R. (1991) 'External networking and innovation in small and medium sized manufacturing firms in Europe', *Technovation*, 11, 2, 93–112.

Rothwell, R. (1994) 'Industrial innovation: success, strategy, trends', in M. Dodgson and R. Rothwell (eds) *The Handbook of Industrial Innovation*, Cheltenham, Edward Elgar.

Saxenian, A. (1990) 'Regional networks and the resurgence of Silicon Valley', *California Management Review*, 33, 1, 89–112.

Saxenian, A (1991) 'The origins and dynamics of production: networks in Silicon Valley', *Research Policy*, 20, 423–37.

Saxenian, A. (1994) *Regional Networks: Industrial Adaptation in Silicon Valley and Route 128*, Cambridge, MA, Harvard University Press.

Schmookler, J. (1966) *Invention and Economic Growth*, Cambridge, MA, Harvard University Press.

Schumpeter, J.A. (1939) *Business Cycles: A Theoretical, Historical and Statistical Analysis of the Capitalist Process*, New York, McGraw-Hill.

Schumpeter, J.A. (1942) *Capitalism, Socialism and Democracy*, New York, McGraw-Hill.

Scitovsky, T. (1963) 'Two concepts of external economies', reprinted in A.N. Agarwala and S.P. Singh (eds) *The Economics of Underdevelopment*, Oxford, Oxford University Press, pp. 295–308.

Scott, A.J. (1982) 'Location patterns and dynamics of industrial activity in the modern metropolis: a review essay', *Urban Studies*, 19, 111–42.

Scott, A.J. (1985) 'Location processes, urbanisation, and territorial development: an exploratory essay', *Environment and Planning A*, 17, 479–501.

Scott, A.J. (1986) 'High technology industry and territorial development: the rise of the Orange County complex 1955–1984', *Urban Geography*, 7, 3–45.

Scott, A.J. (1988a) *Metropolis*, Los Angeles, University of California Press.

Scott, A.J. (1988b) *New Industrial Spaces*, London, Pion.

Scott, A.J. (1989) 'The technopoles of southern California', *UCLA Research Papers in Economic Geography*, No. 1, UCLA, Dept of Geography.

Scott, A.J. (1990) *New Industrial Spaces*, London, Pion.

Scott, A.J. (1993) *Technopolis: High-Technology Industry and Regional Development in Southern California*, Berkeley, CA, University of California Press.

Scott, A.J. and Storper, M. (eds) (1986) *Production, Work and Territory*, London, Unwin Hyman.

Scott, A.J. and Storper, M. (1987) 'High technology industry and regional development: a theoretical critique and reconstruction', *International Social Science Journal*, 112, 215–32.

Simmie, J.M. (ed.) (1996) *Innovation, Networks and Learning Regions?*, London, Jessica Kingsley.

Simmie, J.M. (1998a) 'Innovate or stagnate: economic planning choices for local production nodes in the global economy', *Planning Practice and Research*, 13, 1, 35–51.

Simmie, J.M. (1998b) 'Reasons for the development of "Islands of innovation": evidence from Hertfordshire', *Urban Studies*, 35, 8, 1261–89.

Simmie, J.M. and Hart, D. (1999) 'Innovation projects and local production networks: a case study of Hertfordshire', *European Planning Studies*, 7, 4, 445–62.

Sternberg, R. (1996) 'Reasons for the genesis of high-tech regions – theoretical explanation and empirical evidence', *Geoforum*, 27, 2, 205–23.

Stohr, H.W.B. (1986) 'Regional innovation complexes', papers of the *Regional Science Association*, 59, 29–44.

Storper, M. (1985) 'Oligopoly and the product cycle: essentialism in economic geography', *Economic Geography*, 61, 260–82.

Storper, M. (1986) 'Technology and new regional growth complexes: the economics of discontinuous spatial development', in P. Nijkamp (ed.) *Technological Change, Employment and Spatial Dynamics*, Berlin, Springer Verlag, pp. 46–75.

Storper, M. (1987) 'The new industrial geography', *Urban Geography*, 8, 585–98.

Storper, M. (1991) 'Technology districts and international trade: the limits to globalisation in an age of flexible production', *Graduate School of Urban Planning*, Los Angeles, UCLA.

Storper, M. (1993) 'Regional "worlds" of production: learning and innovation in the technology districts of France, Italy and the USA', *Regional Studies*, 27, 5, 433–55.

Storper, M. (1994a) 'The resurgence of regional economies, ten years later: the region as a nexus of untraded interdependencies', paper presented at the Conference Cities, Enterprises, and Society at the Eve of the XXIst Century, Lille, 16–18 March.

Storper, M. (1994b) 'Institutions of the learning economy', paper presented at the Conference on Employment and Growth in the Knowledge-Based Economy, Copenhagen, 7–8 November.

Storper, M. (1995) 'The resurgence of regional economies, ten years later: the region as a nexus of untraded interdependencies', *European Urban and Regional Studies*, 2, 3, 191–221.

Storper, M. (1997) *The Regional World: Territorial Development in a Global Economy*, New York, Guildford Press.

Storper, M.J. and Harrison, B. (1991) 'Flexibility, hierarchy and regional development: the changing structure of industrial production systems and their forms of governance in the 1990s', *Research Policy*, 20, 407–22.

Sutcliffe, B. (1984) *Hard Times*, London, Pluto.

Teece, D. (1988) 'Technological change and the nature of the firm', in G. Dosi, C. Freeman, G. Silverberg and L. Soete (eds) *Technical Change and Economic Theory*, London, Frances Pinter, pp. 256–81.

3M–NatWest (1999) *Innovation Trends Survey*, 10th anniversary, London, NatWest.

Thwaites, A.T. (1982) 'Some evidence of regional variations in the introduction and diffusion of industrial products and processes within British manufacturing industry', *Regional Studies*, 16, 5, 371–81.

Tichy, G. (1985) 'A sketch of a probabilistic modification of the product-cycle hypothesis to explain the problems of old industrial areas', in A.T. Thwaites and R.P. Oakey (eds) *The Regional Economic Impact of Technological Change*, London, Pinter.

Todtling, F. (1991) 'The geography of innovation: transformation from Fordism towards Postfordism?' paper prepared for the European Science Foundation's RURE Programme, Barcelona, 6–8 September.

Utterback, J.M. (1988) 'Innovation and industrial evolution in manufacturing industries', in B.R. Guile and H. Brooks (eds) *Technology and Global*

Industry: Companies and Nations in the World Economy, Washington, DC, National Academy Press.

Vernon, R. (1966) 'International investment and international trade in the product cycle', *Quarterly Journal of Economics*, 80, 190–207.

Vernon, R. (1979) 'The product cycle hypothesis in a new international environment', *Oxford Bulletin of Economics and Statistics*, 41, 255–67.

Von Hippel, E. (1994) 'Sticky information and the locus of problem solving: implications for innovation', *Management Science*, 40, 429–39.

Weber, A. (1909) *Theory of the Location of Industries*, trans. C.J. Friedrich 1929, Chicago, University of Chicago Press.

Williamson, O.E. (1975) *Markets and Hierarchies*, New York, Free Press.

Williamson, O.E. (1985) *The Economic Institutions of Capitalism*, New York, Free Press.

Yeung, H. (1994) 'Critical reviews of geographical perspectives on business organisations and the organisation of production: towards a network approach', *Progress in Human Geography*, 18, 460–90.

Young, A. (1928) 'Increasing returns and economic progress', *The Economic Journal*, 38, 527–42.

CHAPTER 2

Innovative Clusters and Innovation Processes in the Stuttgart Region

2 Innovative Clusters and Innovation Processes in the Stuttgart Region

Simone Strambach with Annette D'Lorio and Carmen Steinlein

Introduction[1]

It is somewhat surprising that Stuttgart, together with world cities like London or Paris, is among the ten European innovation 'islands' which have dominated the innovation process in Europe for decades. Hilpert (1994) has called these islands the Archipelago of Europe. Simmie (1999) argues persuasively, in line with the explanation of the traditional agglomeration economies, 'that size matters'. Scale advantages in large cities, urbanisation and localisation economies are seen as the main reasons for the clustering of innovative activities in metropolitan regions. Stuttgart is, compared with London and Paris, a much smaller agglomeration. It is therefore surprising that Stuttgart seems to be able to compete with these big international cities in the field of innovation. The fact that Stuttgart is one of these innovative cities in Europe also seems to be astonishing for another reason: large metropolitan regions have increasingly become service economies, but the economic structures of the Stuttgart region are, at the end of the twentieth century, still strongly dominated by manufacturing industry. The aim of this chapter is to identify the specific urban assets Stuttgart has, which can be considered as explanatory factors for the continuing innovative and competitive strengths of the metropolitan region.

Agglomeration economies and location theory offer a more general explanatory framework for the concentration of innovative activities in large metropolitan regions. However, it is difficult to explain specialisations and distinctions between different metropolitan city regions in the field of innovations with these approaches. Although definitions of clusters vary, there is no doubt that the development of industrial and innovative clusters has been an evolutionary one. If we are concerned with identifying

55

the innovation potentials of agglomerations and their urban assets, then dynamic approaches with an evolutionary and institutionalist point of view seem to be more suitable. Porter (1999), also points in this direction when he emphasises that research is needed to distinguish between urban agglomeration economies and cluster agglomeration economies and to explore the way both of these evolve within a country's development and its government policy.

The chapter uses a system-analytic approach. Innovative clusters evolve within national and regional systems of innovation. Common characteristics of the different systems of innovation approaches, identified by Edquist (1997), are among others: innovation and learning at the centre, a holistic and evolutionary perspective and the emphasis on the role of institutions. Empirically, the analytical framework of the 'systems of innovation' approach not only allows regionally differentiated observations to be made, it also allows the interdependent linkages between production and innovation structures and regional governance to be taken into account.

Stuttgart is embedded in the regional innovation system of Baden-Württemberg, which, in turn, is part of Germany's national innovation system. However, just as regional innovation systems are not simply small-scale national systems because they combine elements that are specifically regional, national and even international, so the system of the Stuttgart metropolitan region cannot be seen simply as a smaller-scale blueprint of Baden-Württemberg's regional innovation system (Braczyk et al., 1998; Edquist, 1997; Lundvall and Borras, 1998). The Stuttgart region has developed its own specific core competences which result from the socio-economically integrated interaction and learning processes of firms, institutions, and political actors in the past.

The chapter is divided into four parts. First, the historical development and the socio-economic structures of the Stuttgart region are described. The second section focuses more closely on the innovation potentials of Stuttgart using an interregional comparison with other German agglomerations. The results show that industrial clusters within the region to a large extent determine the innovation profile of the city. It also becomes clear that the institutional set-up, the region-specific profile of semi-public and private suppliers of training and education, the regional research infrastructure and the specialisation profile of the scientific system largely correspond to the industrial technical and technological fields of the R&D-intensive industry branches. From an evolutionary point of view, the regional institutional arrangements make an important, although indirect, contribution to maintaining the technological innovative capacity of the industrial clusters. The third section looks at the empirical results of a survey of innovative enterprises in the region and the relationship between the local environment and the innovation processes of firms. The focal point of the fourth section is new political and economic initiatives in

Stuttgart for promoting both technological and organisational innovations and institutional change at the level of the firms and the region. In this section, changes in governance and institutional structures, which can be very important for the future competitiveness of the city, are considered.

The Stuttgart Region and its Location

The Stuttgart region is situated in the centre of the state of Baden-Württemberg in south western Germany. The region's area is 3,654 km², one-tenth of the area of Baden-Württemberg, and its population is 2.6 million. In contrast to other agglomeration areas like Munich or Hamburg which are dominated by a single very large city, the Stuttgart region has a number of medium-sized cities which have grown up over time around the main centre of Stuttgart and which spread out into the surrounding areas (see Figure 2.1).

Administratively, since 1994 the Stuttgart region has included, in addition to the city of Stuttgart itself, the five middle-level administrative districts – the 'Kreise' – Böblingen, Ludwigsburg, Rems-Murr, Esslingen, and Göppingen. Economically, therefore, the region is polycentric and is made up of 179 independent municipalities. The city of Stuttgart is the political and economic centre of both the region and the state of Baden-Württemberg. Stuttgart itself has various administrative functions and, as the state capital, it is the seat of the state government and the associations in the region.

Figure 2.1. Administrative districts of the Stuttgart region

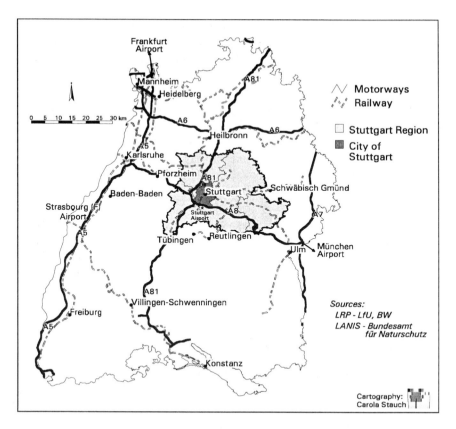

Figure 2.2. Map of the Stuttgart region

The decentralised structure and geographical location meant that the infrastructure in the region began to be developed quite early. The present transport links and the fact that the region is accessible internationally by road, rail, and air are among its obvious advantages. The region is linked to the national transport network by two motorways – the A8 which goes in a west–east direction to the Karlsruhe and Munich conurbations, and the A81 which goes north-east–south-west from Würzburg/Heilbronn to Singen and on into Switzerland. Within the region, a star-shaped pattern of six federal roads converges in Stuttgart and is supplemented by state and local roads (see Figure 2.2).

Stuttgart is integrated into the West–East Marginale rail transport system between Paris–Stuttgart–Munich–Vienna and also has rail connections to eastern Europe, Switzerland, and elsewhere. Since 1991 it has been connected to the high speed railway network – the ICE. The major project 'Stuttgart 21', will increase accessibility when the present rail terminus becomes a through station and the railway lines are transferred underground.

The state's airport, which was extended in 1996 and is still being expanded, will make it possible to fly directly to all German commercial centres and to major centres inside and outside Europe. It is the sixth largest German airport with over 7 million passenger arrivals in 1998. The airport is particularly important for air freight traffic, i.e. the export of high quality investment and consumer goods produced by the industries in the region. It is the fifth largest airport in Germany for air freight with over 74,000 tonnes annually. The regional rail network means that Stuttgart airport is very conveniently situated for connections to the city. The rail project 'Stuttgart 21' will link the Stuttgart airport with the ICE service.

Stuttgart also has two ports. The River Neckar is the most important waterway for the transport of bulk goods and connects the region with the national and west European networks of waterways. The Stuttgart port, which was originally intended mainly for the transport of bulk goods like coal, gravel and sand, is today a modern commercial and industrial port with almost 4 million tonnes of goods volume annually and a central transport hub.

The Historical Development of the Region

The natural conditions in south-west Germany were rather unfavourable for the development of an industrial sector. It lacked important mineral resources like iron and coal and the River Neckar was too small and unavailable to bring them from outside. The mountains and valleys in the area around Stuttgart also made it more difficult to develop the economic area.

However, local people always had the basic Swabian virtues of 'industriousness, reliability and a feeling for quality' (Grotz, 1998, p. 498), combined with strict pietism. They tried to compensate for the natural disadvantages of the location by concentrating on labour and know-how intensive technologies, for example, refining imported raw materials, rather than on the raw material and energy-intensive branches of industry. An enterprise culture of inventors and Swabian 'Tüftler' (tinkerers) was thus established very early in many craft and home production workshops. Things like the nylon stocking, the electric coffee machine, the electric hand drill and the first motor car were developed in the region (IHK, 1996).

The industrialisation of the region in the middle of the nineteenth century began in the eastern part of the city, because it was possible to use the water power of the eastern tributaries of the Neckar (Fils, Lauter, Rems, and Murr), to operate the factories there. At first, most of the factories made consumer goods. After the railway was built at the end of the nineteenth century, raw materials could be brought in more cheaply and the places along the railway line in the eastern valleys profited. Only after the motorways were built and trucks began to be used for transporting materials and goods was economic use also made of the districts to the west, north and south. Unlike in the already densely settled eastern areas, there were large areas available here for settlement and economic development.

After 1945, economic focus shifted to the west where new and modern branches of the investment goods industry were established. The newest industry axis, with large increases in population and jobs, has been developed here in the last few decades. Today, more than three-quarters of the investment goods industry are located on the axis of Stuttgart City and the Böblingen and Esslingen administrative areas. The structural change has meant the stagnation of the old industry axis in the eastern part, which was mainly based on the textile industry.

Population Patterns and Development

Almost 25 per cent of the population of Baden-Württemberg live in the Stuttgart region. With almost 2.6 million inhabitants in 1997, the region is the largest unit in the state in terms of population. Its population density is much higher than in the other metropolitan regions in Germany like Hamburg, Munich and Frankfurt (see Figure 2.2). This is because the region's structure is polycentric with many medium-sized centres of population and industry around the state capital.

The population development in the region was primarily influenced by regional migration, not by natural population change. Up to 1970, the population in the region increased more strongly than the state of Baden-Württemberg as a whole (see Figure 2.3).

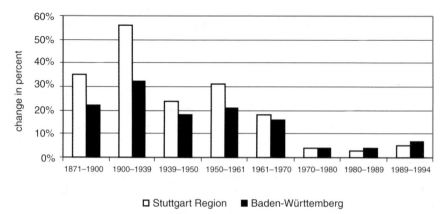

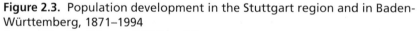

Figure 2.3. Population development in the Stuttgart region and in Baden-Württemberg, 1871–1994
Source: Brachat-Schwarz (1997, p. 32).

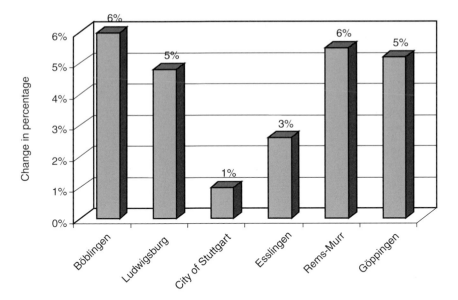

Figure 2.4. Increase in population in the Stuttgart region administrative districts, 1990–96
Source: BBR (1998).

Up to the Second World War the increase in population was concentrated in the city of Stuttgart (Brachat-Schwarz, 1997). Suburbanisation started in the Stuttgart region after the war as a result of better transport connections and the increasing use of motor vehicles as it did in most German centres of population. Suburbanisation still has a strong influence on the development of the region today, as the higher growth rates in the outer districts than in the city core indicate (cf. Figure 2.4).

The demographic patterns and developments in the Stuttgart region differ very little from those in the other German metropolitan regions. The proportion of young people under 18 living in Stuttgart is 19 per cent – 2 per cent higher than in Munich, Frankfurt and Hamburg. The proportion of the older population (65 and over) is lowest in Stuttgart with 14 per cent. The relatively favourable age structure in Stuttgart – the relatively high proportion of younger people and the relatively low proportion of older people – results from the immigration of guest workers since the 1960s, which occurred because industry was so important there (cf. Gaebe, 1997). Since 1970, the number of foreigners living in the Stuttgart region has grown by 86 per cent. The population of the city of Stuttgart increased again between 1989 and 1992 because of the changes in Eastern Europe and the subsequent emigration from there and from the former East Germany. In 1997 around 18 per cent of the 2.6 million people living in the region were foreign nationals (see Figure 2.5) (IHK, 1998b).

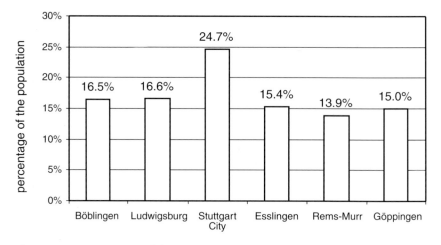

Figure 2.5. Proportion of foreigners in the administrative districts, 1990–96
Source: BBR (1998).

The suburbanisation in the Stuttgart region is reflected in the intra-regional distribution of the age groups, the foreigners, and the household and family patterns. The core city Stuttgart has a higher proportion of older people than the surrounding areas and a lower proportion of children and young people. Stuttgart shows the typical over-ageing which is a feature of core cities. Families with children move to the surrounding areas, while one-person households are concentrated in the city core. The proportion of one-person households in the city of Stuttgart is 47 per cent, well over 10 per cent higher than in the surrounding areas.

The atypical trends in recent years in Stuttgart caused by the changes in eastern Europe since 1993 have given way to the typical trends of conurbations – the shift of the development dynamics to the surrounding areas and the higher growth rates of population in the municipal areas than in the central districts.

Economic Structures and Development: Predominance of Industry

In past years economic development in the Stuttgart region has grown steadily at an above average rate, with high rates of employment and, for a long period, low unemployment levels. An interregional comparison of gross value added puts the Stuttgart region fourth in Germany with DM 52,500 per head. Around 30 per cent of Baden-Württemberg's gross value added is produced in the Stuttgart region. The fact that Stuttgart has had the lowest unemployment in Germany for many years is one indication of its economic strength. Stuttgart had the lowest rate of unemployment of all the major German cities (with more than 500,000 population) up to mid-

1991 with 2.1 per cent.[2] It only lost its top position in 1992 as a result of the crisis at the start of the 1990s, when the job losses in the region were disproportionately high and when its unemployment rate more than doubled. Stuttgart then slipped down to second place after Munich. In 1998 the unemployment rate in the Stuttgart region was 7 per cent which was well below the 12 per cent unemployment rate in Germany as a whole and the 7.7 per cent rate in Baden-Württemberg.

Of the 2.6 million people living in the Stuttgart region, 1.3 million have jobs, over 1 million of them have jobs where social security contributions are compulsory. Job density is comparable to that of Frankfurt and is one of the highest in Germany. In contrast to other metropolitan regions, the Stuttgart region's economic growth, innovative strength and position as an economic location are to a very large extent based on the efficiency of its industry.

Stuttgart has the highest share of people employed in manufacturing industry (see Figure 2.6) in all the conurbations in Germany and thus the lowest degree of tertiarisation. The Stuttgart region continues to be industrially the most dense in Germany even though the share of industrial employment had fallen by over 11 per cent up to 1997 and structural change is making services more and more important. In 1997 the average share of those employed in compulsory social security jobs was 30 per cent in Germany, in Stuttgart the share was almost 41 per cent, higher than in any other German agglomeration area (see Table 2.1).

The main feature of its economic structure is the specialisation in the industry branches of mechanical engineering, electrical engineering/electronics, and vehicle construction. Three-quarters of people employed in manufacturing industry work in these three branches of the investment

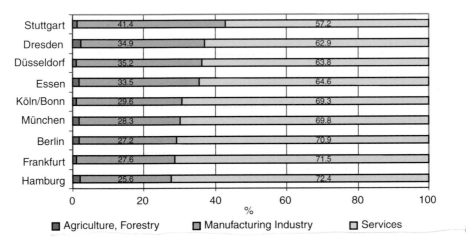

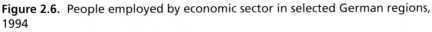

Figure 2.6. People employed by economic sector in selected German regions, 1994
Source: IHK (1998, p. 40), adjusted.

Table 2.1. Social security employees in manufacturing industry branches, 1995

Branch	Stuttgart region		Germany	
	Absolute	%	Absolute	%
Chemicals and oil	9,208	2.2	597,172	7.0
Rubber and plastic	16,316	3.8	415,357	4.8
Mining and quarrying	5,611	1.3	385,347	4.5
Basic metal	16,413	3.9	602,793	7.1
Mechanical engineering, vehicle construction	187,300	44.1	2,689,235	31.5
Electrical engineering, precision engineering	117,306	27.6	1,736,762	20.3
Wood, paper, printing	34,840	8.2	904,247	10.6
Leather, textiles, clothing	15,173	3.6	397,759	4.6
Food, beverages, tobacco	22,449	5.3	818,051	9.6
In total	424,616	100.0	8,546,723	100.0

Source: Statistisches Landesamt, own calculations.

goods industry and they cover almost 40 per cent of industrial firms. The publishing and printing industry, which has had a long tradition in Stuttgart, is still a major branch of industry and provides 8 per cent of industrial employment.

In 1996, Stuttgart had third place, after Munich and Berlin and before Frankfurt, among the four leading cities in Germany where 44 per cent of new books were published.[3] By contrast, the textile and clothing industry, which was important in the development of the region in the initial stages of industrialisation, now plays a much smaller role with a little over 3 per cent of manufacturing employment.

The strong industrial character of the region can also be seen in polarised skills pattern of the workforce. On the one hand, in 1997 the share of highly skilled workers – university and technical university graduates – was 10 per cent in Stuttgart, well above the national average. On the other hand, the share of semi-skilled and unskilled workers was 23 per cent – also well above the national average. This polarisation shows that there is still a large proportion of low-skilled jobs in industry, for example, in motor vehicle assembly and in electrical engineering.

The structure of the industrial firms in the region is a mixture of a few large firms and many small and medium-sized firms. Some 85 per cent of the industrial firms have less than 200 employees, though these provide only 28 per cent of the jobs. Some 56 per cent of employees work in 5 per cent of the firms.[4] The relatively high proportion of exports – almost 40 per cent – is an expression of the strong international competitiveness of the region. Three-quarters of these exports are produced in the three major branches. The concentration on investment goods forced the firms, whose

Table 2.2. Changes in shares of employees in the service sector, 1987–97

	1987 %	1989 %	1991 %	1993 %	1995 %	1997 %
Germany	51.0	51.9	52.9	55.3	57.8*	59.3
Baden-Württemberg	43.7	44.7	45.7	48.5	50.6	52.0
Stuttgart region	43.6	44.7	45.6	49.0	51.6	52.4

Note: * Includes East Germany – the new German states.
Source: Statistics of employees contributing to social security, Bundesanstalt für Arbeit, own calculations.

products are highly specialised, to adapt early on to geographically large markets. The rate of exports of the electrical technology industry is low compared to that of mechanical engineering and vehicle construction. This indicates the large supply networks that link the firms. A large share of the production of the electronics branch is supplied to the automobile industry whose products are then exported. Many smaller branches in the region which produce specialised textile and plastic products are also export dependent in this same roundabout way.

The converse of this industrial strength is the structural weakness in the service sector that is associated with it. At the end of the 1980s and the middle of the 1990s the share of employees contributing to social security in the service sector was below the national average in the Stuttgart region (see Table 2.2). In Germany as a whole over half of employees contributing to social security were working in the service sector by 1987, but both in the state of Baden-Württemberg and in the Stuttgart region this figure was only reached in 1995.

Sectoral differentiation of the service branches shows that banking and insurance is the only segment of services which is relatively strongly represented in Stuttgart. Its share of employment in 1997 is higher than both the national average and the share in Baden-Württemberg (see Table 2.3). The percentage of jobs in all the other service segments in Stuttgart is below the average German level.

The dynamic growth and concentration tendencies of the knowledge-intensive business services increasingly determine the structures and developments in the metropolitan regions. Stuttgart is less concentrated in this segment in terms of employment than the metropolitan regions in other countries, although here, too, knowledge-intensive services are the growth engines. In 1997 around 13 per cent of people employed in the services sector in the region were working in the knowledge-intensive services (Strambach, 1997b).

In any interpretation of the sectoral structure of services it must be recognised that, when workers are classified in terms of activities rather than sectors, i.e. in functional terms, the services share in the region is

Simone Strambach

Table 2.3. Social security employees in the Stuttgart region compared with Baden-Württemberg and Germany, 1997

Branches	Stuttgart region		Baden-Württemberg		Germany	
	Absolute	%	Absolute	%	Absolute	%
Agriculture, forestry	6,880	0.7	27,900	0.8	350,600	1.3
Energy industry	8,717	0.9	34,800	1.0	461,000	1.7
Manufacturing industry	413,653	40.6	1,464,100	40.0	8,102,200	29.9
Building and construction	55,579	5.5	224,200	6.1	2,073,200	7.7
Trade	128,987	12.7	473,000	12.9	3,779,800	13.9
Transport and communications	43,836	4.3	140,700	3.9	1,408,600	5.2
Banking and insurance	52,981	5.2	147,100	4.0	1,046,200	3.9
Services	222,980	21.9	855,000	23.4	7,113,200	26.2
Public organisations	30,748	3.0	83,300	2.3	833,700	3.1
Authorities, social insurance	55,220	5.4	240,600	5.6	1,940,800	7.2
In total	1,019,581	100	3,654,700	100	27,112,300	100

Source: Brachat-Schwarz and Deckarm (1997, p. 50f); IHK (1998, p. 5), adjusted; Statist. Bundesamt (1998).

considerably higher. Tertiarisation has taken place within the sectors but the statistics do not capture this development at all satisfactorily. In the secondary sector, many people now employed in industrial firms perform service functions; that is, they no longer carry out direct productive activities. In the statistics, however, these people are assigned to manufacturing industry. Thus it is not quite correct to speak of a general services deficiency compared to other metropolitan areas. The significant difference is that the business service functions are organised differently in the Stuttgart region. Far more of them are performed within the firm than in other metropolitan regions and independent service firms (Strambach, 1997a) perform fewer.

This appears to be the result of the particular economic structure in the Stuttgart region, whose success in the world market is determined by the export-oriented core industries producing technology and service-intensive products. The strength of the industrial sector and the weakness of the service sector appear to be the two sides of a single coin.

Summarising, the economic development indicators for Stuttgart show that the industrial specialisation in the past decades has had decidedly favourable effects. Despite the massive reduction in employment during the recession at the start of the 1990s, the Stuttgart region still has a relatively strong labour market with high levels of employment and unemployment remaining low. The economic strengths of the region can also be seen in its focus on, and strength in, exports. In 1996 the region had, in absolute terms, the largest foreign sales in the manufacturing sector of all agglomeration areas in Germany with DM 42 billion, and the third highest export rate of 37.1 per cent, which, in 1997, rose to 41 per cent (IHK, 1998).

Stuttgart: The Core Region of the Innovation System of Baden-Württemberg

Recent research into innovation has focused almost entirely on Baden-Württemberg as a whole. In the spatial innovation discussion Baden-Württemberg has become well known, first as an industrial district model, and actually as a successful regional innovation system.[5] As a subject for innovation research, Stuttgart has not yet received the same attention as Baden-Württemberg. Nevertheless, for more than two decades the economic and political centre of Baden-Württemberg and the engine of its economic growth has been Stuttgart and the region around it. Baden-Württemberg, as a state in the German federal system, is a single governance area so that institutions in the industry, education, and technology policies relate to it as an entity. However, Baden-Württemberg is not economically homogeneous – it includes rural areas as well as four agglomerations. Very different technological and sectoral specialisations are characteristic of these conurbations. Different lines of development have been pursued in the process of structural change and these are important from the point of view of the distribution of, and explanation for, the regional innovation potential. Empirically, therefore, it does not appear appropriate to consider Baden-Württemberg as a single industrial district as was often done in the past. This is particularly so as the empirical studies on which the classification of the state as an industrial district are based often only relate to the core region Stuttgart (for example, Schmitz, 1992) and are then carried over to the state as a whole.[6]

In what follows, the special place of Stuttgart in the innovation system of Baden-Württemberg will be identified using innovation indicators, and the innovation potential of the Stuttgart region will be described using an interregional comparison with selected German agglomerations.

Highly Integrated Industrial Clusters: The Drive for Successful Economic Growth and Innovativeness

The main feature of the Stuttgart region's economic structure is its concentration on the industry branches of mechanical engineering, electrical engineering/electronics, and vehicle construction. These branches can be grouped into two industrial clusters, one based on the automobile industry and the other on mechanical engineering. The electrical engineering/

67

electronics branches are oriented towards these two clusters. Simmie and Sennett (1999) point out that definitions of clusters differ considerably. The models include a range from high degrees of local economic and social interactions to simple co-location. In the following, the term 'cluster' is used in a broad manner as the concentration of a group of industries *with a functional affinity*, which do not have necessarily tight regional linkages. The clusters make up the industrial core of the region and provide more than half the industrial employment. The vehicle construction cluster consists primarily of large firms, the mechanical engineering cluster of medium-level firms, defined not so much in terms of the firm size – many of the firms now have more than the quantitative criterion of 500 employees – but rather in terms of the qualitative aspects of management structure and firm culture.

Well-known firms such as Daimler-Benz and Porsche in the automobile cluster, or Bosch in the electronics branch, have their origins in the Stuttgart region and carry out their global operations from here. In the electronics industry there are, in addition to Bosch, numerous subsidiaries of multinational firms, such as IBM, Hewlett Packard, SEL/Alcatel, whose German headquarters are situated in the region. The highly integrated structure, the stability of the supplier relationships, and the close co-operative relationships between the firms – vertical rather than horizontal – have been stressed as the main features of the region which affect its competitiveness, particularly in empirical regional science studies made at the end of the 1980s and the beginning of the 1990s (Sabel *et al.*, 1987; Morgan, 1992; Schmitz, 1992; Cooke and Morgan, 1994). They are the result of product specialisation, which makes it necessary for firms to buy individual parts and components from other specialists.

Indicators for the Regional Innovation Potential of Stuttgart

The national innovation system in Germany is characterised by a regionally differentiated distribution of innovation potential. There are not only interregional differences between the metropolitan areas and the peripheries but, as already mentioned, there are different kinds of emphases and lines of development within the metropolitan regions themselves.[7] The distribution of R&D activities in the German innovation system is more polycentric than in the national innovation systems in France and Great Britain where they are heavily concentrated in the capital city regions (see Table 2.4).

Regional innovation potentials in the Munich, Stuttgart, Frankfurt, and Rhine–Ruhr regions are determined by a wide range of technology-intensive branches of industry and this gives these regions their prominent place in the German agglomeration areas (NIW/ZEW, 1998). The *regional*

Table 2.4. International comparison of regional concentrations of the national R&D employment

France	%	United Kingdom	%	Germany	%
Paris/Ile-de-France	52.5	London	44.9	München	12.6
		Oxford	6.4	Stuttgart	11.5
				Frankfurt	8.3
				Rhein-Neckar	5.6
				Köln	4.9
				Berlin	4.2
				Nürnberg/	3.7
				Erlangen	
R&D Employees	52.5	R&D Employees	51.3	R&D Employees	50.8

Source: NIW/ZEW (1998, p. 19), adjusted.

innovation indicators show that for the Stuttgart region the three core sectors are the main determinants of Stuttgart's innovation potential and are responsible for the outstanding position of the metropolitan region in the regional innovation system of Baden-Württemberg.

The DM 13.7 billion spent on R&D by the economy in Baden-Württemberg in 1995 was the highest of all the states. More than a quarter of the federal research expenditure of the economy was concentrated in Baden-Württemberg.[8] The focal point in Baden-Württemberg is clearly in the Stuttgart region. The firms in the region provide 54 per cent, or more than half, of the internal R&D expenditure of the whole state.[9] An intraregional comparison at the *Kreis* level shows that the city of Stuttgart has the top position with DM 3.75 billion spent on R&D by industry,[10] followed by the *Kreis* Böblingen, which is also part of the Stuttgart region, with DM 1.79 billion. The firms' high commitment to research shows that there is a significant potential for innovation and it is an important factor for the competitiveness of the Stuttgart region.

The region's 7.6 per cent share of R&D employment in manufacturing industry as a whole is clearly above the state and federal averages. Research- and development-intensive industry branches, the so-called 'high tech' industries, are considered to be very important for the regional innovative strengths (Sternberg, 1996). An interregional comparison of the number of research-intensive industries in the West German agglomeration areas in 1996 shows the sectoral specialisation in innovations in the Stuttgart region. Most of the West German agglomeration areas are characterised by one, or at most two, sectoral focal points in research-intensive industries. Stuttgart, on the other hand, has three state-of-the-art technology areas and is only surpassed by the Munich region. The latter is the only conurbation which has five of the seven research-intensive industry branches.[11] The three R&D-intensive industries in Stuttgart, mechanical engineering, road vehicle construction and electronics, carry exceptionally

Simone Strambach

Table 2.5. Scientist intensity in research-intensive industries in West German agglomeration areas, 1996

Scientist intensity*	Mechanical engineering %	Vehicle construction %	Electronics %
Stuttgart region	8.1	8.3	15.6
Munich region	9.9	6.8	21.8
Agglomeration areas	7.3	4.7	12.2

Note: * Share of natural scientists and engineers in total employment in manufacturing industry.
Source: NIW/ZEW, 1998, p. 31 (adjusted).

heavy weight and Stuttgart is the leading region for road vehicle construction in West Germany (cf. NIW/ZEW, 1998).

The scientist intensity indicator (the share of natural scientists and engineers in total employment in manufacturing) explains Stuttgart's innovation potential in the industrial clusters (see Table 2.5). The proportion of scientists in road vehicle construction in the Stuttgart region is higher than in the Munich region and clearly above the average of the German population centres. The proportions of scientists in the other two sectors in Stuttgart, mechanical engineering and electronics, are above the federal average.

The patent applications output indicator allows conclusions to be drawn about the innovation orientation of the economy and firms of the Stuttgart region. The international criterion for innovation applies to a patent application and this criterion requires the innovation to be at a high level. Studies of patent intensity in Germany show that Baden-Württemberg, with 98 patents per 100,000 population, had the most applications of all states in 1997, i.e. well above the national average of 55 patent applications. Approximately 36 per cent of the applications in Baden-Württemberg were in the Stuttgart region. The fact that over 81 per cent of the patent applications in the Stuttgart labour market region are produced by the economy clearly indicates the importance of applied industrial research there (Greif, 1998). The patent analysis shows that, compared both to Germany and to the world as a whole, the Stuttgart region specialises in innovations in the technical areas vehicle construction, mechanical engineering – especially motors, turbines and transport – and electronics. The patent applications in Baden-Württemberg also show the concentration of the firms in the individual technical areas (see Table 2.6).

It is evident that the chief actors among the firms are located in the Stuttgart region.[12]

- In electro-technology the dominant position of Robert Bosch GmbH in the sub-field electricity was evident. It and its subsidiary ANT–Nachrichtentechnik made around 23 per cent of the patent applications in 1992.

70

Table 2.6. Patent applications, 1997, according to technical area in the Stuttgart region

Technical areas of patent applications	Stuttgart region %	National average %
Vehicles, ships, aircraft	17.7	8.8
Motors, turbines, transport	12.4	5.1
Electronics	9.6	8.3
Measuring, testing, optics	7.6	7.6
General mechanical engineering	5.8	5.8

Source: Greif (1998, p. 77), adjusted.

- In the telecommunications field the group of three firms – SEL/Alcatel, Robert Bosch GmbH and Daimler-Benz AG (now Daimler-Chrysler) – led the patent applications.

- In the computing area the IBM subsidiary in the Stuttgart region carried out most of its own research. The parent firm in the USA made a lot of the applications but the inventors were residents of Baden-Württemberg.

- In the semiconductor field, the Daimler-Benz subsidiary Telefunken and Robert Bosch GmbH made applications as did the research establishments of the Frauenhofer Gesellschaft, the Institut für Mikroelektronic in Stuttgart and the Max-Planck-Gesellschaft.

The biggest patent applicants in the Stuttgart labour market region are the firms Robert Bosch GmbH (with 1,508 patent applications in 1997) and DaimlerChrysler AG (with 683 patents) in 1997). These two firms are very important not only for the technological innovations in the Stuttgart region and in Baden-Württemberg, but also for Germany as a whole. In terms of patent applications, Robert Bosch GmbH has second place in Germany and DaimlerChrysler fifth place (Greif, 1998). More than half of the 28 largest firms applying for patents in the region are located outside Stuttgart. This spatial distribution indicates the importance of the surrounding districts for the city of Stuttgart with respect to innovations.

It can be concluded that the Stuttgart region has a top position in research and technology-intensive industrial branches both in Baden-Württemberg and in an interregional comparison of the German agglomeration areas. The sectoral specialisation of innovations in the three dominant core industrial sectors, the highly skilled human resources, and the research commitment of the firms are significant comparative innovation advantages.

Institutional Environment: A Crucial but Hidden Factor in Innovativeness and Competitiveness

Evolutionary development is a feature of innovative clusters. Porter (1996, 1999) emphasises that the formation of clusters and their growth can be

Simone Strambach

supported by specialised infrastructures and institutions. In particular institutions, which are concerned with knowledge creation and knowledge diffusion, are crucial for sustaining industrial competitiveness. From the following analysis of the structure of the institutional set-up in the Stuttgart region, it can be seen that four dimensions of the institutional environment determine the industrial technology and science-based innovation profile of the regional economy.

1. The *concentrated regional research infrastructure*; in addition to eighteen universities and applied science universities and two technically oriented universities in the region, there are a large number of scientific-technological institutes and establishments in and around Stuttgart whose fields of activity focus on applied research. The research scene contains two Max Planck Institutes, six Institutes of the Frauenhofer Gesellschaft, industrial research by the municipality, the Akademie für Technikfolgen-abschätzung (Academy for Technology Assessment), the research centre of the Deutsche Forschungsanstalt für Luft- und Raumtechnik (German Air and Space Technology Research Institute), the universities' contractual research establishments and a technology centre.

It is not just the concentration of regional research institutions that is important for creating the comparative innovative advantages of the industry sector. Another important element is the technology, natural science and engineering orientation of the scientific system in the Stuttgart region, which, compared to other regions in Germany, is exceptional. The *specialisation profile of the scientific system* corresponds to a very large extent to the industrial technical and technological fields of the R&D-intensive industry branches. The science system produces innovative basic and applied knowledge, which is relevant for the industrial sectors of the region. In this way synergy effects and numerous overlapping areas and interfaces between the public research capacities and those of the business firms are established which are necessary for the reciprocal learning and interaction processes. The fact that the universities make use of external funds is an indication of the interdependence between the science system and the economic system. Not only do the two universities in Stuttgart have the biggest expenditures on R&D in Baden-Württemberg relative to the number of students, the University of Stuttgart also receives a far greater amount of external funds than any other university in the state. Engineering sciences get 86 per cent of the external financing given to the different faculties. The engineering sciences faculty at the University of Stuttgart received DM170 million in external funds in 1996, by far the largest amount in Baden-Württemberg. It can be concluded that, because the suppliers of the external funds include large business firms, collective learning processes between the actors in the economic and science systems are involved.

2. The *occupational training and further education systems*, which guarantee diversified quality production by the highly qualified profes-

72

sional workforce, are a strength of the German innovation system. Overlapping, interconnected qualification structures of skilled workers, technicians and engineers have been built up by the prevailing dual training system which ensures the transfer of technology-oriented knowledge and technical capabilities to the production process (Naschold, 1996).

Although there are no serious regional disparities in the quality standard of the occupational training and further education systems in Germany, it is nevertheless possible to identify a region-specific profile of semi-public and private suppliers of education in Stuttgart. The supply is directed towards the industrial base and the requirements of the large and medium-sized firms in the manufacturing sector of the region. The education centre of the Engineering Association of Württemberg provides an example here. It is the oldest education centre of the Association of German Engineers – VDI – and was established in 1946. Between 20,000 and 30,000 participants attend seminars and lectures at the centre each year. The clientele of the public or semi-public suppliers of technical education are usually self-employed engineers and employees of industrial firms. The connection between the large industrial firms and the institutions is a close one so that the education suppliers are quickly informed of the firms' qualification requirements. This learning process takes different forms. Executives and qualified employees of the industrial firms give lectures or act as instructors and tutors at the seminars. Interdisciplinary seminars are set up for specialised innovative fields of knowledge by bringing together the expertise of practitioners and scientists.

Another special feature of the region is the *Berufsakademie* – BA (Academy for Vocational Training) which was set up in 1974 on the initiative of companies in Stuttgart initially as a model project. In contrast to university studies, the goal of the *Berufsakademie* is to supplement the professional scientific qualifications of the students with practice-oriented vocational training. This is achieved by offering courses of study alternately in the academy and the firm. Setting up the courses of study required close co-operation between the state, which subsidises the academy, and industry, which makes training places available. Because the project proved so successful, the *Berufsakademie* was made a regular establishment in 1992. It has been providing an alternative to university study since 1995, although only in Baden-Württemberg. In this state the diploma awarded by the BA has the same value as a degree from a technical university and thus counts as the completion of tertiary education. The *Berufsakademie* in Baden-Württemberg thus has a special status as, in the other states that have taken over this model, the diploma awarded by the BA only counts as the completion of secondary education. At present over 4,000 firms are participating in the vocational training of students, most of them in the Stuttgart area. This is a further indication of the companies' engagement in the training and further education of the workforce. Like the dual system in the secondary area, the institution of the *Berufsakademie* in the tertiary area ensures that the specific knowledge needs of the firms and the new skill requirements of the workforce are quickly integrated with vocational training. The close links between the provision of theoretical knowledge and the direct process of learning on the job can have only beneficial effects as a catalyst for innovation.

3. The decentrally organised knowledge and technology transfer structure for SMEs, which is a prominent example in the *Green Book for Innovation*. There is a long tradition of sponsoring innovativeness among SMEs in the regional innovation system of Baden-Württemberg. In the 1970s the regional supply of intermediary consulting services was already being developed. The head offices of the most important intermediary institutions like the Chambers of Handicrafts, the Chambers of Commerce and Industry (IHKs), the German Rationalisation Board (RKW) and the headquarters of the Steinbeis Foundation for Economic Development, became concentrated in the Stuttgart region as the political and economic centre of the state. The Stuttgart region has 35 Steinbeis transfer centres, the greatest concentration of these centres. From an evolutionary point of view, the support structures have made a contribution to the development of competitiveness of the SMEs in the past years.

4. The specific labour market institutions and regulations, which are expressed in the stable co-operative employer–employee relationships and which are characteristic for the national innovation system in Germany. They promote the investment in human capital by the firms.

To summarise, the analysis shows that the institutional set-up, the region-specific profile of semi-public and private suppliers of training and education, the regional research infrastructure and the specialisation profile of the scientific system correspond in no small way to the industrial technical and technological knowledge fields of the R&D-intensive industry clusters. From a dynamic point of view, it can be said that the co-evolution of a cluster specific infrastructure in the region is a result of past interaction processes between firms, political actors, public and semi-public institutions.

Innovative Clusters and Innovation Processes in the Stuttgart Region: Empirical Results

Selection of the Sample

Databanks of innovation prizewinners were used to ensure that the firms in the sample were innovative ones. The first source for the selection of the sample of firms were the databanks of the European innovation programme BRITE-EuRamIII. Some 57 per cent of the Baden-Württemberg firms listed in the BRITE awards are located in the Stuttgart region. Here,

Table 2.7. Innovation award winners in the Stuttgart region

Awards	Numbers	Percentage of sample
Brite-EuRamIII	12	37.5
Top 100 Baden-Württemberg	8	25.0
Rudolf Eberle Prize	5	15.6
Adalbert Seifriz Prize	3	9.4
Patent applicants	4	12.5
Total N	32	100.0

Source: Own survey.

Stuttgart's strong position in the state in terms of innovative activities and the importance of the global players in the region are also evident. Some 74 per cent of the winners located in the Stuttgart region are departments and subsidiaries of DaimlerChrysler and Bosch; only 12 of them are independent firms. It was not possible to obtain a sufficiently large sample from the BRITE award winners so local databanks were also used for this purpose. These provide lists of firms that have won the Rudolf Eberle Prize or the Adalbert Seifriz Prize, firms that are among the 28 largest patent applicants in the Stuttgart region, and firms in the Baden-Württemberg Top 100 (see Table 2.7).[13]

Innovation Types and Innovation Characteristics

Most of the innovations introduced (up to two-thirds) are product innovations (see Table 2.8). The small proportion of process innovations can be explained by the fact that the study concentrates on technological

Table 2.8. Innovation type and novelty ranking of the innovations introduced

Innovation type	Total sample		Of which:		
	N	%	small firms < 20 empl. (%)	medium firms 20–499 empl. (%)	large firms ≥ 500 empl. (%)
Product innovation	21	65.6	9.3	31.3	25.0
Process innovation	11	34.4	6.2	9.3	18.8
Innovation novelty					
New to the world	20	62.5	9.4	15.6	37.5
New to this country	3	9.3	3.1	6.2	–
New to your sector	7	21.9	3.1	15.6	3.2
New to your firm	2	6.3	–	3.2	3.1
Total N	32	100.0	15.6	40.6	43.8

Source: Own survey.

innovation by industrial firms. Services firms, whose innovative behaviour differs considerably from that of the firms in manufacturing industry, were not represented in the study sample. With regard to the novelty of the innovations, 63 per cent of the firms said that they were world firsts. Almost 22 per cent said that they were new for the sector. The categories 'new for Germany' or 'new for the firm' were insignificant.

These results emphasise the international focus of the firms and correspond with the export orientation of the industrial sector in the Stuttgart region. They also support the regional patent analysis conclusion that the innovations made in the Stuttgart region are of a very high standard. The requirements in terms of specialised technological competences and accumulated experience for the development of the innovations are considerable, as can be seen from the development time and the expected lifetimes of the innovations. Almost every second firm (47 per cent) envisaged a lifespan for the innovations of between five and ten years. A quarter of the firms even expected a lifetime of more than ten years (see Table 2.9). None of the firms thought that the innovation would have a life of less than one year, or of only two to three years.

Correspondingly, the development time needed is also relatively long. A quarter of the innovations required a development time of between three and five years. It took between five and ten years for almost 10 per cent of the innovations to be ready. Included among them were innovation projects of a firm in the electronics branch which required a development time of ten years, and a product innovation which took another three years before it was ready to go into production. It can be seen that the products of high technology have a very long development time and a relatively long time is needed before they are ready to be put on the market. This means a high level of uncertainty for the firms because the time at which the product is put on the market has a decisive influence on the potential sales of the innovation.

These kinds of research activities and resources mostly involved large companies with more than 5,000 employees engaged in R&D. They were about 10 per cent of the firms in the random sample. However, half of the

Table 2.9. Expected lifetime of the innovations introduced

Lifetime of the innovation	N	%
Less than 1 year	0	–
1 to 2 years	2	6.3
2 to 3 years	0	–
3 to 5 years	7	21.9
5 to 10 years	15	46.9
More than 10 years	8	25.0
Total N	32	100.0

Source: Own survey.

Table 2.10. Number of employees and principal economic activity of the firms surveyed

Principal economic activity	N	Total %	Small firms < 20 empl. (%)	Medium firms 20–499 empl. (%)	Large firms ≥ 500 empl. (%)
Pulp, paper, paper products	1	3.1	–	3.1	–
Construction	2	6.2	3.1	3.1	–
Fabricated metal products	2	6.3	–	–	6.3
Machinery n.e.c.	11	34.4	–	15.6	18.8
Electrical machinery	7	21.9	3.1	3.2	15.6
Computer services	5	15.6	3.1	9.4	3.1
Architectural, engineering	4	12.5	6.3	6.2	–
Total N	32		15.6	40.6	43.8

Source: Own survey.

innovative firms employed fewer than twenty people in R&D (see Table 2.10). This is an indication of the innovative ability of the medium-sized industrial firms in the region that has already been described.

For almost 60 per cent of the firms, customer requirements and the changed market demands were the main reasons for developing innovations. The customers were said to be by far the most important co-operation partners, know-how was shared with them and they were brought in as advisers. Close contact with the customers is also particularly important for reducing uncertainty in the innovation process. This shows the firms' orientation towards the individual customer and their high degree of specialisation, both of which are very important for the development of innovations and thus for the competitiveness of the firms.

The firms see technical feasibility as the main risk associated with the development of innovations. The financial risks are said to be only secondary. The competitive strength of the firms in the Stuttgart region is also evident from the fact that the costs of the innovations are almost entirely paid for out of the firms' own retained profits. Other financial sources or the use of special loans are unimportant for covering costs. Because the small amount of risk capital is characteristic not only of the regional innovation system of Baden-Württemberg, but also of the national one, the firms' own financial strength has been, and still is, a necessary prerequisite for the development of innovations.

The firms attempt to protect their innovations from competitors primarily through their temporal lead. Some 88 per cent of the firms see the time factor as the best protection for their innovations. Patent applications to secure property rights in the innovation take second place (66 per cent). Registered brand names and trade marks, which in Germany are only relevant for non-technical innovations, are unimportant. Patents have a relatively high value for the kind of technological innovations of industrial firms that are examined here. This was already obvious from the large number of patent applications in the Stuttgart region and is partly the result of the fact that the products of high technologies have a relatively long life-cycle. In other areas of innovation, for example with service firms in the software branch, patents play a minor role because the length of some of the innovation cycles of the product or process innovations is only about six months. However, even the industrial firms in the survey consider that innovations can no longer be protected by complexity of the product design or by ensuring that they are kept secret. These results show that the rapid changes in technologies and the global production of information and knowledge are making the innovation cycle even shorter. What counts is the time to market – speed is what ensures the benefits from the innovations for the longest time.

Human Capital, Technological Qualifications and Tacit Knowledge: The Basis of Comparative Innovative Advantages

For developing innovations, the firms in the Stuttgart region rely mainly on their own permanent staff and their knowledge and experience. This is evident from the fact that hardly any new staff were recruited for the innovations. No one new was employed in finance, marketing, management or training. These areas of knowledge generally appear to be quite unimportant for the technological innovations because these are so highly specialised. The most important qualifications and competences for the innovations are in the technological areas and in production processes. The employees who participate in the development of innovations are almost entirely technological experts, followed by experts in production processes (see Table 2.11). For example, in 69 per cent of the firms,

Table 2.11. Share of new employees for the innovations in selected fields of knowledge

Field of knowledge	0%	1–25%	26–50%	51–75%	76–100%	N
Finance	100	–	–	–	–	32
Marketing	100	–	–	–	–	32
Management	100	–	–	–	–	32
Training/Personnel	100	–	–	–	–	32
Technology	90.6	6.3	–	3.1	–	32
Production process	96.9	3.1	–	–	–	32

Source: Own survey.

between 76 per cent and 100 per cent of the employees involved were experts in the technological area. These people are also professionally very highly qualified as can be seen from the large proportion of graduates, especially in technological fields. Indeed, new employees are hardly ever used in the knowledge areas relevant to the innovations. The hiring of new employees for development activities is very unusual.

Technological input from external suppliers also plays a subordinate role for the development of innovations. One-third of the firms give an external technological input of less than 25 per cent and no firms use an external input of more than 50 per cent for the development of innovations. Co-operation partners are also considered to be relatively unimportant for innovation. For almost half the firms, customers make up the only groups, which, as already mentioned, are valued highly as co-operation partners. Two-thirds of the firms consider the information flows within the firm itself to be the most important information source for innovation, followed, after a long gap, by books, technical journals, universities and technical universities.

The firms in the Stuttgart region do most of their research and development in house and, for this purpose, mainly invest in the human capital of their own employees. This can also be seen from the fact that, in order to overcome the main risk of technical feasibility, the firms say that, apart from developing prototypes, using their own employees is their main way of reducing uncertainty and ensuring that research and development are successful. These employees, their experience, potential, and tacit knowledge are the most important resources for creating specialised technological innovations. These results indicate the relatively stable co-operative labour relations of employers and employees which are characteristic of both Baden-Württemberg's regional innovation system and the national system. They underline the interdependent relationship between the innovation potential of the firms and their socio-economic embeddedness. In contrast to the labour market institutions and the organisation of the innovation systems in the UK or the USA, which promote the transmission of knowledge between firms through the exchange of employees, the comparatively stable employer–employee relationships in the German system promote the firm internal accumulation of experiential knowledge and competences.

How Relevant is Local Embeddedness for the Innovative Firms at the End of the 1990s?

Local embeddedness of the firms is one possible explanatory factor for the fact that innovative activities are clustered in regions. Attempts to explain this embeddedness empirically often examine the locational factors of the area and the local co-operation, supplier, and customer relationships that exist there.

Simone Strambach

Table 2.12. Importance of external persons and institutions as collaborators and as sources of information for innovations

Importance of external collaborators	Not important (%)	Moderately important (%)	Very important (%)	Mean score*
Clients or customers	40.6	12.5	46.9	3.03
Universities or other HEIs	62.5	12.5	25.1	2.16
Suppliers	59.4	25.0	15.6	2.16
Other firms within the group	71.9	9.4	18.8	1.84
Research associations, independent research and technology organisations	90.6	6.3	3.1	1.28
Competitors	96.8	–	3.2	1.26
Private non-profit organisations	90.6	9.3	–	1.25
Consultancy services	90.6	9.3	–	1.22
Government research establishment	96.9	3.1	–	1.16
Importance of external sources of information				
Universities or other HEIs	65.5	–	34.4	2.16
Other firms within the group	65.6	12.5	21.9	2.03
Consultancy firms	81.3	12.5	6.3	1.53
Private non-profit research institutes	84.4	9.4	6.3	1.44
Government research establishments	87.5	6.3	6.3	1.41
Trade associations	93.8	6.3	–	1.13
Research and technology associations	93.8	6.3	–	1.13

Note: * Mean score on a scale from 1 (least important) to 5 (most important).
Source: Own survey.

The empirical results show little evidence for intensive and locally confined co-operation relationships between the firms in the Stuttgart region (see Table 2.12). Only the customers are estimated by 47 per cent of the enterprises as important co-operation partners, although these are not primarily resident in the local area. Just 3 per cent of the enterprises have the major part (over 76 per cent) of its main clients for innovation in the local market. No co-operative relationships with local research and development organisations or other public and private consulting services were indicated as being important. According to the innovative firms these institutions are not relevant external sources of information for the development of highly specialised innovations. Only one-third of the firms ranked the universities and the applied science universities as important external

Table 2.13. Importance of location factors – reasons for location of innovative firms in the Stuttgart region

Factors*	Factor description	Mean score°
Factor 4	Professional labour market	3.69
	Availability of professional experts to recruit	3.69
Factor 2	Regional Transportation System	3.53
	Good access to national road network	3.97
	Good access to major airport	3.88
	Good rail connections	2.78
	Low levels of traffic congestion	3.50
Factor 5	Industrial production factors	3.29
	Availability of skilled manual labour	3.42
	Proximity of suppliers	3.38
	Cost of labour	3.06
Factor 6	Local scientific knowledge, and sources of information	2.59
	Proximity of sources of information	2.87
	Contributions from universities	2.31
Factor 1	General and specialised business support, and financial support	1.99
	Access to private general business services	1.94
	Proximity of business services	1.90
	Access to private specialised business services	1.77
	Contributions from TECs	1.72
	Access to financial capital	2.65
Factor 3	Local industrial knowledge and experience	1.64
	Contributions from Business LINKS	1.44
	Local public business support services	1.35
	Presence of friends	1.37
	Presence of ex-colleagues	1.28
	Proximity of collaborators	2.77

Notes: * The share of whole explained variance is 76%.
° Mean score on a scale from 1 (least important) to 5 (most important).
Source: Own survey.

information sources and only a quarter of them think that universities are important collaborators in the innovation process.

The results of the factor analysis (see Table 2.13) on the evaluation of the meaning of the location factors show that both local industrial knowledge (factor 3) and general specialised business (factor 1) are quite unimportant for the enterprises. The evaluation is based on a ranking scale running from 1 not important to 5 very important. The contribution of local public business support services, the access and the proximity to private business services, or local support based on social relationships resulting from the presence of friends and former colleagues were not

Table 2.14. Location of main customers, suppliers, and competitors*

Location	Local (%)	Regional (%)	National (%)	European (%)	USA (%)	Japanese (%)	Pacific Rim (%)
Customers	64.4	43.7	87.5	84.4	71.0	43.7	15.6
Suppliers	83.4	45.8	62.5	75.0	25.0	16.7	16.7
Competitors	28.1	15.6	50.0	37.5	31.3	25.0	3.1

Note: * All positive replies.
Source: Own survey.

considered to be significant. The local scientific knowledge of universities (factor 6), too, is seen as only moderately important (2.59).

Absolutely essential for the successful development of the enterprises' innovations in Stuttgart is the user–producer interaction (Lundvall, 1988) and the learning processes connected with it. The location of the customers for whom the innovations are developed show that both local clients and customers in international markets are the targets for innovations (see Table 2.14). The main markets for the innovations are those in Germany and Europe, followed by the US and Japanese markets and the regional market. Around 64 per cent of the firms also have customers in the region, but the regional market has become less important relative to international markets, as can be seen from the fact that the share of customers in international markets is often 20 percentage points higher. Looking at the supplying enterprises' locations for innovations, it is obvious that these are not limited to the local markets. The majority of the innovative companies (83 per cent) have supplier relationships within the Stuttgart region and 75 per cent of the enterprises also function as suppliers within Europe.

The question here is, how can this paradox be explained? On the one hand, Stuttgart has for a long time been considered to be one of the most innovative regions in Europe, on the other hand, the innovative firms considered the existing institutional environment and the support structures of the region to be relatively unimportant for them directly. There is little evidence for the importance of the local embeddedness of the local firms in terms of the close relationships with other local firms in the innovation process.

It can be seen from the existing customer and supplier linkages in Stuttgart that the innovations of the enterprises are sold in many different markets and therefore that local, national and international linkage are increasingly being used simultaneously. The empirical results of the interviews provide a snapshot of the innovation processes of the enterprises in Stuttgart at the end of the 1990s. The main features of the current economic situation include increasing internationalisation of customers, acceleration of change in the globalisation process through market liberalisation and deregulation, through more complex and more expensive technologies, and increasing diffusion of information and knowledge. The emerging knowledge economy, the success and the competitiveness of innovative enterprises seem to be less dependent on tight local linkages to other companies than on whether the enterprises succeed in adapting themselves flexibly to the needs of the key customers distributed over the different national and international markets. The results point out that, with the innovation cycles getting shorter, it becomes more important to use local, national and international input flexibly in the innovation process. Urban infrastructure services, which support the information and communication processes of the firms and enable them to have quick access to the international markets and customers, have now become necessary and almost self-evident, conditions that the metropolitan areas must offer the innovative firms. This can be seen from the fact that both the innovative enterprises in Stuttgart and the companies in London have evaluated the transport system, especially the airport, as an essential location factor in those cities (see Table 2.13 (factor 2); Simmie and Sennett, 1999).

To conclude from the survey results that, in the globalisation process, local environment and localised capabilities are no longer important for the innovative enterprises in Stuttgart is not absolutely correct. The territorial embeddedness of firms is a complex phenomenon and cannot be equated with close local linkages. Localised input–output relations or traded interdependencies (Dosi, 1988; Storper, 1995) are only one part of region-specific assets. Innovative clusters develop over the years and these dynamic developments cannot be grasped by a static research design. However, from an evolutionary point of view, there are some indicators for the localised capabilities and the local embeddedness of the innovative firms.

Examining the structures of the firms shows that the branch and firm size structures of the innovation prizewinners surveyed reflect the economic structures of the industrial clusters in the region. The majority are medium-sized firms in the mechanical engineering and electrical branches, only a minority are large firms. The long-term competitiveness of the industrial firms and their roots in the region are evident, among other things, from the fact that more than half of the innovation prizewinners are old, well-established firms (see Table 2.15). These were founded before 1950, most of them even before the Second World War. The oldest of the firms surveyed was founded in 1880. The majority of the SMEs are older firms in traditional industry sectors rather than newly established firms in innovative segments like biotechnology.

Nevertheless, they are able to compete successfully with high quality innovations in international markets, as the large proportion of innovations that are new to the world showed. The firms compete with their innovations in international markets and most of them must survive against competition in various regions simultaneously (see Table 2.15). Competition from the Stuttgart region or from Baden-Württemberg is not very relevant.

Some 72 per cent of the firms say that they have no competitors in the region and over 84 per cent of them have no competitors for their

Table 2.15. Year of establishment of the firms surveyed

Year firm was started	N	%
Before 1950	16	50.0
1951–1960	–	–
1961–1970	4	12.5
1971–1980	3	9.4
1981–1990	9	28.1
After 1991	–	–
Total N	32	100.0

Source: Own survey.

innovations in Baden-Württemberg. Competition primarily comes from all over Germany, from Europe, or from the USA. A quarter of the firms also face competition from Japan.

It is evident from the assessments made of the locational factors in Stuttgart that the competitive advantages of the innovative firms increasingly result from the availability of professional experts (factor 4) and the existing industrial production factors (factor 5) such as the skilled manual labour, the proximity of suppliers and the cost of labour in the metropolitan region. The results show that the specific local knowledge base represents a significant resource for the companies. The institutional analysis (cf. Chapter 1) has shown that the region-specific profile of the supporting institutional environment that promoted the accumulation of knowledge largely corresponds with the industrial technical and technological knowledge fields of the R&D-intensive industry clusters. Overlapping, interconnected qualification structures have been built up and this ensures the transfer of technology-oriented knowledge and technical capabilities to the production process. The established communication channels between the industrial firms and the semi-public training institutions ensure that the education suppliers are quickly informed about the firms' qualification requirements. In this manner, numerous overlapping areas and interfaces have come into existence, which create many opportunities for knowledge spill-overs and synergy effects between the different actors in the innovation system.

The nature of the local knowledge base means that it can be considered as a collective asset, consisting mostly of tacit knowledge and, as Storper (1995) points out, it is an intangible aspect of a territorial or regional economy that underlies innovative, flexible agglomerations. The basis of the continuing innovative and competitive capacity of the firms is the highly skilled human capital and the technological skills potential. Although it is not easy to validate this empirically, from a systems perspective the regional institutional arrangements make an important, but indirect, contribution to the provision and maintenance of the necessary local knowledge and skills potential.

The Current Restructuring Process: Redefining Competitiveness of an Industrial Region

At the start of the 1990s the world recession was also affecting Baden-Württemberg and the Stuttgart region. This crisis situation shows that, during global changes a given top position in technological fields is no guarantee for the future competitiveness of the region. Even the competitive advantages of the industrial clusters that have grown up over the years can collapse when changes in the environment are extreme. This decline also shows that a particular institutional set-up cannot promote innovative developments permanently because of the path dependence of learning processes and the resulting tendency towards rigidity. The importance of 'untraded interdependencies' in securing learning and innovation advantage are accentuated in interregional competition (Asheim and Dunford, 1997). Storper (1995, 1997) considers the region as a key necessary element in the 'supply architecture' for learning and innovation. A part of the explanation for the central role of regions is, in his opinion, in its 'untraded interdependencies' (like the labour market, regional conventions, norms and values, public and semi-public institutions) which attach to the process of economic and organisational learning and co-ordination. Looked at dynamically, it can be observed that the innovative advantages resulting from untraded independencies are partly limited by the co-evolution of core rigidities in the Stuttgart region.[14]

The political, economic and scientific actors' recognition of the crisis at the start of the 1990s was the starting point for a variety of initiatives and measures directed towards restoring and promoting regional competitiveness. No doubts have been expressed about the importance of institutional change and institutional learning in the recent discussions about the learning economy (Lundvall and Johnson, 1994). However, the question of how new innovation and co-operation networks and a new collective stock of knowledge can be developed within a well-established industrial and institutional structure is still largely an open one. Gregersen and Johnson (1997, p. 482) pointed out that most socio-economic processes couldn't be designed, planned and implemented in terms of a one-dimensional rationality. This is because institutions, as products of collective learning processes, are not just the intended result of the strategies of public and private actors but are, to different degrees, not intended at all (see, for example, Dosi, 1988).

In the following, first, the rigidities evident in the Stuttgart region are described and, second, the measures and initiatives of the current restructuring processes, aimed at tapping the innovational potential available through the organisation of collective communication and learning processes at the regional level, are shown.

85

Simone Strambach

Loss of Competitiveness during the Globalisation Process in the 1990s

At the start of the 1990s the industrial strengths of the region began to seem like weaknesses. Saturation trends and intensified international competition in the predominant investment goods branches, particularly from the export-oriented threshold countries in South East Asia, resulted in the loss of their traditional market shares. The characteristic key industries of the Stuttgart region were caught up in a cyclical and structural crisis that caused a large fall in employment in the export-intensive manufacturing branches. The structural changes led to a loss of 168,117 jobs (4.3 per cent) in Baden-Württemberg between 1991 and 1995. The Stuttgart region was particularly badly hit by the crisis. Almost half of the state's job losses occurred here. Between 1992 and 1995 almost 97,000 jobs were lost (−8.5 per cent). In the mechanical engineering, vehicle construction and electrical engineering branches alone 56,000 jobs were lost.

The rigidities in the Stuttgart region, which had become established over the years and which caused lock-in effects, showed up as a result of the crisis and the economic collapse at the start of the 1990s. Reinforcing elements in three areas were recognised:

- A functional lock-in: the strong linkages between the three core branches in the two industrial clusters that are very important for the Stuttgart region meant that the crisis in these industry sectors affected the whole region. The effects were even more widespread – because Stuttgart is the economic centre of Baden-Württemberg the collapse of these core sectors had negative effects for the whole state (Bracyk *et al.*, 1996; Schienstock, 1997).

- A political lock-in: political interventions were primarily oriented towards strengthening the industrial core sectors. Comprehensive structures and networks of politics, science and the economy have long since been established. These are tailored to particular technological fields and branches of industry and innovative developments in other branches are impeded. The weak position in the major new key technologies and industry fields, like microelectronics, in sections of information technology, in important new materials, and in biotechnology is seen as the main deficiency (cf. Staatsministerium Baden-Württemberg, 1993; Wirtschaftsministerium Baden-Württemberg, 1996).

- A cognitive lock-in: the correspondence between the production and innovation profiles shows that it was primarily the orientation towards industry and technological innovation that directed the learning processes in the Stuttgart region for many years. While there were numerous attempts made to improve technological competitiveness, hardly any attention was paid to organisational and services innovations. Empirical studies therefore indicate that there are serious deficiencies in these areas of knowledge.

The developments in the Stuttgart region at the start of the 1990s have shown that, in the current process of globalisation, deciding whether the economic structure indicators at the firm and regional levels are strong or weak is becoming more and more dubious and misleading. A major reason for this is that the global structural changes and significant changes in the innovation processes are tightly interwoven. In the knowledge economy, knowledge is increasingly becoming a strategic resource for the creation of value while, at the same time, the international generation of knowledge and the networking opportunities of the information and communication technologies are reducing the half-life value of the knowledge. This not only means that the existing comparative advantages of the industrial clusters in particular specialised technological fields of knowledge are being more rapidly undermined, it also means that the supporting institutional environment which promoted the accumulation of knowledge is becoming less important for the support of firms' innovativeness and competitiveness. Consideration of regional competitiveness shows clearly that redefining competitiveness for the Stuttgart region does not only involve reconstructing the present regional innovation profile, which, as before, is determined by the 'mature' industrial clusters, and promoting the development of new fields of technology. The additional challenge is to simultaneously stimulate the collective learning processes that will bring about the parallel changes in the diversified institutional scene. Here, it is not only necessary to introduce these innovative collective learning processes at the firm level, it is also necessary to promote organisational learning at the system level of the Stuttgart region.

New Institution-Building at the Strategic Policy Level in the Region and the State Baden-Württemberg

The government of Baden-Württemberg has taken the leading role in the present restructuring process in the Stuttgart region. While it is true that this government had in the past a significant influence on the developments in the state's key region, the strategies since the middle of the 1990s have been based on a more complete understanding of innovation and are thus not like past initiatives, which mainly focused on technology transfer. Another difference is that the measures are no longer mostly implemented from the top down, they are now directed towards promoting bottom-up initiatives and self-organising processes.

The convening of the future-oriented commission 'Wirtschaft 2000' (Economy 2000) provided the starting point for the new positioning. Actors with competences and expertise in economy, science, politics, and society from all over Germany were brought together in this committee. The goal of the 'future commission' is to identify the innovation deficit in the economic structure of Baden-Württemberg and the Stuttgart region and work out recommendations for action by the state government. The present regional adjustment process is based on the committee's suggestion that a double strategy, which combines restructuring the 'mature industry clusters' with promoting new technology fields, should be used.

Two new institutions were set up to support the restructuring process at the start of the 1990s:

1. The *Akademie für Technikfolgenabschätzung Baden-Württemberg* (Academy for Technological Assessment) situated in Stuttgart. This scientific institute is financed by the state and is composed of social scientists as well as natural scientists and engineers. The reason for the interdisciplinary nature of the academy is to enable greater account to be taken of the social relationships in studying and evaluating innovations and technologies, something that tended to be neglected in the past. In addition, the academy has the explicit task of initiating public discussion on the results of technology, its opportunities and risks, for example, by setting up and moderating topics for discussion and project-specific networks. Because the academy, as a scientific institution, is not answerable to any business interests, it should be within its competence to bring together different economic and social interest groups for particular projects. Part of its function is to open up previously closed networks and to get new communication and learning processes started, which in turn can stimulate innovation potential.

2. In 1994 the Innovation Council was set up as an institution by the Baden-Württemberg government. The Innovation Council brings together members from leading firms, from science, and from technology transfer. The function of this institution is to monitor the technological and economic development procedures and to advise the state government directly about the strategic directions of the research, technology and economic policies, about the framework conditions relevant to innovation, and about public relations activities targeted towards improving the climate for innovation. By carrying out its task of indicating the co-ordination needed in the research, technology, and economic policies, the council will be able to create new linkages, communications, and exchanges between previously separated policy areas.

These two institutions should help to loosen the rigidities and thus contribute to the diffusion of the currently available knowledge through new ways of interaction besides the traditional channels of communication and interaction.

Initiating Institutional Change at the Territorial Level: The Establishment of the Stuttgart Region Association to Support and Maintain Competitiveness

The establishment of the 'Stuttgart Region' Association as an inter-municipal decision-making body with legislative responsibilities and its own regional parliament by the government of Baden-Württemberg in Spring 1994 is clearly an important institutional innovation. This organisational innovation provides an institutional framework in which the political and administrative activities for the region as a territorial entity can be carried out. Previously, this had not been possible because the metropolitan region of Stuttgart consisted of 179 independent municipalities, which, although combined into five administrative districts, under the German system of regional organisation had sovereignty for planning at the local level. With the growing complexity of the areas of responsibility for economy, settlement, transport, and environment that occurred in all the agglomeration areas, problem-solving approaches were colliding more and more frequently with the extremely fragmented policy and administration structures. General approaches to solving problems frequently foundered at the municipal borders or required lengthy communication and negotiating processes. Intraregional competition between the municipalities often resulted in zero sum games for the region as a whole and thus to locational disadvantage.

The establishment of 'Region Stuttgart' as a territorial association is an institutional innovation that is still unique in Germany. From the point of view of organisational learning, the advantage of this institutional change is that it enables communication and decision-making processes to be speeded up, thus enhancing the adjustment and reaction capabilities of the regional system. Moreover, problems of the regional development can generally be targeted and completely solved. The new institutional framework can, of course, not get rid of intraregional competition completely, but it can limit it. The external 'pressure' for the municipal actors to co-operate can, from a long-term perspective, have beneficial effects for the emergence of a common regional consciousness. To this extent, it can be assumed that there will be positive effects for regional competitiveness associated with this institutional change.

Initiating New Industrial Clusters: Mobilisation of Self-organising Processes to Link and Utilise Regional Competences

The structural innovation deficits that were found in the Stuttgart region have resulted in a large number of initiatives and measures being taken which are directed towards building up innovation networks and promoting the establishment of clusters in the new fields of technology like microelectronics, in some areas of information technology, and in cross-sectoral biotechnology. The following points are important with respect to how collective learning at the regional level can be initiated so as to develop new industrial clusters.

- The initiatives focus on bringing together the different competences, abilities, and experiences that have become established in the various branches and in different fields of technology. The starting point for building up innovative clusters is the existing regional stock of knowledge of the firms. The potential innovation networks, however, do not target the territorial aspects.

- The measures thus not only focus on linking the firms' stocks of know-how but, at the same time, they try to integrate competences from various social areas (education, science, politics, and the public) and to tie them together in specific projects with the firms. This has the advantage that the non-technical conditions for the transformation of knowledge into innovations are also taken into account. As was evident from the development of the clusters in the region that are already established, their competitiveness can be promoted by a cluster-specific infrastructure in the area of occupational training and further education or by specific regulations. By linking different groups of social actors, the necessary institutional innovations will be promoted in parallel with the technological innovations.

- The regional direction and co-ordination of the decentralised learning processes takes place through leading models like BioRegion, ServiceRegion, or MediaRegion Stuttgart. These models act as catalysts for initiating the interaction processes. Resources are made available through these models, but the actors themselves actually organise the topics and projects. The models thus have an action-oriented and co-ordinating function for the self-organisation processes of the actors at the regional level.

- For example, under the model MediaRegion Stuttgart, initiatives which focus on linking existing competences in the media and communications business area and on boosting innovation networks are tied together. The aim is to bring together the printing and publishing industry, which has a long tradition in the region, the service industries in the areas of advertising, public relations, film and television, and Internet providers and hardware and software firms. The actors themselves will develop joint projects and identify innovative areas of co-operation through regular meetings and workshops. New provision for occupational training and further education has already been created and measures have been developed to improve the conditions for the media and communications sector in the region. Examples here are the setting up of the Venture Capital Fund and consulting establishments especially for the media sector. In addition, working parties have co-operated in developing projects and ideas for multimedia applications.

Whether ultimately permanent competitive innovative clusters will emerge from these various initiatives must for the present remain an open question.

Conclusion

It can be concluded that the innovative potential of the Stuttgart region is determined by sectoral specialisation in R&D-intensive industry branches, by the large proportion of qualified human resources in these branches, and by the large amount of research engaged in the region not only by the global players but also by the small and medium-sized firms. The regional institutional set-up is, an important element, which, from the system point of view, makes a significant, though indirect, contribution to maintaining the technological innovative capability, especially by providing the greatest potential of highly qualified human capital in the technical and technological fields of knowledge. The correspondence between the technology, natural science, and engineering orientation of the knowledge system, the technical and technological fields of the particular industrial branches, and the overlapping and interconnected occupational training and further education structures in the region guarantees the transfer of the technical and technological knowledge to products and production processes. If we look at the situation in the Stuttgart region at the start of the 1990s, another factor that is important for the innovativeness and competitiveness of the region becomes apparent – the capacity to organise learning processes. The reflections about, and interpretations of, this problem situation, and the kind and extent of the measures initiated make it possible to conclude that the ability to organise learning processes, to create new institutions and organisational forms to support the exchange of communication and knowledge in the different economic, political, and social areas, even though difficult to comprehend, can be seen as a further strength of the region.

Notes

1. The author is grateful for the support of Dipl. Geo. Annette D'Lorio in the part of the data collection and the efficient help of Dipl. Geo. Carmen Steinlein with the handling of the data and during the project. The study comes out of a wider project on *Innovative Clusters and the Competitiveness of Cities in the UK and Europe*, co-ordinated by Professor James Simmie and financed by the ESRC.
2. Landeshauptstadt Stuttgart, Statistisches Amt (eds) (1999a).
3. IHK (1998, p. 49).
4. IHK (1996).
5. Braczyk *et al.* (1998), Cooke and Morgan (1994), Sable *et al.* (1987), Schmitz (1992).

6. Schienstock and Steffens (1995) ask quite justifiably whether it would not be more appropriate to divide Baden-Württemberg into different districts for classification purposes. Unfortunately they do not follow up this differentiated approach.
7. For detailed results on the regional level NIW/ZEW (1998). Sternberg (1996) shows the regional concentration of R&D-intensive industry branches for West Germany at the administrative district level.
8. The figures are based on the calculations of the Stifterverband für die Deutsche Wissenschaft, Landeshauptstadt Stuttgart, Statistisches Amt (1999b), Landesregierung (1996).
9. IHK (1996).
10. Here the research expenditures of the global players are assigned not only to the headquarters in Stuttgart but also to all locations where the companies carry out their research.
11. NIW/ZEW (1998).
12. In this study the corporate concentrations were calculated by means of Gini coefficients (see Ifo 1995, p. 68).
13. The Rudolf Eberle Prize was established in 1984 by the Baden-Württemberg State Ministry for Economy, Industry, Medium-Sized Companies and Technology. The ministry awards this innovation prize to SMEs which have had 'commendable success in developing new products and processes or in applying modern technologies to products, production or services'. The Adalbert Seifriz Prize of the Baden-Württemberg Handicrafts Convention is one of the major innovation prizes in Germany. The firms in the Baden-Württemberg Top 100 are distinguished by their high level of innovativeness. Innovations must be reported from both the main activities and the supporting activities.
14. Nelson (1994) provides evidence for the co-evolution of technologies, organisational forms and supporting institutions.

References

Asheim, B. and Dunford, M. (1997) 'Regional futures', *Regional Studies* 31, 5, 445–55.

Brachat-Schwarz, W. and Deckarm, M. (1997) 'Langfristige Bevölkerungsentwicklung in der Region Stuttgart 1871–1994', in W. Gaebe (ed.) *Struktur und Dynamik in der Region Stuttgart*, Stuttgart, Verlag Eugen Ulmer.

Braczyk, H.-J., Cooke, P. and Heidenreich, M. (eds) (1998) *Regional Innovation Systems*, London, UCL Press.

Braczyk, H.-J., Schienstock, G. and Steffensen, B. (1996) 'Die Regionalökonomie Baden-Württembergs – Ursachen und Grenzen des Erfolgs', in H.-J. Braczyk and G. Schienstock (eds) *Kurswechsel in der Industrie*, Stuttgart, Kohlhammer Verlag.

Bundesamt für Bauwesen und Raumordnung (BBR) (1998) *Indikatoren und Karten zur Raumentwicklung*, CD-ROM vol. 1, Bonn, Berichte des BBR.

Cooke, P. and Morgan, K. (1994) 'The regional innovation system in Baden-Württemberg', *International Journal of Technology Management* 9, 3+4, 394–429.

Dosi, G. (1988) 'The nature of the innovative process', in G. Dosi, C. Freeman, R. Nelson, G. Silverberg and L. Soete (eds) *Technical Change and Economic Theory*, London, Pinter.

Edquist, C. (ed.) (1997) *Systems of Innovation: Technologies, Institutions and Organizations*, London, Pinter.

Gaebe, W. (ed.) (1997) *Struktur und Dynamik in der Region Stuttgart*, Stuttgart, Verlag Eugen Ulmer.

Gregersen, B. and Johnson, B. (1997) 'Learning economies, innovation systems and European integration', *Regional Studies*, 31, 5, 479–90.

Greif, S. (1998) 'Der Stuttgarter Raum im Patentgeschehen der Bundesrepublik Deutschland', in Landeshauptstadt Stuttgart (ed.) *Statistik und Informationsmanagement*, 3, 57, 67–78.

Grotz, R. (1998) 'Die Industrie im Wirtschaftsraum Stuttgart', in E. Kulke (ed.) *Wirtschaftsgeographie Deutschlands*, Stuttgart, Klett-Perthes Verlag.

Hilpert, U. (1994) 'Archipel Europa: Regionalisierung internationaler Innovationsprozesse als Problem politisch induzierter sozio-ökonomischer Entwicklung', in U. Hilpert (ed.) *Zwischen Scylla und Charybdis? Zum Problem staatlicher Politik und nicht-intendierter Konsequenzen*, Opladen, Westdeutscher Verlag.

Ifo Institut für Wirtschaftsforschung (ed.) (1995) *Der Wirtschafts- und Forschungsstandort Baden-Württemberg: Potentiale und Perspektiven*, Munich, Ifo Studien zur Strukturforschung 19/I.

IHK Region Stuttgart (ed.) (1996) *Die Wirtschaftsregion Stuttgart*, Stuttgart, IHK.

IHK Region Stuttgart (1998) *Statistik 98. Die Wirtschaft Baden-Württembergs und der Region Stuttgart*, Stuttgart, IHK.

Landeshauptstadt Stuttgart, Statistisches Amt (ed.) (1999a) 'Arbeitslosenquoten am 31.12.1998', *Statistik und Informationsmanagement*, 4, 58, 79.

Landeshauptstadt Stuttgart, Statistisches Amt (ed.) (1999b) 'Forschungsregion Stuttgart', *Statistik und Informationsmanagement*, 4, 58, 84–91.

Landesregierung Baden-Württemberg, Statistishes Landesamt (ed.) (1996) 'Personal und Ausgaben für Forschung und Entwicklung an den Hochschulen in Baden-Württemberg', *Statistisch-prognostischer Bericht*, 1996, 71–80.

Lundvall, B.-A. (1988) 'Innovation as an interactive process: from user–producer interaction to the national systems of innovation', in G. Dosi, C. Freeman, R. Nelson, G. Silverberg and L. Soete (eds) *Technical Change and Economic Theory*, London, Pinter, pp. 348–69.

Lundvall, B.-A. and Borras, S. (1998) 'The globalising learning economy: implications for innovation policy', paper for European Commission, Science Research Development, Studies Targeted Socio-economic Research, Luxembourg, European Commission.

Lundvall, B.-A. and Johnson, B. (1994) 'The learning economy', *Journal of Industry Studies*, 1, 2, 23–42.

Morgan, K. (1992) 'Innovating by networking: new models of corporate and regional development', in M. Dunford and G. Kafkalas (eds) *Cities and Regions in the New Europe: The Global–local Interplay and Spatial Development Strategies*, New York, Belhaven Press and Halsted Press.

Morgan, K. (1997) 'The learning region: institutions, innovation, and regional renewal', *Regional Studies*, 31, 5, 491–503.

Naschold, F. (1996) 'Jenseits des baden-württembergischen "Exceptionalism": Strukturprobleme der deutschen Industrie', in H.-J. Braczyk and G. Schienstock (eds) *Kurswechsel in der Industrie*, Stuttgart, Kohlhammer Verlag.

Nelson, R. (1994) *The Co-evolution of Technology: Industrial Structures and Supporting Institutions*, Industrial and Corporate Change.

NIW/ZEW (eds) (1998) *Zur regionalen Konzentration von Innovationspotentialen in Deutschland*, Studie im Auftrag des BMBF, Dokumentation No. 98–09, Mannheim, Zentrum für Europäische Wirtschaftsforschung (ZEW).

Porter, M. (1996) 'Competitive advantage, agglomeration economies, and regional policy', *International Regional Science Review*, 19, 1 and 2, 85–94.

Porter, M. (1999) 'Unternehmen können von regionaler Vernetzung profitieren. Trotz Globalisierung liegen viele langfristigen Wettbewerbsvorteile direkt vor der Haustür', *Harvard Business Manager*, 1, 51–63.

Sabel, C., Kern, H. and Herrigel, G. (1987) 'Regional prosperities compared: Massachusetts and Baden-Württemberg', *Economy and Society*, 18, 374–404.

Schienstock, G. (1997) 'The transformation of regional governance: institutional lock-ins and the development of lean production in Baden-Württemberg', in R. Whitley and P.H. Kristensen (eds) *Governance at Work: The Social Regulation of Economic Relations*, Paris, European Science Foundation.

Schienstock, G. and Steffens, U. (1995) 'Lean Production als Leitbild der Restrukturierung einer Region – die Wirtschaft Baden-Württembergs im Wandel', in J. Fischer and S. Gensior (eds) *Netzspannung: Trends in der sozialen und technischen Vernetzung von Arbeit*, Berlin, Edition Sigma.

Schmitz, H. (1992) 'Industrial districts: model and reality in Baden-Württemberg, Germany', in F. Pyke and W. Sengenberger (eds) *Industrial Districts and Local Economic Regeneration*, Geneva, International Institute for Labour Studies.

Simmie, J. (1999) 'Innovative clusters: global or local linkages?', paper presented at the International Conference of the Regional Science Association, Regional Potentials in an Integrating Europe, Bilbao, 18–21 September 1999.

Simmie, J. and Sennett, J. (1999) 'Innovative clusters: theoretical explanations and why size matters', *National Institute Economic Review*, 170, 87–98.

Staatsministerium Baden-Württemberg (ed.) (1993) *Aufbruch aus der Krise*, Bericht der Zukunftskommission Wirtschaft 2000, Stuttgart.

Sternberg, R. (1996) 'Regionale Spezialisierung und räumliche Konzentration FuE-intensiver Wirtschaftszweige in den Kreisen Westdeutschlands – Indizien für Industriedistrikte?', *Berichte zur deutschen Landeskunde*, 70, 1, 133–55.

Storper, M. (1995) 'The resurgence of regional economies, ten years later: the region as a nexus of untraded interdependencies', *European Urban and Regional Studies*, 2, 3, 191–221.

Storper, M. (1997) *The Regional World: Territorial Development in a Global Economy*, New York, The Guilford Press.

Strambach, S. (1997a) 'Wissensintensive unternehmensorientierte Dienstleistungen – ihre Bedeutung für die Innovations- und Wettbewerbsfähigkeit Deutschlands', in Deutsches Institut für Wirtschaftsforschung (DIW) (ed.) *Vierteljahrshefte zur Wirtschaftforschung*, 2, 66, 230–42.

Strambach, S. (1997b) 'Die Rolle wissensintensiver unternehmensorientierter Dienstleistungen im Strukturwandel der Region Stuttgart', in W. Gaebe (ed.) *Struktur und Dynamik in der Region Stuttgart*, Stuttgart.

Wirtschaftsministerium Baden-Württemberg (1996) *Informationen aus dem Wirtschaftsministerium*, Stuttgart.

CHAPTER 3

Milan: Dynamic Urbanisation Economies vs. Milieu Economies

3 Milan

Dynamic Urbanisation Economies vs. Milieu Economies

Roberta Capello with Alessandra Faggian and Daniele Villa Veronelli

Introduction

The aim of the chapter is to explain the tendency of innovation activity to cluster in a few metropolitan areas. Urban areas are regarded as 'creativity centres', and recently labelled 'islands of innovation' which induce economic progress and technological innovation (Davelaar and Nijkamp, 1990; European Commission, 1995; Hingel, 1992; Simmie, 1998). The main explanation for their success is that agglomeration economies are much higher than elsewhere, so that the metropolitan area is often conceived as the breeding place for new activities.

Agglomeration economies, in fact, have always been conceived not only as the economic explanation of efficiency in urban production;[1] the advantages of large-scale production manifest themselves also in terms of greater innovative capacity and industrial growth. Thanks to the presence of specialised services, of a 'technological environment' represented by R&D centres, of intense inter-industry linkages, of a large and sophisticated demand for new products, large cities have been defined as 'incubators' of new ideas, of new entrepreneurial spirit, of industrial dynamics. Since the work of Hoover (1937), scale advantages in cities have been classified into three main well-known categories: (a) internal economies of scale, where the advantages stem from the size of the single firms; (b) location economies, where the advantages stem from the size of the industry; and (c) urbanisation economies, where the advantages stem from the size of the city. More recently, a fourth category has been suggested, i.e. globalisation economies; in this case, the advantages firms receive stem from the size of the international market in which firms operate. Linkages with clients and suppliers in foreign markets are crucial to the commercial success of innovative new products and services (Simmie, 1998; Simmie and Sennett, 1999).

In this sense, agglomeration economies operate not only as vehicles for

the achievement of greater static efficiency, but as mechanisms for reducing uncertainty and risks in innovative processes, and in this sense
become the determinants for greater entrepreneurial creativity and industrial innovation. Dynamic urbanisation economies are the basis of three
main urban processes: the generally higher rate of new firms in cities (the
'incubator hypothesis'), the location dynamics of new products, which in
large cities can find a more diversified market for their start-up phase (the
'product life-cycle' theory), and the dynamics of innovation processes in
general.

If a consensus exists on the importance of dynamic urbanisation
economies on innovative processes, more recently a new stream of literature has put forward the question whether firms located in large cities are
more influenced by dynamic urbanisation economies in their innovative
activities, or whether they take advantage of a spatially concentrated location in specialised production systems, generally known in the literature as
(dynamic) location economies.[2] The tendency of high-tech manufacturing
firms to locate in central areas, and in areas where a high density of firms
of the same sector are already located, leaves open the question whether
firms are more influenced in their innovative activities by urbanisation
economies rather than location economies.

The role played by dynamic urbanisation economies rather than by
dynamic location economies on the innovative activity of firms in an urban
area is the subject matter of this chapter, which is mainly of an empirical
nature. The interest of this kind of analysis lies in the particular location
patterns followed by high-tech manufacturing firms and services in the
metropolitan area of Milan, where specific parts of the metropolitan area
become the preferred location for high-tech firms. A legitimate question is
whether in these areas firms have more advantage in their innovative activity from diversified knowledge spill-over, stemming from a central location, or from specialised knowledge spill-over, typical of a specialised area
of small and medium firms.

The chapter is structured as follows. Next, the case study area of Milan
is presented, through the description of its economic performance, and its
innovative activity. From the description of the location patterns of the
high-tech industry, a tendency towards an industrial clustering of small
and medium-sized firms emerges, and raises the question of the determinants of firms' innovative activity. Then the concepts of dynamic urbanisation economies and of milieu economies and their impact on the
innovative activities of firms are presented. The sample of the empirical
analysis and the results obtained from the empirical analysis on the metropolitan area of Milan are then discussed.

Major Characteristics of the Metropolitan Area of Milan
Historical Development Patterns

The geographical area where the empirical analysis has been undertaken is the metropolitan area of Milan. The economic leadership of this area dates back to the mid-nineteenth century. In this period intense industrialisation developed in Northern Italy and some industries, such as chemical, mechanical and iron industry, started expanding very quickly to substitute for the traditional silk and cotton sectors. In contrast to the textile industry, which prefers a decentralised location to exploit low labour costs, the new sectors showed a stronger tendency towards urban settlements to take advantage of economies of scale, financial and commercial services, infrastructure and skilled labour. In this period of transition from an agro-industrial economy to an industrial system, Milan consolidated its leading role as a financial and business pole.

From a location point of view a great difference soon appeared between the north and the south of the area. Thanks to public investments in roads and railway, the northern sub-area received the early industrial settlement, while in the Southern sub-area important agricultural investments were made. As a result, the north started growing more quickly, while the south became one of the most productive agricultural areas in Europe, but this hampered possible industrial development in this area.

In the first decade of the twentieth century a new industrial area developed in the northern outskirts of Milan, along Milan–Sesto S. Giovanni

Figure 3.1. The metropolitan area of Milan*
Note: * The lines correspond to the motorways; the direction is indicated with the name of the main town.

axis (see Figure 3.1). Three large firms, Breda (mechanical), Marelli (mechanical engineering) and Pirelli (tyres) moved from the core of the city to the suburbs where land rent was lower and more space for industrial plants' settlement was available.

During the 1930s the extension of the railway system in the direction of Sesto and Monza made still more profitable the decentralisation of the firms from the centre towards the Northern part of the city. Even though the centre of Milan held the supremacy in the share of industrial employees until the beginning of the 1950s, in these decades the northern part of the Milan metropolitan area witnessed a high growth rate of industrial employees.

Between 1952 and 1961 the industrial leadership of the centre, though confirmed by the absolute values, diminished through time. Though the rate of growth of industrial employees in the North was not so high as the previous period, this area remained still the most dynamic. In the following ten-year period the situation started changing. Characterised by scale diseconomies, due to congestion, high rents and growing use of private cars, the centre of Milan lost industrial employment. Also the Northern sub-area started having lower growth rates than in the past, while the north-east, characterised by more innovative sectors, became the most attractive area for new industrial settlements, shown by 20 per cent of industrial employment growth.

In the period between 1972 and 1981 there was a completely opposite situation to the one in 1936–51. The south, thanks to low rents and freely available floorspace, became an attractive area for new industrial settlements; the north, where mature industrial sectors were located, experienced negative industrial employment growth; the north-eastern sub-area went on growing thanks to its typical features, like space to grow, good communication infrastructures, amenities, that new industries, particularly high-tech, look for (Camagni and Rabellotti, 1988).

After 1981 the metropolitan area of Milan became more oriented towards tertiary specialisation. As Table 3.1 reveals, in the period 1981–91 the industrial sector shows a decrease of −19.21 per cent. This result is due especially to the crisis of the traditional manufacturing industry which lost more than 200,000 employees during this decade (−23.01 per cent). In contrast, service activities register a considerable development, with a growth rate of 24.78 per cent in the ten-year period. This is especially true for advanced service activities (e.g. credit, finance, insurance, computer services), traditionally found in the centre of the city, for accessibility and environmental quality reasons. The agricultural sector witnesses a decisive increase in this period, with a growth rate of 208 per cent in ten years; however, most of this effect is explained by statistical reasons, because of the very low starting value of 1981 (Table 3.1).

As a result of the historical development patterns, the metropolitan area of Milan nowadays presents the following territorial profile:

Table 3.1. Employment in 1981 and 1991 in the metropolitan area of Milan by sectors

Sector	Total employment in 1981	Total employment in 1991	Growth rate 1981/91 (%)
Primary sector	397	1,226	208.82
Agriculture	397	1,226	208.82
Industrial sector	1,081,689	873,946	−19.21
Extractive industry	6,116	9,279	51.72
Manufacturing industry	981,518	755,687	−23.01
Energy, gas and water industry	7,768	15,394	98.17
Constructions	86,287	93,586	8.46
Tertiary sector	698,303	871,369	24.78
Commerce	340,821	356,694	4.66
Hotels and restaurants	51,379	70,786	37.77
Transport	79,412	63,990	−19.42
Finance and insurance	97,041	129,289	33.23
Other services (e.g. informatics, estate activities, public sector)	129,650	250,610	93.30

- the north, characterised by the old industrial sectors showing signs of crisis;

- the north-east that seems to be the favoured location of new high-tech sectors;

- the south, still agricultural, but with a high rate of industrial and service development;

- the centre, specialised in advanced service activities.

Economic Profile

Milan lies in one of the most dynamic regions of Italy, the Lombardy region. The region accounts for more than 15 per cent of the national population and 9 per cent of the national territory. Some 20 per cent of national GDP is produced in this region: 24 per cent of the national industrial employment is located in this region, and even 31 per cent of high-tech national employment takes place in Lombardy (see Table 3.2).

The metropolitan area of Milan,[3] in its turn, accounts for 44 per cent of the regional population and 11.5 per cent of the regional territory. Taking into account that the metropolitan area of Milan encompasses only 1.2 per cent of national agricultural employment and 9.7 per cent of national

Roberta Capello

Table 3.2. The metropolitan area of Milan

	Metro-politan area of Milan	Metro-politan area/ Lombardy (%)	Metro-politan area/ Italy (%)	Lombardy/ Italy (%)
Population	3,922,710	44	7	16
Square km	2,762	11	0.9	8
Agriculture (employment)	1,305	14	1.3	9
High-tech industry (employment):	64,376	73	23	31
Computer and office equipments	8,241	82	32	39
Radio and TLC equipments	35,720	81	25	31
Medical, measure and optical equip.	20,415	59	17	29
Traditional manufacturing industry	633,347	40	10	24
Advanced services:	409,656	62	13	20
Transport sector	98,022	57	9	15
Monetary and financial services	90,500	66	16	24
Real estate	12,394	52	15	28
Computer services	31,910	70	17	25
Legal services	46,610	63	15	23
Services to firms	125,699	62	14	23
R&D activities	4,521	73	10	14

Source: National Census, 1991.

traditional industrial employment, its good economic performance may also be estimated by other indicators.

The industrial productivity in the area is much higher than the national and the regional level, and is one of the highest among the ten most important metropolitan areas of Italy[4] (Figure 3.2). In line with the regional profile, the metropolitan area has a very high share of high-tech industry employment; this area, in fact, accounts for more than 22 per cent of the national employment in advanced industries, and nearly 72 per cent of the regional employment. Moreover, 12.8 per cent of national advanced service employment is present in the area, which grows to 62 per cent when compared to the regional level.

The area demonstrates a strong specialisation in both advanced services and high-tech industries: there is a high presence of metal products, mechanical equipment and textile industry, but also of all high-tech industries, higher than the national average. Monetary and financial services represent the most important category of advanced service in which the metropolitan area of Milan is specialised, an expected result giving the fact that Milan is the international financial city of Italy, and the location of the international stock exchange.

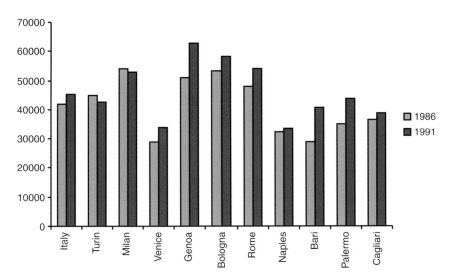

Figure 3.2. Industrial productivity in Italian metropolitan areas, 1986 and 1991 (thousands of lire)
Source: Camagni and Capello (1998).

Location Patterns of High-tech Industry

The technological dynamics of the region are probably the result of the technological climate characterising the metropolitan area of Milan. Many indicators suggest that the level of scientific activity in the metropolitan area is definitively high when compared to the national average.

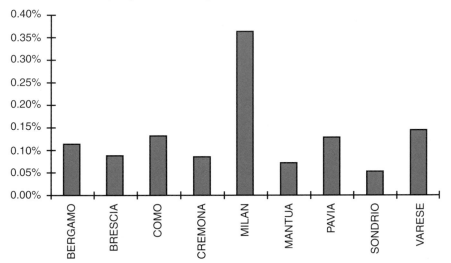

Figure 3.3. Patent intensity in Lombardy provinces*
* The variable has been calculated as the number of patents for each region between 1986 and 1991 on the number of industrial employees.

Figure 3.3 shows the patent intensity in the provinces of the Lombardy region; the metropolitan area of Milan has a patent intensity which is more than double that of the other areas. Moreover, if compared with the other fourteen metropolitan areas in Italy, the metropolitan area of Milan has once again an outstanding innovative performance; Milan has the highest patent intensity among all metropolitan areas, followed by Turin and Bologna. Moreover, the metropolitan area of Milan is the location of a number of research centres: as well as universities, a lot of autonomous research centres are present in the area (CISE, applied physics and techno-logy; Mario Negri, pharmaceutics and biology; Assoreni, chemistry and applied engineering; IRB, new material tests, just to mention a few) (Camagni and Rabellotti, 1988).

The outstanding performance of the metropolitan area of Milan with respect to the other Italian metropolitan areas is not astonishing. Milan is in fact the largest metropolitan area in Italy,[5] specialised in advanced financial services, requiring strong international connections: its size, its position in the national and international urban hierarchy and its func-tional role generate locational benefits to existing firms, attract new ones, but also stimulate innovative activities in firms in order to compete on the international markets.

Another indicator of the good innovative performance is the high share of high-tech activities, being nearly 23 per cent of the national employment in high-tech industries located in the metropolitan area of Milan. Definitely, high-tech industry may be seen as a strategic factor in the development tra-jectory of the metropolitan area of Milan; in terms of spatial patterns, high-tech firms may represent the countervailing element with respect to the inevitable relocation of traditional industries in peripheral areas of the city.

The spatial dynamics of high-tech firms is analysed on the basis of census data in 1981 and 1991. Many studies have already tried to identify objective criteria to isolate high-tech sectors from the other traditional industrial sectors. Some of the approaches present in the literature use, as a proxy for high-tech capacity, some indicators such as:

- high R&D expenditure;

- considerable share of highly qualified labour forces, such as researchers, engineers, technicians;

- rapid growth in sales, output and employment.

(Glasmeier et al., 1983)

However, none of these indicators is fully satisfactory for the definition of high-tech industries and all have the problem of being difficult to measure.

Another method of defining high-tech sectors, more subjective in its nature, but at the same time more operative, is to analyse the nature of firms' output. Following this criterion, it is possible to assume that high-

Table 3.3. Detailed census classes of the high-tech sector

High-tech industries	Share of employees in the metropolitan area of Milan on the national value (%)
High-tech industry	
Office machines, computers and data-processing production	32.2
Communications equipment and radio and TV appliances production	25.5
Medical, precision, optical instruments and watches production	17.3
High-tech services	
Computers and data-processing services	17.6
R&D activities	10.4
Total	19.9

tech sectors are those sectors whose products are 'core products inside the dominant technological paradigm, that of information technologies' (Camagni and Rabellotti, 1988). This criterion is the one applied to this study to define the high-tech industry. In Table 3.3 we present the categories of industries as they appear in the Industrial Census, which we included in the high-tech industry, divided between manufacturing and service industry.

A high regional diversification exists in the location patterns of high-tech industry, which may suggest a tendency of high-tech industry to locate in metropolitan areas. For this reason, the share of high-tech industry has been calculated for the fourteen most important metropolitan areas in Italy. As Figure 3.4 shows, however, also at the metropolitan level there is a great difference in the location patterns of high-tech industries, Milan playing the leading role also in this respect.

The location patterns of the high-tech industry in the metropolitan area of Milan are presented in Figures 3.5 and 3.6, representing 1981 and 1992 data respectively. The comparison between the two years highlights the

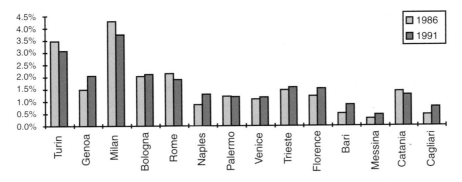

Figure 3.4. Share of high-tech employees in the different metropolitan areas

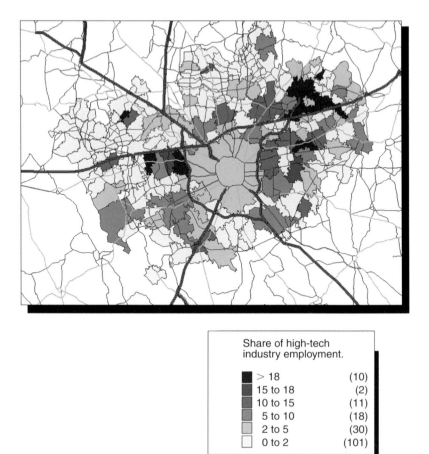

Share of high-tech
industry employment.

■	> 18	(10)
■	15 to 18	(2)
■	10 to 15	(11)
■	5 to 10	(18)
■	2 to 5	(30)
□	0 to 2	(101)

Figure 3.5. Share of high-tech employment industry, 1981

changes in the location patterns of high-tech firms in the decade; the following tendencies emerge:

- a concentration in the core areas, witnessed by an increase of the share of high-tech firms located in the core of Milan and by the constant presence near Monza (the first most important city after Milan in the area) of a high share of high-tech firms;

- a city-edge development around Milan, especially in the north and north-eastern part of the town, in line with the decentralisation tendency of the residential and industrial activities in the area (Camagni, 1995);

- an increasing location pattern along the main north-eastern axis, characterised by the presence of motorways, a ring motorway connecting them, and two underground lines connecting the area with the city centre of Milan.

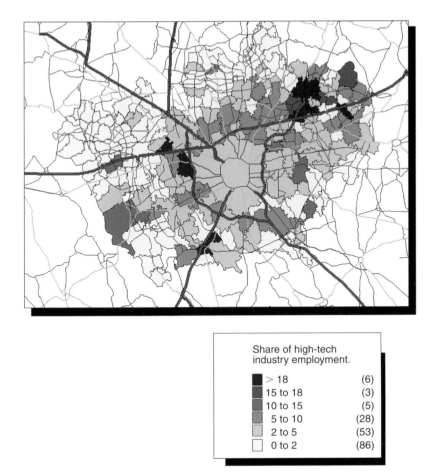

Share of high-tech industry employment.	
> 18	(6)
15 to 18	(3)
10 to 15	(5)
5 to 10	(28)
2 to 5	(53)
0 to 2	(86)

Figure 3.6. Share of high-tech employment industry, 1992

Within the core area of Milan, the main result that emerges in the location of high-tech firms is that the highest density of high-tech firms is in the north-western and north-eastern parts of Milan, the latter being the starting point of the north-eastern axis at the metropolitan level (see Figure 3.7). These results support a qualitative analysis run ten years ago in the same area (Camagni and Rabellotti, 1988), which envisaged the existence of a 'Milan Innovation Field' (MIF) in the north-eastern part of the town thanks to the high density of high-tech firms. Also the south-western part of the town seems to be an attractive location for high-tech firms, more than the central or southern parts of the town, the former being the natural location of advanced tertiary activities, the latter being traditionally a more agricultural area. The same spatial patterns are confirmed for R&D activities: a tendency towards the centre of Milan and towards the north-eastern axis between Milan and Monza, the same axis which emerges as one of the most preferred locations of high-tech firms.

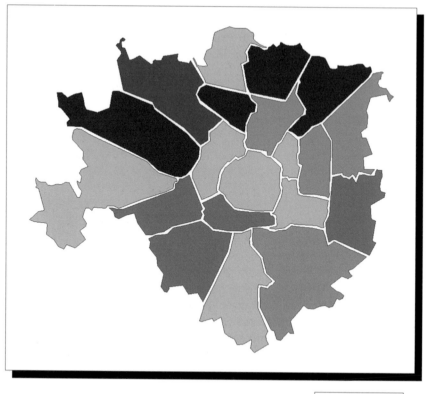

Share of high-tech
industry employment.
■	8 to 13	(4)
■	6 to 8	(1)
■	4 to 6	(4)
■	3 to 4	(4)
□	1 to 3	(7)

Figure 3.7. Share of high-tech employment industry in the core of Milan

Dynamic Urbanisation Economies and Milieu Economies: Research Issues

An urban location provides innovative firms with particular advantages, which can be interpreted as the determinants of the tendency of innovation to cluster in cities, namely accessibility (and physical proximity) to the following:

- infrastructure, and social capital in general;

- a vast input market;

- a vast output market;

- a vast supply of diversified business services;

- a vast and diversified labour market, highly skilled and qualified;

- general information and know-how.

A large consensus exists on the presence of these advantages in cities, which go under the name of (dynamic) urbanisation economies. However, a question emerges on whether innovation in urban areas is also influenced by the presence of dynamic location economies, i.e. by those advantages stemming from the presence of a vast production market of the same industry.

The concept of dynamic location advantages has been stressed by the GREMI, which has emphasised the role of dynamic economies in the innovation activities of clusters of small and highly specialised medium-sized firms.[6] This theory is the dynamic counterpart of the concept of 'industrial districts' or 'system areas' developed in the 1970s in the framework of the endogenous growth theory: local efficiency factors, like geographical and organisational proximity, external economies promoting a sort of industrial atmosphere, are overcome by more dynamic spatial elements like dynamic synergies and collective learning, which explain innovation processes at the spatial level. In a milieu, the more traditional and static elements of Smithian division of labour, of Marshallian externalities, generated by a common industrial culture and by dense input–output exchanges, co-exist with more dynamic elements, like Schumpeterian entrepreneurial spirits enhanced by long-standing and specific skills and by wide imitation possibilities, learning by doing and by using *à la Arrow*, cross-fertilisation processes *à la Freeman*, generating systems of integrated and incremental innovations (Camagni, 1991).

In the milieu, the innovative activity of firms is thus supported by location economies, also called 'milieu economies', which are the dynamic counterpart of the traditional economies of scale taking place within an industry. Cumulative and collective learning processes enhance local creativity and innovative output, through the informal exchange of information and of specialised knowledge. The processes of collective learning take place through the following.

- continuity in collecting knowledge over time, embedded in stable linkages with local suppliers and customers, and a stable local labour market;

- synergies between local actors, which guarantee the transfer of knowledge in the local area, in the form of innovative cooperation between customers and suppliers, of spin-off mechanisms, of labour force turnover.

(Camagni, 1991; Capello, 1999a, 1999b)

Milieu economies thus find their sources in:

Proximity to and synergy with:
- innovative local suppliers and customers;
- qualified and specialised labour market;
- local competitors.

Socialisation processes of:
- specialised knowledge cumulated in the local labour market;
- information (transcoding of new information);
- specialised human capital.

The main differences with urbanisation economies are the following:

- On one hand, the indivisibility element characterising the urban environment, which generates advantages only on the basis of the physical dimension of the urban market, and of the economies of scale accompanying the supply of physical and social capital. These advantages are typical only of the city;

- On the other hand, the diversified nature of urban knowledge, vs. the highly specialised nature of the knowledge cumulated in the milieu.

When specialised and highly innovative small and medium-sized firms cluster in a particular area of the city, as is the case of the high-tech industry in the north-eastern part of Milan, an interesting question emerges on whether the innovative activities of these firms is more influenced by dynamic urbanisation economies, i.e. by the more traditional advantages stemming from an urban atmosphere, like the access to infrastructure, physical capital overheads, diversified knowledge, presence of international airports, or by milieu economies, i.e. by collective learning of specialised knowledge, by socialisation processes of local specialised human capital.

It has been argued that industry-scale effects are not fundamentally different from city-size effects; they are just more specialised and confer benefits primarily on firms within a single industry (Satterthwaite, 1992). The issue of whether urban dynamic efficiency is associated with urbanisation economies or milieu economies has instead important implications: as suggested by Sveikauskas et al. (1988), if productivity is associated with city size, efficiency in production suggests that most production should be concentrated in the largest cities. On the other hand, if greater productivity stems from industry size, then a process of decentralisation, in which particular industries agglomerate in particular locations, is feasible.

This problem has also been put forward by a recent stream of literature related to industrial economics. The debate is concerned with the question whether specialised or diversified knowledge spill-overs can better explain innovation activities and technological change in spatially concentrated production systems (Feldman and Audretsch, 1999).

The tendency of high-tech industry in the metropolitan area of Milan to locate in a specific part of the city stresses the interest need for an empirical analysis, to analyse the following research issues:

- whether the north-eastern part of Milan works as a highly innovative specialised area, where intense informal interactions among economic agents, exchange of informal information and know-how, and where processes of collective learning take place and influence positively the innovative activity of local firms;

- whether firms in the metropolitan area of Milan take advantage more of dynamic urbanisation economies rather than milieu economies;

- whether different behavioural patterns exist in the way firms benefit from urbanisation or location economies, which can be related to structural characteristics like their size. It is in fact our impression that milieu economies are more strategic for small firms, which overcome some of the limits related to their size, by decreasing production and transaction costs, and by reducing uncertainty of innovation activities through socialising the processes of knowledge, and of strategic information.

The results of the empirical analysis are presented in the next sections.

The Sample Structure and Some Research Results

The analysis was run on a sample of thirty-five firms, located in the metropolitan area of Milan, belonging to different sectors of the economy, both manufacturing and services. These were selected according to the criteria outlined in the introduction. Table 3.4 presents the sample characteristics. Just a little more than a half (54.3 per cent) of firms are located in the

Table 3.4. Sample characteristics

	Total sample (%)	Of which: NE (%)	NE and HT (%)	Large in NE (%)	Small in NE (%)
North East	54	–	89	58	37
Product innovation	66	61	71	35	71
Small firms	55	37	35	–	–
Medium firms	23	23	29	–	–
Large firms	23	37	35		–
Private firms	97	53	94	29	100
Public firms	3	47	6	100	0
High-tech sectors	63	50	–	14	89
North East and High-tech	49	89	–	–	–
Award	37	69	61	54	15

Notes: NE = north-eastern part of Milan; HT = high-tech industry.

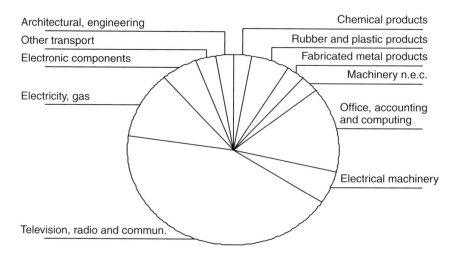

Figure 3.8. Principal economic activity of the sample firms

north-eastern part of the metropolitan area of Milan, and only just a little more than a half are firms with less than 50 employees. Nearly all our sample firms are private firms, and 62.9 per cent belong to the high-tech industry, defined in Table 3.2. The industry composition of the firms' sample is presented in Figure 3.8. High-tech industry is represented by the television, radio and communications manufacturing sector (more than 42 per cent), and by office, accounting and computing machines (14.3 per cent), while electricity, gas and water supply and electrical machinery are the largest represented sectors in our sample.

Interestingly enough, 89.5 per cent of our firms located in the north-east belong to the high-tech sector, and in this sector and in this area the highest innovative firms are located. In fact, 70.6 per cent of firms have developed product innovations, and this percentage increases to 71.4 per cent if only small firms in the high-tech areas are included.

The common questionnaire has been administered to these firms, with the intention of collecting information on the following:

- the innovation developed;

- the geographical proximity to customers, suppliers and competitors;

- the forms of cooperation developed for the innovation activity;

- the people involved in the innovation activity;

- the sources of information used for the innovation activity;

- the financial sources for the innovation;

- the strategic contacts for their innovation activity;

- the importance of location factors in their innovation activities.

Table 3.5. Innovation type and novelty

	Total sample (%)	Of which: small firms (%)	Firms in the North East (%)	High-tech firms in the North East (%)
Product innovation	66	69	74	71
Process innovation	34	31	26	29
Innovation novelty:				
New to the world	40	50	25	28
New to this country	3	0	6	6
New to the sector	20	19	19	22
New to the firm	37	31	50	44

The data collected through the questionnaire provide useful information on the kinds of innovation developed, on the determinants of innovation activities within Milanese firms and on the importance of the location of firms on their innovation activity. The latter is the main research issue this chapter investigates. The chapter in fact aims at defining the main determinants of innovation in the Milanese firms, and in particular, to understand whether firms' location advantages are primarily represented by the proximity to other firms of the same industry, to suppliers and customers, to specialised services (location or milieu economies) or whether they stem from the location in an advanced and large metropolitan area, like the one of Milan (urbanisation economies).

Table 3.5 shows the types of innovation developed by the firms' sample and the degree of novelty. The share of product innovation is greater than process innovation, and this is especially true for the north-east and for the high-tech industry in the north-east of Milan. In terms of innovation novelty, according to the respondents, 40 per cent of innovation is new to the world, and 37 per cent to the firm, while only 3 per cent new to the country. The high degree of novelty in the innovation applies to both large and small firms (50 per cent for each) and not particularly the north-east or the high-tech sector in the north-east.

Table 3.6 presents the location of the main suppliers, customers and competitors of the firms in the sample. Interestingly enough, 34 per cent of the firms' sample have their main suppliers located in the area (in less than 50 kilometres), and 58 per cent of these firms are located in the north-east and belong to the high-tech sector; these results suggest that a sort of filière economy exists in the north-eastern part of Milan, linked to the high-tech industry. Moreover, 86 per cent of the firms' sample replied that their main competitors are both at the regional and at the national level, and all of them are located in the north-east and belong to the high-tech industry. The presence of most of their competitors in the region strengthens the idea of a city region characterised by a high density of firms of the same

Table 3.6. Location of main suppliers, customers and competitors*

	Total sample (%)	Of which: small firms (%)	Firms in the North East (%)	High-tech firms in the North East (%)
Local:				
Suppliers	34	33	50	50
Customers	6	50	50	50
Competitors	9	33	67	67
Regional				
Suppliers	3	100	100	100
Customers	3	0	0	0
Competitors	86	43	100	100
National				
Suppliers	6	0	100	100
Customers	3	0	0	0
Competitors	86	43	100	100
European				
Suppliers	14	40	40	40
Customers	3	0	100	0
Competitors	6	0	0	0
American				
Suppliers	0	0	0	0
Customers	0	0	0	0
Competitors	3	0	3	3

Note: * Share of positive replies regarding the location of most of their suppliers, competitors and customers (more than 76%).

industry and by a high regional and national competition. Customers are instead spread around, with no particular location.

The main sources of information for the innovation activities of the firms' sample are the suppliers (26 per cent) and other firms of the same industry (29 per cent), followed by customers (11 per cent) (Table 3.7). Interestingly enough, those firms having replied that other firms of the same industry are important information channels are all located in the north-east. Competitors or firms of the same group do not represent an important channel for acquiring information on innovation.

Suppliers play an important role also as channels for knowledge acquisition for the innovation activity, representing one of the most important channels (26 per cent of replies). Technicians also play an important role (29 per cent), while more informal knowledge acquisition channels, like ex-colleagues or friends, do not play any role (Table 3.8).

Table 3.9 shows that the informal contacts with ex-colleagues and friends do not play an important role, while suppliers on the contrary seem to be a very important contact for the innovation activities of our firms: 43 per cent have underlined the importance of contacts with suppliers,

Table 3.7. The most important information channels for the innovation activity

	Total sample (%)	Of which: small firms (%)	Firms in the North East (%)	High-tech firms in the North East (%)
Suppliers	26	67	54	56
Customers	11	75	75	75
Competitors	9	100	100	44
Other firms within the group	6	100	100	100
Other firms	29	70	70	60

Note: Share of replies of scores 3 = moderate, 4 = important, 5 = very important.

Table 3.8. The most important channels of knowledge for the innovation activity

	Total sample (%)	Of which: small firms (%)	Firms in the North East (%)	High-tech firms in the North East (%)
Customers	9	42	67	67
Competitors	6	100	67	45
Suppliers	26	67	56	44
Friends	0	–	–	–
Ex-colleagues	3	0	0	0
Experts	9	67	100	67
Technicians	29	50	50	50

Note: Share of replies of scores 3 = moderate, 4 = important, 5 = very important.

Table 3.9. The most important contacts for the innovation activities

	Total sample (%)	Of which: small firms (%)	Firms in the North East (%)	High-tech firms in the North East (%)
Contacts with university and research centres	23	62	62	50
Contacts with suppliers, customers and competitors	43	33	60	60
Contacts with other collaborators	8.6	33	33	33
Contacts with friends and ex-colleagues	6	0	50	50

Note: Share of replies of scores 3 = moderate, 4 = important, 5 = very important.

customers and competitors, more than half of which are located in the north-east of Milan.

As far as the strategic location factors for the innovation activities of the firms' sample are concerned, the results are interesting; different behavioural patterns emerge between large and small firms, and between firms located in the north-east and elsewhere in Milan. Looking at the total sample, both traditional urbanisation economies, like access to good international infrastructure, and milieu economies, such as the availability of professional experts to recruit, of skilled and specialised manual labour, and proximity to suppliers and collaborators, seem to be important in the innovation activity of firms. However, some more interesting results emerge from the analysis, when the replies are analysed for different categories of firms (Table 3.10):

- Small firms in general seem to benefit from both urbanisation and milieu economies more than large firms do. The percentage of positive replies is higher for most of the different sources of agglomeration economies. However, the difference with the replies provided by large firms is greater for what concerns milieu economies: small firms seem to prefer milieu economies much more than large firms. Between urbanisation and milieu economies, large firms seem to appreciate urbanisation economies more.

- Firms in the north-eastern part of Milan seem to appreciate milieu economies more than firms located elsewhere: availability of professional experts to recruit locally, availability of skilled manual labour, proximity to suppliers and collaborators are highly appreciated.

- If we divide our sample between small and large firms in the north-east, small firms appreciate milieu economies much more than urbanisation economies. Interestingly enough, large firms are more in favour of urbanisation economies, like good infrastructure connections.

From these results a clear difference emerges between large and small firms, and between firms located in the north-east and elsewhere in the degree of appreciation of the different sources of advantages: this means that *both the size of the firm and the location play a role in defining the sources of metropolitan advantages for firms' creativity.*

The Determinants of Innovative Activity: Evidence from the Metropolitan Area of Milan

Methodology: Factor and Cluster Analyses

The methodology used to describe the determinants of innovation activity in our firm sample is a cluster analysis. Cluster analysis allows us to determine whether the firms of our sample fall into distinct groups or clusters in

Table 3.10. The importance of location factors in the decision to set up a new firm and develop an innovation in the region

	Total sample (%)	Of which: small firms (<49 empl.) (%)	Medium-size firms (50–249) (%)	Large firms (>250) (%)	BRITE award (%)	North East (%)	North East and high-tech (%)	Small firms in the North East (%)	Large firms in the North East (%)
Urbanisation economies:									
Access to private general business services	40	64	7	29	38	32	29	43	27
Cost of premises	0	–	–	–	23	16	18	29	9
Proximity to business services	26	56	11	33	23	10	12	14	9
Proximity to sources of information	17	50	33	17	–	5	6	14	–
Access to financial capital	9	67	33	–	–	–	–	–	–
Good access to the centre of Milan	3	100	–	–	38	37	35	29	45
Good rail connection	43	47	27	27	46	37	35	29	45
Good access to national road network	49	53	24	23	54	42	41	29	54
Good access to major airport	49	47	24	29	–	16	18	14	18
Contributions from universities	20	43	14	43	8	–	6	14	–
Location (or milieu) economies:									
Availability of professional experts to recruit	86	57	20	23	85	79	76	86	82
Availability of skilled manual labour	49	65	29	6	23	42	47	57	36
Access to private specialised services	34	67	17	17	31	26	29	29	27
Proximity to customers	23	62	25	13	38	42	41	57	26
Proximity to suppliers	43	33	33	13	15	16	12	14	9
Proximity to competitors	6	50	–	50	38	68	76	71	64
Proximity to collaborators	66	56	30	13	23	26	23	29	27
Local public business support services	17	33	67	0	23	21	23	14	27
Contribution from TECS	11	25	25	50	15	16	17	14	18
Contribution to business links	17	50	33	17	46	32	35	29	36
The presence of ex-colleagues	9	67	33	–	–	5	6	14	–
The presence of friends	3	100	–	–	–	5	12	18	–

Note: Replies of scores 3 = moderate, 4 = important, 5 = very important.

terms of the variables considered, and, if so, to determine the number of groups or clusters and their membership. Clusters of firms are formed on the basis of the variables we think can influence the behaviour of firms in their innovation activities, with the aim of identifying the structural characteristics of the innovation behaviour shared by each group.

The variables characterising innovation behaviours are a relatively high number: they include the structural features of firms, their size, their location, the type of innovation they develop, the nature of these firms, as well as the financial channels, the information channels, the knowledge acquisition, the contacts firms have with the external world (suppliers, customers, competitors, other firms). All these variables are present in our questionnaire, and provide the database on which the analysis of the different innovative behaviours is run.

However, before entering the behavioural analysis, another methodological step is needed. In fact, the number of variables which are in the questionnaire and can enter the behavioural analysis is quite large. In order to reduce them without losing too much of their explanatory power, factor analysis is run.

Factor analysis is a statistical technique used to identify a relatively small number of factors that can be used to represent relationships among sets of many interrelated variables. Factor analysis has the primary objective of simplifying the description of the innovative behaviours of firms. It identifies a relatively small number of underlying principal elements or factors that explain the correlations among a set of variables; in other words, it summarises a large number of variables and translates them into a smaller number of derived variables or factors.

The basic assumption of factor analysis is that underlying dimensions, or factors, can be used to explain complex phenomena. The goal of factor analysis is thus to identify the not directly observable factors based on a set of observable variables, reducing their number without losing too much of their explanatory power.[7]

From our questionnaire, many variables could be used to describe the following:

- firms' characteristics: growth, size, location in the area of Milan (north-eastern part or elsewhere), type of innovation (new in the sector, in the world, in the firm), nature of the firm (public or private);

- location of suppliers, customers and competitors (local, regional, national, European and American);

- location factors, in terms of urbanisation economies, such as the presence of infrastructure provision, of general business services, of financial capital, of general information, and milieu economies, the presence of local suppliers, customers and competitors stimulating the innovative activity, of a scientific atmosphere, of trust and informal cooperation provided by friends and ex-colleagues in the innovative activity;

- contacts developed by firms in the innovation activity, with suppliers, customers, business services, and informal contacts with friends and ex-colleagues;

- sources of finance for the innovative activity, such as European or other forms of grants to the research, loans; formal venture capital and other industrial forms of finance;

- sources of information important for the innovative activity, such as public information, specialised information, generic information, private information, club information;

- sources of cooperation for the innovative activity, i.e. with other firms of the group, with research centres, with suppliers and customers, with experts.

Research Hypothesis

The research hypothesis we would like to test in this part of the analysis is whether firms located in the north-east appreciate milieu economies rather than urbanisation economies. Thus, in the metropolitan area of Milan we expect heterogeneous behaviour from firms regarding their appreciation of local advantages in their innovative activity. This hypothesis is tested through the cluster analysis. The results are presented in Table 3.11. Four main clusters explain the behaviour of our firms' sample:

- the first cluster depicts the behaviour of firms having won the BRITE award and being world leader in their innovative activity. Some of them are located in the north-east, mainly high-tech firms. Their leadership in the innovation developed is also witnessed by low process innovations developed. The main contacts they have are formal and external contacts. Because of the nature of the BRITE award, the finances for these innovations are mostly European, and the cooperation developed for the innovation is with other firms. Given the high scientific value of these projects, it is not surprising that an important source of information for this group of firms comes from research institutes. Other information sources for their innovation are mainly from other firms of the group, and mostly of a public (governmental) nature. These firms manifest a clear appreciation of the traditional urbanisation economies, such as the presence of advanced financial services, proximity to the centre of Milan and to advanced and international infrastructure networks.

- the second cluster characterises the group of catching-up firms. They have a high rate of innovation processes, as expected, and act in a

Table 3.11. Cluster analysis on firms' importance of urbanisation and milieu economies in their innovative activity*

Factors	1 cluster	2 clusters	3 clusters	4 clusters	Mean value
BRITE award-winning firms	**1.07**	*−0.97*	−0.04	−0.44	0.02
Formal contacts for innovation	**0.28**	−0.04	*−0.64*	−0.47	−0.01
Cooperation with other firms (network cooperation)	**0.19**	−0.03	−0.16	*−0.39*	0.01
European finance channels	**0.77**	−0.63	**0.15**	*−0.81*	0.02
Public information	**0.32**	−0.21	*−0.21*	−0.49	0.01
Information from research centres	**0.61**	−0.36	*−0.50*	−0.19	0.00
Proximity to advanced business services	**0.08**	0.01	−0.27	0.25	−0.05
Proximity to information sources	**0.02**	−0.04	−0.00	−0.34	−0.02
Proximity to the centre of Milan	**0.25**	−0.50	−0.20	*−0.61*	−0.02
Proximity to universities and research centres	**0.40**	−0.15	−0.38	−0.10	−0.11
Process innovative firms	−0.08	**0.36**	**0.33**	−0.07	0.13
Private finance channels	*−0.07*	**0.21**	−0.20	−0.24	0.00
Governmental finance	−0.11	**0.24**	−0.16	−0.22	0.00
Contacts with trade association	−0.19	**0.37**	*−0.27*	−0.22	0.00
Proximity to a qualified local labour market	−0.12	**0.59**	−1.24	*−0.21*	−0.03
Informal contacts for innovation	0.00	**0.16**	**−0.45**	−0.16	−0.00
Information from the press	0.02	**0.26**	**−0.54**	−0.41	0.01
National customers and competitors	*−0.36*	**0.47**	0.02	−0.08	0.02
Catching-up firms	0.33	**0.67**	*−1.91*	*−1.91*	−0.00
Small high-tech firms in the North East	0.17	−0.18	**1.11**	*−1.11*	0.03
Cooperation with competitors	**0.27**	−0.40	**0.58**	−0.17	0.00
Proximity to specialised services	−0.27	0.25	**0.28**	−0.64	0.00
Proximity to customers and suppliers	−0.28	−0.06	**0.52**	−0.22	0.02
Local suppliers	−0.26	0.23	*−0.66*	**0.57**	−0.04
National suppliers	−0.31	0.09	0.11	**0.83**	−0.00
European suppliers	0.19	−0.13	−0.56	**0.68**	−0.01
Cooperation with suppliers	−0.23	**0.44**	−1.02	**0.50**	−0.00
Cooperation with governmental bodies	0.27	−0.18	−0.15	−0.16	0.00
Good quality of life	−0.22	0.18	−0.44	*−0.79*	−0.05

Note: * Values characterising clusters are in bold, for the positive aspects, and in italics, for the negative aspects.

national market, their competitors and customers being mainly national. Their channels of information are mainly informal, and the sources of finance of their innovation are traditional, from banks and joint ventures, or of a public nature. Sources of information are traditional trades union information channels and public channels, like the press. They do not particularly appreciate either urbanisation or milieu economies, with the expection of a highly qualified labour market, which can assure the catching-up process. Interestingly enough, they do not appreciate the proximity to the centre of Milan.

- the third cluster depicts the behaviour of small firms located in the north-east, which are catching-up firms with respect to innovation processes. They seem to act primarily on a local market and having customers and competitors at the local level, and not at the European level. Cooperation for the innovation is developed mainly on the basis of cooperation with local competitors. Information channels are similar to the first group, and are mainly information from other firms of the group. These firms seem to prefer milieu economies rather than urbanisation economies: proximity to customers and suppliers is extremely important in their innovative activity, as well as the presence of specialised business services.

- the fourth cluster is characterised by large firms not located in the north-east, developing product innovation and not being catching-up firms. They have both national and local suppliers and act on a European market. The main cooperation channels for the development of their innovations are their suppliers. Concerning their judgement on urbanisation rather than milieu economies, they seem to prefer the former, being highly interested in quality of life in general, and in proximity to the centre of Milan.

The cluster analysis shows that firms undoubtedly have a different behaviour in the way they appreciate urbanisation rather than milieu economies. The main results from this analysis is that firms in the north-east are more in favour of milieu economies than firms located elsewhere. A second result is that smaller firms seem to be attracted more by milieu economies, while large firms seem to appreciate urbanisation economies more.

An interesting and meaningful result is the distribution of firms among the three statistical clusters obtained: more than 41.3 per cent of our sample firms belong to the first cluster, 38.2 per cent to the second, 11.7 per cent to the third and the remaining 8.8 per cent to the fourth. In the metropolitan area of Milan, the prevailing behaviour seems to be the ones of leading firms, which appreciate the metropolitan location for their traditional urbanisation advantages provided by the existence of advanced infrastructure networks, by advanced services and by proximity to an advanced urban centre. Another high percentage of our firms behave like catching-up firms, which appreciate the high quality of the labour market probably as a channel for innovative processes to take place, through processes of reverse engineering. A small share of firms has a milieu behaviour, appreciating milieu economies more than urbanisation economies: interestingly enough, these firms are located in the north-east.

Homogeneity and Diversity of Firms in the High-tech Milieu

The results of the previous cluster analysis suggest that firms located in the north-east manifest a milieu behaviour. The research question in this part of the study is whether homogeneity of firm behaviours rather than diversity exist in the north-east. Our hypothesis is that firms appreciate urbanisation rather than milieu economies not only according to their location, but also to their size. In this sense, we expect a different behaviour in the appreciation of urbanisation economies and location economies even in the north-eastern part of the metropolitan area, since large firms are by definition not dependent on milieu economies, and more oriented towards the highly qualified and advanced functions provided by a metropolitan area.

For this reason, we ran a second cluster analysis, with the aim of finding out the different behaviours of large versus small firms in the north-eastern part of Milan. The cluster analysis is run on the basis of the factor analysis already presented, with the only exception that we run a new factor analysis on firms' characteristics; the new factor analysis is able to emphasise more the characteristics we are interested in.

The results of the new cluster analysis are presented in Table 3.12. Four clusters emerge from the analysis:

- The first cluster represents small firms located in the north-east as leaders in the sector, with a remarkable networking behaviour. They act mostly in a local market, their customers and competitors being mainly local. They behave as if they are in a milieu, with strong cooperation with suppliers and customers as far as their innovative activity is concerned, their strategic cooperation channel is a networking behaviour with other firms, which represent also the main channels of information. Other more public information sources are not of interest for these kinds of firms.

- The second cluster is represented by large firms located in the north-east. They act in a national market, and most of them are winners of the BRITE award. They appreciate the scientific climate of the area, since their most important sources of information are local research centres and universities. They appreciate agglomeration economies of

Table 3.12. Cluster analysis on diversity or homogeneity in the north-eastern part of Milan*

Factors	1 cluster	2 clusters	3 clusters	4 clusters	Mean value
Small firms in the North East	**0.06**	−0.31	**1.82**	−0.46	0.03
Formal contacts for innovation	**0.24**	0.00	−0.13	−0.26	−0.05
Cooperation with other firms (network cooperation)	**0.26**	−0.13	−0.37	−0.18	−0.10
Good quality of life	**0.18**	−0.05	−0.42	**0.16**	0.01
Cooperation with suppliers	**0.34**	−0.19	−0.24	−0.01	−0.31
BRITE award-winning firms	−0.16	**1.11**	0.14	−0.99	0.03
Large firms in the North East	−0.11	**0.44**	−0.77	0.04	0.02
National suppliers	0.08	**0.40**	0.06	−0.46	0.01
Informal contacts for innovation	−0.42	**0.59**	−0.48	−0.04	0.02
European finance channels	0.01	**0.14**	0.36	−0.42	−0.03
Contacts with trade association	−0.23	**0.32**	−0.23	−0.05	0.00
Information from the press	−0.54	**0.24**	−0.04	−0.00	−0.04
Proximity to specialised services	−0.33	**0.59**	−0.01	−0.37	0.00
Local customers and competitors	0.11	0.09	**0.27**	−0.19	0.03
Cooperation with competitors	0.26	0.09	**0.39**	−0.42	0.00
Cooperation with governmental bodies	−0.23	−0.07	**0.84**	−0.08	0.02
Private finance channels	−0.20	−0.07	**0.96**	−0.21	0.00
Proximity to customers and suppliers	−0.29	−0.22	**0.74**	0.08	0.00
Proximity to universities and research centres	−0.31	−0.17	**0.98**	−0.21	−0.04
Information from research centres	−0.21	**0.23**	0.24	−0.16	0.01
Process innovative firms	0.15	−0.09	0.21	**0.34**	0.14
Imitating firms	−1.93	0.36	0.53	**0.62**	0.00
Local suppliers	−0.52	0.25	−0.39	**0.36**	0.03
National customers and competitors	−0.36	0.04	−0.44	**0.43**	0.01
European suppliers	−0.10	−0.03	−0.23	**0.11**	−0.03
Governmental finance	−0.17	−0.15	−0.13	**0.33**	0.00
Public information	−0.15	−0.28	0.27	**0.32**	0.02
Proximity to advanced business services	−0.07	−0.07	−0.56	**0.37**	−0.00
Proximity to a information channels	−0.31	0.05	−0.02	**0.26**	0.03
Proximity to a qualified local labour market	−0.52	0.07	−0.45	**0.31**	−0.05
Proximity to the city centre	−0.02	−0.34	0.13	**0.22**	−0.02

Note: * Values characterising clusters are in bold, for the positive aspects, and in italics, for the negative aspects.

the large city, since they emphasise the importance of the proximity to the city centre. However, they also seem to appreciate the highly specialised business services offered in the area.

- The third cluster depicts a group of small firms located in the north-east with a mainly incremental innovation activity. These firms have a local market, and appreciate in a particular way the proximity to suppliers and customers, the presence of specialised business services and the scientific climate of the presence of universities for their innovation activity.

- The fourth cluster represents large firms located outside the north-east with a mainly incremental innovation activity. These firms work in an international market and appreciate urbanisation economies for their innovation activity: the presence of advanced services, of a qualified labour market, the proximity to the centre of Milan, to good infrastructure networks, to a high quality of services (like schools, hospitals). On the contrary, they are not at all interested in the presence of specialised business services.

The results seem to emphasise the following:

- firms in the north-east appreciate milieu economies for their innovative activity more than firms located somewhere else in the metropolitan area of Milan;

- within firms located in the north-east, small firms appreciate milieu economies more than large firms do, and these latter seem to appreciate also urbanisation economies.

A high diversity of behaviour exists in the appreciation of agglomeration advantages on the innovation activity of firms. The behaviours greatly depends on two elements: the size of the firm, and the location of the firm within the metropolitan area. Small firm size and location in areas where a high concentration of firms of the same sector exists seem to characterise firms which appreciate milieu economies also in large metropolitan areas, more than urbanisation economies.

Conclusion

The aim of this chapter has been to find out the advantages firms achieve in their innovative activity when they locate in large metropolitan areas. In particular, the empirical analysis is developed on the metropolitan area of Milan. A vast literature exists on the advantages of an urban location on dynamic efficiency of firms; highly qualified and diversified input market, of output, proximity to international networks, to qualified business services. All these are labelled in the literature as 'urbanisation economies'.

Our work has gone a step further, by trying to capture at the empirical level the role played by urbanisation economies in the innovation activity of firms or by milieu economies, i.e. those economies stemming from the spatial clustering of highly specialised firms, which share a common and highly specialised labour market, specialised business services, and mechanisms of collective learning put in place through intense exchange of information with suppliers and customers and through a high turnover of the labour market.

Our aim was thus to see whether firms located in the metropolitan area of Milan benefit more from urbanisation economies rather than milieu economies in their innovation activity. The analysis was facilitated by the fact that in the north-eastern part of Milan a high concentration of high-tech firms is present, which represents a spatial clustering of high-tech firms.

The main research issues have been:

- whether the north-eastern part of Milan works as a highly innovative specialised area, where intense informal interactions among economic agents, exchange of informal information and know-how, and where processes of collective learning take place and positively influence the innovative activity of local firms;

- whether firms in the metropolitan area of Milan take advantage more of dynamic urbanisation economies rather than milieu economies;

- whether different behavioural patterns exist in the way firms appreciate urbanisation or location economies, which can be related to structural characteristics like their size. It is in fact our impression that milieu economies are more significant for small firms, which overcome some of the limits related to their size, by decreasing production and transaction costs, and by reducing uncertainty of innovation activities through socialisation processes of knowledge and of strategic information.

The results may be synthesised as follows:

- concerning the north-eastern part of the metropolitan area of Milan, firms benefit from milieu economies;

- however, there is not a homogeneous behaviour in appreciating milieu economies in the north-east. Large firms located in the north-east seem to prefer advantages related to the size of the city.

- in general, we can reasonably argue that the size of the firm plays a role in the definition of the advantages firms prefer: large firms are more influenced by urbanisation economies, small firms by milieu economies.

The results presented in this chapter are, however, of a descriptive nature. An interesting and necessary further research direction is to investigate the same issues with more interpretative and advanced statistical analyses. Many methodological problems have to be solved for an interpretative analysis, such as the treatment of discrete variables in models requiring continuous variables, and the application of advanced econometric technics (like panel data) in the case of random samples.

Notes

1. See, among others, Alonso (1971); Mera (1973); Henderson (1974); Segal (1976); Marelli (1981); Ladd (1992); Catin (1991); Rousseaux and Proud'homme (1992); Rousseaux (1995); Capello (1998).
2. Born with the work of Weber (1929), the theory on location economies finds its refinements and improvements in the field of location theory to the works of Hoover (1937 and 1948), Lösch (1954), Isard (1956), Koopmans (1957), Jacobs (1969) and Bos (1965), just to quote some of them. Empirical analyses are present in Shefer (1973); Sveikauskas (1975); Carlino (1980); Mills (1970); Moomaw (1983) and Henderson (1985).
3. In this work, the metropolitan area of Milan coincides with the administrative boundaries of the Province of Milan. Therefore, the data concerning the metropolitan area are at a provincial level.
4. The ten metropolitan areas are: Milan, Rome, Venice, Bologna, Turin, Naples, Cagliari, Palermo, Genoa, Bari.
5. The metropolitan area of Milan has a population of 3,991,710 and is larger than the metropolitan area of Rome, which has 3,200,000 inhabitants. These data refer to 1996.
6. For the GREMI literature, see among others Aydalot (1986); Aydalot and Keeble (1988); Camagni (1991); Maillat *et al.* (1993); Ratti *et al.* (1997).
7. The use of factor and cluster analysis to local districts theory is not new: see, for example, Rabellotti (1997); Rabellotti and Schmitz (1999); Capello (1999a, 1999b).

References

Alonso, W. (1971) 'The economies of urban size', *Papers and Proceedings of the Regional Science Association*, 26, 67–83.

Aydalot, Ph. (ed.) (1986) *Milieux Innovateurs en Europe*, Paris, GREMI.

Aydalot, Ph. and Keeble, D. (eds) (1988) *High Technology Industry and Innovative Environment*, London, Routledge.

Bos, H. (1965) *Spatial Dispersion of Economic Activities*, Rotterdam, Rotterdam University Press.

Camagni, R. (1991) 'Local "milieu", uncertainty and innovation networks: towards a new dynamic theory of economic space', in R. Camagni (ed.) *Innovation Networks: Spatial Perspective*, London, Belhaven Press, pp. 121–44.

Camagni, R. (1995) 'L'organizzazione socio-economica del territorio lombardo e la sua recente evoluzione', in *Rapporto IReR '95 – Rapporto di Legislatura 1995–2000*, Milano, IRER.

Camagni, R. and Capello, R. (1998) 'Innovation and performance in SMEs in Italy: the relevance of spatial aspects', *Competition and Change*, 3, 69–106.

Camagni, R. and Rabellotti, R. (1988) 'Innovation and territory: the Milan high-tech innovation field', in Ph. Aydalot (ed.), *Milieux Innovateurs en Europe*, Paris, GREMI, pp. 101–28.

Capello, R. (1998) 'Economies d'échelle et taille urbaine: théorie et études empiriques révisités', *Revue d'Economie Régionale et Urbaine*, 1, 43–62.

Capello, R. (1999a) 'Spatial transfer of knowledge in high-technology milieux: learning vs. collective learning processes', *Regional Studies*, 33, 4, 353–65.

Capello, R. (1999b) 'SMEs clustering and factor productivity: a milieu production function model', *European Planning Studies*, 7, 6, 719–35.

Capello, R. and Faggian, A. (1998) 'Innovation and performance in the Milan area: spatial patterns of high-tech activities', paper presented at the International Workshop on innovation clusters and competitive cities in Europe, Cambridge, UK, 8 December.

Carlino, G. (1980) 'Contrast in agglomeration: New York and Pittsburgh reconsidered', *Urban Studies*, 17, 343–51.

Catin, M. (1991) 'Economie d'agglomération et gains de productivité', *Revue d'Economie Régionale et Urbaine*, 5, 565–98.

Davelaar, E. and Nijkamp, P. (1990) 'Industrial innovation and spatial systems: the impact of producer services', in H. Ewers and J. Allesch (eds) *Innovation and Regional Development*, Berlin, de Gruyter, pp. 83–122.

European Commission (1995), *Green Paper on Innovation*, Luxembourg, EC.

Feldman, M. and Audretsch, D. (1999) 'Innovation in cities: science-based diversity, specialisation and localised competition', *European Economic Review*, 43, 409–29.

Glasmeier, A.K., Hall, P. and Markusen, A.R. (1983) *Defining High Technology Industries*, Working Paper No. 407, Berkeley, CA, Institute of Urban and Regional Development, University of California.

Henderson, J. (1974) 'The sizes and types of cities', *The American Economic Review*, 64, 640–56.

Henderson, J. (1985) *Economies, Theory and the Cities*, Orlando, Academic Press.

Hoover, E. (1937) *Location Theory and the Shoe and Leather Industries*, Cambridge, MA, Harvard University Press.

Hoover, E. (1948) *The Location of Economic Activity*, New York, McGraw-Hill.

Isard, W. (1956) *Location and Space Economy*, New York, John Wiley.

ISTAT (1991) *Industry National Census*, Rome, ISTAT.

ISTAT (1996) *Intermediate Industry National Census*, Rome, ISTAT.

Jacobs, J. (1969) *The Economy of Cities*, New York, Random House.

Koopmans, T. (1957) *Three Essays on the State of Economic Science*, New York, McGraw-Hill.

Ladd, H. (1992) 'Population growth, density and the costs of providing public services', *Urban Studies*, 29, 2, 237–95.

Lösch, A. (1954) *The Economies of Location*, New Haven, CT, Yale University Press.

Maillat, D., Quévit, M. and Senn, L. (1993) *Réseaux d'innovation et milieux innovateurs: un pari pour le développement régional*, Neuchatel, EDES.

Marelli, E. (1981) 'Optimal city size, the productivity of cities and urban production functions', *Sistemi Urbani*, 1–2, 149–63.

Mera, K. (1973) 'On the urban agglomeration and economic efficiency', *Economic Development and Cultural Change*, 21, 309–24.

Mills, E. (1970) 'Urban density functions', *Urban Studies*, 7, 5–20.

Moomaw, R. (1983) 'Is population scale worthless surrogate for Business agglomeration?', *Regional Science and Urban Economics*, 13, 525–45.

Rabellotti, R. (1997) *External Economies and Cooperation in Industrial Districts: A Comparison of Italy and Mexico*, London, Macmillan.

Rabellotti, R. and Schmitz, H. (1999) 'The internal heterogeneity of industrial districts in Italy, Brazil and Mexico', *Regional Studies*, 33.2, 97–108.

Ratti, R., Bramanti, A. and Gordon, R. (eds) (1997) *The Dynamics of Innovative Regions: The GREMI Approach*, Aldershot, Avebury.

Rousseaux, M.P. (1995) 'Y a-t-il une surproductivité de l'Ile de France?', in M. Savy and P. Veltz (eds) *Economie Globale et Réinvention du Local*, Paris, DATAR/Editions de l'Aube, pp. 157–67.

Rousseaux, M.P. and Proud'homme, R. (1992) *Les Bénéfices de la Concentration Parisienne*, Paris, L'OEIL-IAURIF.

Satterthwaite, M. (1992) 'High-growth industries and uneven distribution', in E. Mills and F. McDonald (eds) *Sources of Metropolitan Growth*, New Brunswick, New Jersey, Center for Urban Policy Research, pp. 39–50.

Segal, D. (1976) 'Are there returns to scale in city size?', *Review of Economics and Statistics*, 58, 250–339.

Shefer, D. (1973) 'Localisation economies in SMSA's: a production function analysis', *Journal of Regional Science*, 13, 55–64.

Simmie, J. (1998) 'Reasons for the development of "islands of innovation": evidence from Hertfordshire', *Urban Studies*, 8, 1261–89.

Simmie, J. and Hart, D. (1999) 'Innovation projects and local production networks: a case study from Hertfordshire', *European Planning Studies*, 7, 4, 445–62.

Simmie, J. and Sennett, J. (1999) 'Innovative clusters: global or local linkages', *National Institute Economic Review*, 170, 87–98.

Sveikauskas, L. (1975) 'The productivity of city size', *Quarterly Journal of Economics*, 89, 393–413.

Sveikauskas, L., Gowdy, J. and Funk, M. (1988) 'Urban productivity: city size or industry size', *Journal of Regional Science*, 28, 2, 185–202.

Weber, A. (1929) *Theory of the Location of Industries*, Chicago, Chicago University Press.

CHAPTER 4

Innovation in the Amsterdam Region

4 Innovation in the Amsterdam Region

Walter J.J. Manshanden and Jan G. Lambooy[1]

Introduction

Since the early 1980s innovation has been an important topic of researchers and policy-makers in the Netherlands. The reason for this interest was the country's economic sluggishness in the 1970s and early 1980s, referred to internationally as 'Hollanditis'. Important political and economic choices needed to be made at the time. On the one hand, the post-war welfare state and levels of public spending had reached their peak. On the other hand, the economic crisis, only partly due to the oil crises, was wreaking havoc in the market sector. In 1982 public debt as a percentage of GNP reached critical levels. In the Netherlands the general cause of this crisis has been cited as tight regulation and the institutionalised position of the labour unions which had resulted in spiralling rates of wage growth and inflation.

In these years it became clear that economic policy would need to be changed fundamentally. The most important measure of attempting to revive the market by deregulation and liberalisation has been well documented. The renewed policy interest in the relationship between innovation and urban recovery, initiated by the White Paper 'Innovatie' by the Ministries of Economic Affairs and Scientific Board of Government Policy (1979) and the White Paper 'Greep op de stad? (Hold on the City) (Lambooy *et al.*, 1982), has received less attention in the literature. Since the publication of the White Papers a greater priority has been placed on the socio-economic problems in the cities in the Netherlands and the level of innovation in the manufacturing industry. The purpose of this chapter is to examine these twin phenomena.

In the Netherlands, a number of institutions have been established to boost innovation. Besides opportunities for large firms, the 'Innovation Centrum' was developed as an instrument to stimulate innovation in small and medium-sized firms. Also cities with large universities began to develop science parks. This did not aim to copy the blueprint of Silicon Valley, but aimed to develop institutions at the interface of academic knowledge and the market. This was exemplified by the Science Park in Amsterdam which has seen several hundred start-ups in the ICT sector, resulting from the Centre of Mathematics and Informatica[2] of the University of Amsterdam. Also firms in biotechnology have become established. The policy of this Centre is decided by the university, which has been aiming to concentrate all science faculties (the Beta Cluster) along the beltway in the eastern part of Amsterdam. The university cooperates with an international bank and the city council to fulfil this goal.

This chapter is the outcome of an international research project that aimed to collect comparable data[3] in five European metropolitan regions. The main aim is to find evidence of a new economic situation in these cities in the late 1990s, especially in relation to the dominant sources of economic change, including processes of innovation. This chapter on Amsterdam follows the common approach taken in each city study. First, the Amsterdam Metropolitan Region is described. Besides some historical facts, attention is mainly focused on the economic development of the urban region. In the next section, evidence on innovation and technological change in this region, compared with the rest of the Netherlands, is considered. In the third section the findings of the comparable survey of innovative firms are shown. The last section will set out the main lessons and conclusions to emerge.

Major Characteristics of the Amsterdam Metropolitan Region

Amsterdam is the capital of the Netherlands. The origins of the city date back to the twelfth century, when trade along the coasts of the North Sea and the Baltics developed. The main centre of European trade had been shifting from the North Italian cities towards North-west Europe, where many cities were developing on the basis of trade and access to water transport (Pirenne, 1925). During the 80-year war with the Spanish, the city of Amsterdam developed very quickly. The main reason for this was that the cities in the Netherlands offered a liberal and tolerant climate that attracted many people who had previously been persecuted because of religion or political ideas. Whereas other European regions nearly collapsed under the burden of the noblesse, the Netherlands also offered a liberal economic climate that attracted capital and trade, especially from Antwerp, that was occupied by the Spanish. During and after the 80-year war, the Netherlands experienced a Golden Age, in which Amsterdam flourished and fulfilled a key role.

Description of the Region and its Location

Amsterdam became the main trade centre in Europe, where all kinds of goods were stored and distributed. Among other Dutch cities (for example,

Hoorn) Amsterdam had a predominant role in the trade to the Far East. The Vereenigde Oostindische Compagnie (VOC), the United East Indies Company, was founded. This was a global multinational with stockholders. Together with growing international trade, Amsterdam developed as the most important financial centre in the seventeenth century. Not only was the first stock exchange founded in Amsterdam, developed on the need to share risk in the dangerous trade, but also a market for financial derivatives like futures and options developed in order to hedge against long-term risk. Also cities in the Netherlands did not thrive on the surrounding land, that was mostly wet in wintertime and easy to defend, but on trade. This is why population density was able to reach high levels as early as the sixteenth and seventeenth centuries. The Netherlands, including Amsterdam, began to lose its key role in European economic development in the late seventeenth and early eighteenth centuries, when England developed as the main power in Europe. It is not surprising that New Amsterdam was exchanged with the English to be renamed New York, for an insignificant area in Latin America.

The legacy of the Amsterdam Golden Age needs to be considered with respect to the topic in question. First, we have to stress the fact that the lack of central power (absolutism) in the Netherlands contributed to the dispersed nature of the Dutch population. By the seventeenth century Amsterdam was by far the largest city in the Netherlands. However, the industrial revolution of the nineteenth century did not affect Amsterdam as it did other cities. In the nineteenth century, when the economic base of Amsterdam was eroded in relative terms, other cities like The Hague, Rotterdam and Utrecht were growing at a faster pace.

The history of Amsterdam explains why this small city in international terms still has a unique, open-minded, tolerant and liberal international climate. It also explains why the main economic sectors are now trade, transport and finance, and why manufacturing industries have a secondary position. Furthermore, the kind of manufacturing industries which dominate such as printing and publishing also date back to the Golden Age. These industries thrived on the lack of censorship. Other important industries were timber (shipping), food and paint (shipping). These industries developed on the large-scale use of windmills around the city, especially in Zaandam, at the northwest of Amsterdam and part of Amsterdam Region.

The Amsterdam Economy

Population

At present, the population of Amsterdam is 700,000 inhabitants while the entire region has some 1.2 m inhabitants. The economic region as defined in the Foundation Amsterdam Economic Forecasts extends from the

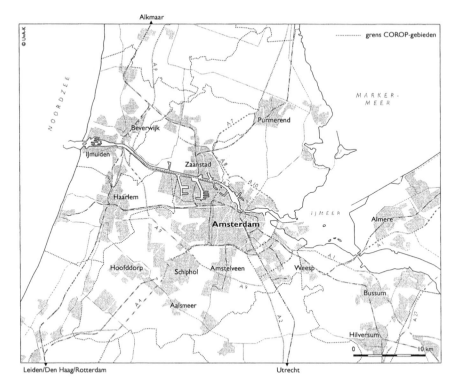

Figure 4.1. The Amsterdam Region

IJsselmeer in the east towards the North Sea coast (see Figure 4.1). If a functional region is defined based on the spatial extent of commuting, the region would extend somewhat more to the east, comprising Hilversum, and to the north, some of the province of North Holland. The maximum accepted commuting trip in the Netherlands is about one hour (one way), which explains why the functional region or the daily urban system is relatively small compared to London or Paris.

Production

As a percentage of national production, the Amsterdam economy amounted to 5.7 per cent in 1998 (Table 4.1). In 1970 this percentage was 8.75 per cent. The Region of Amsterdam amounted to 13.3 per cent whereas in 1970 this was 15.2 per cent. This indicates two crucial facts. First, as a proportion of the entire Dutch economy, the regional economy of the capital is relatively small. Second, this decreased after 1970. This reduction in the city of Amsterdam is larger (−3 per cent) than of the region as a whole (−2 per cent). Figures like this are a sign of the large-scale suburbanisation that took place in the urban system of the Randstad

Table 4.1. Production in the Netherlands, Amsterdam and the Amsterdam Region

The Netherlands	1998 ABS	1970–83 %	1984–98 %	1970–98 %
agriculture	44074	4.0	1.2	2.5
industry	399326	2.1	2.8	2.5
building	80129	−1.3	3.1	1.0
wholesale/transport	157823	3.0	4.5	3.8
fin. and business services	130485	3.8	5.4	4.7
comm. consumer serv.	92887	1.6	3.8	2.7
real estate	60788	5.5	3.5	4.4
non-profit services	162775	2.9	1.7	2.2
total production	1128285	2.3	3.2	2.8
Amsterdam	**1998 ABS**	**1970–83 %**	**1984–98 %**	**1970–98 %**
agriculture	51	1.6	−1.1	0.2
industry	12491	−2.6	1.4	−0.5
building	2581	−1.9	1.5	−0.1
wholesale/transport	10287	−0.7	2.8	1.2
fin. and business services	18103	2.7	3.4	3.1
comm. consumer serv.	6133	−0.5	1.7	0.7
real estate	3049	3.3	3.4	3.4
non-profit services	11931	1.9	1.5	1.7
total production	64625	0.0	2.3	1.2
Amsterdam Region	**1998 ABS**	**1970–83 %**	**1984–98 %**	**1970–98 %**
agriculture	1284	1.6	1.7	1.6
industry	35921	−0.8	2.1	0.8
building	7273	−2.7	2.5	0.1
wholesale/transport	38810	2.7	5.7	4.3
fin. and business services	26697	3.3	4.2	3.8
comm. consumer serv.	12941	0.7	2.9	1.9
real estate	7192	5.0	3.4	4.1
non-profit services	19635	2.4	1.6	2.0
total production	149753	1.1	3.3	2.3

Source: SEO/databank Amsterdam Economic Forecasts.

and the economic opportunities that areas outside the large cities provided such as space and accessibility. As with most other cities in the Western world, a lack of space and increasing congestion has limited the economic development of Amsterdam.

In the period 1970–83, the average production growth rate in Amsterdam was exactly zero. However, the period 1984–98 saw a relative recovery with an average annual growth of 2.3 per cent. This is not only better than the earlier period, but also relatively improved compared to the national figure. In the first period, the difference in growth of annual production between Amsterdam and the national figure was 2.3 per cent. In the second period this decreased to 0.9 per cent. This relative improvement is largely due to sectoral shifts. If the growth differential between the two periods is measured, it turns out that apart from agriculture and the non-profit services, all market sectors contributed to this better performance. The policy change in the Netherlands towards economic liberalisation and moderate wage growth shows up. If we consider the sectoral composition of the change in production growth, we observe that industry showed the largest growth differential between the two periods of 4 per cent. Industry is followed by building (difference of 3.4 per cent), wholesale, transport (3.5 per cent) and commercial consumer services (2.2 per cent). Financial and business services did not show up as having a large growth differential. The reason for this is that this sector was successful during the 1970s.

The Amsterdam Region developed at a very moderate pace during the 1970s but growth levels accelerated during the 1980s to the national level. With regards to the sectoral composition, the same picture as Amsterdam emerges. However, whereas industry performed better in Amsterdam after 1983, it is the building sector that shows the largest growth differential in the entire region. This is probably caused by higher investment levels in the period 1983–98, especially investment in the Schiphol Airport Area and the so-called South axis, where there was a boom in real estate development.

In summary, the city and the region performed better compared to national figures in the period 1983–98. One explanation for this better performance is that suburbanisation slowed down in the 1980s. There was a negative relationship between economic growth and the size of the city in the Netherlands in this period (Van der Vegt and Manshanden, 1996). This can be explained by agglomeration disadvantages such as the lack of space and congestion. However, firms cannot leave the city twice and the remaining firms performed better during the 1980s and 1990s.

Employment

With regards to employment levels, a somewhat similar picture emerges. We have to bear in mind that the difference between production and employment consists of *labour productivity* and the *extent of part-time work*. During the 1970s, production growth was accompanied by relatively high labour productivity growth (Figure 4.2). By the same token, part-time work had not yet developed by then. Total employment figures therefore decreased in Amsterdam during the period 1970–83 (Table 4.2). In industry, building, wholesale and commercial consumer services employment declined severely while the non-profit services – that is, the extension of government spending – grew at a faster rate. In industry, the failures of large firms and productivity growth (rationalisation) in the remaining firms resulted in severe job losses. This job loss continued during the period 1983–98 as the fast rate of productivity growth con-

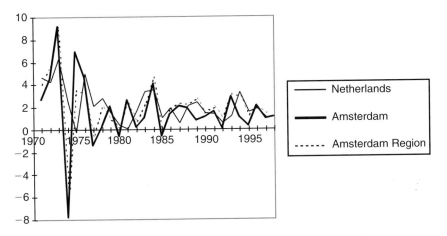

Figure 4.2. Labour productivity growth, annual growth, 1970–98
Source: SEO/databank Amsterdam Economic Forecasts.

tinued. This applied to the nation-wide economy as well as to the Amsterdam Region (Table 4.3). Moreover, part-time work was not as widespread in manufacturing industries as it was in the commercial services.

In the period 1983–98, employment exploded in the financial and business services sector. Apart from real estate this sector shows an average annual growth rate in employment of 3.8 per cent during these fifteen years. In the Amsterdam Region this figure is even higher (4.8 per cent annually). The reason for this is the low and even declining productivity growth in the financial and business services sector during the 1980s and 1990s and the large increase in part-time work in this sector. The increase in part-time work is also a substantial explanation for the employment growth in commercial consumer services and non-profit services.

A Renewed Regional Economy?

In the course of the period 1970–98, the regional economy became more labour-intensive. In the 1980s the pattern reverted to a slow employment growth, followed by acceleration of growth in the 1990s. Even in the 1994–95 downturn, the growth of employment remained on a positive trend. However, a new phenomenon is that since the mid-1990s the growth of employment in the city of Amsterdam is no longer behind the figure of the entire region. An important reason for this is the rate of labour productivity growth which declined in this period. If the sectoral decomposition of labour productivity is taken into consideration, the difference among sectors seems to be more important than among regions. In other words, the sectoral figures do not differ significantly in each region. In general, labour productivity is higher in those sectors where capital intensity (and the pace of innovation) are high such as agriculture,

Table 4.2. Employment in the Netherlands, Amsterdam and the Amsterdam Region (× 1000)

The Netherlands	1998 ABS	1970–83 %	1984–98 %	1970–98 %
agriculture	329	−1.2	−0.1	−0.7
industry	1036	−2.2	−0.3	−1.2
building	443	−3.1	1.3	−0.9
wholesale/transport	882	0.2	2.0	1.1
fin. and business services	907	2.7	5.5	4.1
comm. consumer serv.	1439	0.0	2.7	1.4
real estate	41	4.1	3.0	3.5
non-profit services	1914	3.1	1.2	2.1
total production	6992	0.1	1.7	0.9
Amsterdam	**1998 ABS**	**1970–83 %**	**1984–98 %**	**1970–98 %**
agriculture	1	−7.2	1.3	−2.7
industry	40	−5.1	−1.4	−3.1
building	15	−4.6	−0.2	−2.3
wholesale/transport	65	−2.6	0.5	−0.9
fin. and business services	115	0.6	3.7	2.3
comm. consumer serv.	100	−1.5	1.1	−0.1
real estate	4	2.0	3.8	3.0
non-profit services	152	2.2	1.4	1.8
total production	492	−1.2	1.3	0.2
Amsterdam Region	**1998 ABS**	**1970–83 %**	**1984–98 %**	**1970–98 %**
agriculture	14	−2.2	0.4	−0.9
industry	107	−3.5	−1.2	−2.3
building	41	−4.1	0.4	−1.7
wholesale/transport	166	−0.4	1.8	0.8
fin. and business services	187	1.4	4.8	3.2
comm. consumer serv.	207	−0.6	1.7	0.6
real estate	7	2.8	3.8	3.4
non-profit services	252	2.7	1.6	2.1
total production	980	−0.5	1.7	0.7

Source: SEO/databank Amsterdam Economic Forecasts.

manufacturing industries and wholesale and transport. Financial and business services have the lowest productivity levels in the market sector (Table 4.3). The only remarkable figure is that of the labour productivity of wholesale and transport in the Amsterdam Region. This is most probably due to investment developments in relation to Schiphol Airport.

Specialisation among Industries

The more urbanised a region is, the more the regional economy is dominated by service industries (Richardson, 1973). This is caused by the existence of scale economies that favour the local production and consumption

Table 4.3. Growth rate labour productivity, average 1970–1998

	The Netherlands	Amsterdam	Amsterdam Region
agriculture	3.5	3.7	2.9
industry	3.9	3.3	3.5
building	1.9	2.4	2.0
wholesale/transport	2.8	2.4	3.7
fin. and business services	0.6	1.0	0.8
comm. consumer serv.	1.8	1.4	1.7
real estate	0.9	0.6	0.9
non-profit services	0.5	0.5	0.5
total production	2.1	1.5	2.0

Source: SEO/databank Amsterdam Economic Forecasts.

of services, and agglomeration disadvantages for manufacturing industries, that need space and accessibility to international markets. As far as these characteristics are concerned, the production structure of the Amsterdam Region is as regional economic theory predicts: dominated by the service sector. Manufacturing industries such as Ford (car industry), NDSM (ship-building), Fokker (aircraft) and many smaller industrial firms have either failed or left the region.

Which manufacturing industries have predominantly remained in Amsterdam and the region? In Amsterdam itself, printing and publishing is the most dominant industry (Table 4.4). The headquarters of this activity are located in the centre of Amsterdam. The strong position of this industry dates back to the Golden Age, and it can also be described as an 'urban activity' tied to service industries like translating, writing and marketing.

Table 4.4. Specialisation index for the Amsterdam Region and City, based on production, 1996

	Amsterdam Region	Amsterdam
food	25	10
food, other	102	71
drinks/tobacco	81	119
textile/clothing	74	58
timber/building materials	33	22
printing and publishing	165	235
crude oil	8	5
chemical	66	44
steel	340	0
metals/machines	60	39
electrotechn.	42	31
transport	46	55

Source: SEO/databank Amsterdam Economic Forecasts.

Another industry that has a strong position in Amsterdam is drinks and tobacco. The main activity here is the production of beer by a leading brand, Heineken, that has its headquarters in the centre of Amsterdam. All other industrial sectors are under-represented in Amsterdam, especially those sectors that belong to the so-called high-tech industrial sectors, where innovative activity is relatively high.

In the Amsterdam Region, the picture is somewhat different. In general, the concentration indices are higher (table 4.4). The main industry in the region is the steel industry, dominated by the Hoogovens steelmills in IJmuiden (nowadays Corus after a merger with British Steel). Printing and publishing are also spatially concentrated in the region, as is the food industry (non-animal). The under-representation, in relative terms, of most of the manufacturing industries in the Amsterdam Region follows from the predominance of the service sector (the concentration index compares the relative share of a sector in the region with the national relative share).

Innovation in the Amsterdam Economy

A Geography of Innovation: Amsterdam in the Randstad

The Netherlands is a fascinating laboratory for researchers on innovation. The Netherlands does not have a dominant urban core like other European countries. One should speak of an urban continuum with varying density and parts having specific economic specialisations. Accordingly, as is shown in the previous section, the Netherlands and especially Amsterdam, developed an economy based on trade, transport, finance and insurance and specific business services. Meanwhile, the manufacturing industries were developing in the Netherlands in the south-east of the Netherlands. Consequently, in absolute terms, innovation is concentrated in that area (Poot et al., 1997).

Budil-Nadvornikova and Kleinknecht (1993) described regional innovation patterns in the Netherlands in detail. They concluded that the number of product innovations out of every 1,000 companies was highest in the Outer Rotterdam area, the location of Europe's largest harbour. The second highest is South-East Noord-Brabant, where Philips Electronics and ASM Lithography, a world leader in the production of wafer steppers and a spin-off from Philips Electronics have their factories and laboratories. Accordingly, many suburban areas in the Randstad and the so-called intermediary zone accommodate the most innovative industrial firms. The Green Heart, Utrecht and South-East Noord-Brabant especially stand out. This is observed in the study by Hilpert (1992), in which the Amsterdam/Rotterdam area is mentioned as one of the most innovative urban regions in Europe. Planners refer to this area as the Randstad. In functional or regional-economic terms, however, this can hardly be conceived

Table 4.5. Number of innovations by 1,000 firms by geographical area in the Netherlands

	All	Modern	Traditional	Services
The Netherlands	1.81	28.43	2.53	0.62
Utrecht	3.73	51.93	4.88	1.74
Alkmaar	2.33	62.28	0.00	0.25
Zaanstreek	*0.40*	*2.91*	*0.00*	*0.23*
Haarlem	*1.12*	*19.67*	*0.00*	*0.55*
IJmond	*0.72*	*8.58*	*0.00*	*0.11*
Amsterdam City	*1.21*	*16.97*	*2.29*	*0.72*
Amsterdam, outer area	*2.65*	*42.14*	*2.82*	*1.01*
't Gooi	1.92	20.41	1.76	1.22
Leiden	0.76	4.77	0.00	0.66
Den Haag	2.02	59.38	5.17	0.36
Delft	2.73	42.64	0.00	0.14
East S-Holland	4.81	48.45	0.00	3.07
Rotterdam	0.75	13.97	1.34	0.20
Rotterdam, outer area	6.85	93.66	6.04	2.32
Southeast S-Holland	3.27	41.32	3.19	1.10

Note: Amsterdam Region in italic.
Source: Budil-Nadvornikova and Kleinknecht (1993).

as one urban entity; it consists of three large cities situated at close proximity. Each of them has its own daily urban system and specific regional economic features.

Within the Randstad, modern innovative manufacturing industries are mainly concentrated in south-east South Holland and outer Rotterdam. Only in the Ring of Amsterdam there is a more than average level of innovative activity by industrial firms. If the number of product innovations out of every 1,000 firms is considered (Table 4.5), it is clear that the Amsterdam Region is below the national average. In general, within the Randstad the most urbanised areas have a low innovation rate, whereas the more suburban parts have the highest innovation rates. If the logarithm of population density in each COROP region in Table 4.5 is plotted against the innovation rate, it is clear that a negative relationship exists (Figure 4.3).

Within the urban system of the Netherlands, it seems that the less congested areas in the Randstad benefit from the proximity of the big cities (agglomeration advantages) and the large market potential of the Randstad (Brouwer *et al.*, 1999). Within the Randstad, companies tend to avoid the large cities, preferring to establish themselves in the less congested areas of the Green Heart. There, they do have the benefit of the market potential of the Randstad as a whole within a 100 km range that contains a market of some 10 million people. The Randstad as a whole contains less manufacturing firms in relative terms, but those firms are more innovative, as Brouwer *et al.* (1999) have shown.

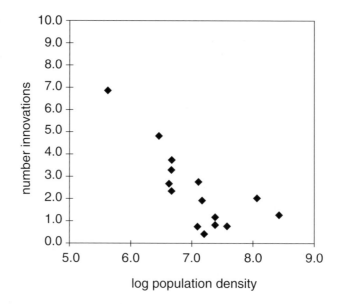

Figure 4.3. Population density in the COROP regions of the Randstad and innovation rate
Source: Budil-Nadvornikova and Kleinknecht (1993).

In so far as agglomeration economies exist, the very question is of course why this is so when communication technology is supposedly allowing information to be more ubiquitous. Moreover, with regard to innovative firms, there tends to be more contact with regular clients in export markets than there is with clients in local markets. These distant clients tend to provide more information to the innovative firm than clients nearby (Manshanden, 1996). Innovation is strongly triggered by the demand side of the firm, but there are strong indications that this is not influenced by agglomeration economies or forces nearby. However, Brouwer *et al.* (1999) showed that agglomeration economies do influence the innovativeness of firms. This follows the assumption that supply factors that influence the innovative level of manufacturing firms have a spatial bias, not demand factors. The next sections address this apparent paradox.

SMEs in the Amsterdam Region: Innovation and Clustering

The Supply of Knowledge

According to evolutionary economics it is knowledge, in the end, which determines what will happen in the future, since R&D and resulting innovations are built on that knowledge (Lambooy, 1997). We therefore need to consider what kinds of knowledge are available in the Amsterdam

Region. Previous research has indicated where the technological areas of knowledge supply lie in the Amsterdam Region. For example, Manshanden (1998) drew up an inventory of knowledge supply. We could also make use of extended regional sources such as the Knowledge Book Amsterdam and the Knowledge Circle Amsterdam. These sources originate from initiatives in Amsterdam in the late 1980s when the importance of knowledge was recognised (Knight, 1986). This result is an elaborated body of quantitative and qualitative data that mainly covers the Amsterdam Region.

The supply of knowledge is measured in man years by academics, consultants, researchers, teachers and professors at universities and high schools, research institutions, manufacturing firms and service firms. Because the Knowledge Circle Amsterdam only selected large firms, SMEs are not included in this inventory. A further limitation is that comparisons with the Netherlands were not possible because we did not have at our disposal a similar source for the whole country. For this reason only the absolute supply of knowledge in North Holland has been analysed. All man years, given in the sources and academic guides, are counted and classified by technological area (see Table 4.6).

The data show that the supply of knowledge in North Holland is concentrated in a few technological areas, listed below, and is negligible in most other areas:

- medical sector;
- economics and management;
- information software;
- data transmission systems;
- leisure, tourism and art;
- design/synthesis/processing low molecular compounds;
- transport and traffic systems;
- management environment/safety/health.

The kind of knowledge available in the Amsterdam Region is therefore characteristic of an urban region dominated by the economic sources of services and consumer markets. The supply results from the demand for knowledge from the headquarters, banks and the business services, that are abundant in the region. Knowledge of the medical services and the leisure–tourism/art sector results from the consumer market in the region. The knowledge of design/synthesis/processing low molecular compounds results from the presence of Royal Dutch/Shell Laboratories in Amsterdam. The knowledge of transport and traffic systems results from the

Table 4.6. Supply of knowledge in North Holland

R&D investments in man years Technological areas	Universities and high school	Research institutions	Industry	Services	Total
1 Cultivation cattle/fish/crops	0	0	0	0	0
2 Exploring/producing minerals	0	0	0	0	0
3 Design/synthesis/process low molecular	50	0	1,020	0	1,070
4 Design/synthesis/process high molecular	50	0	580	0	630
5 production/process/applying metals	9	120	500	0	620
6 Surface/thin layer/film	0	120	250	0	370
7 Biological processes	80	180	0	0	260
8 Design/production durable goods	0	0	0	0	0
9 Engineering production systems	20	120	0	0	140
10 Manufacturing	20	0	10	0	30
11 Measuring/control processes	0	120	0	0	120
12 Testing product quality	0	0	0	0	0
13 Design/production integrated circuits	0	0	0	0	0
14 Information systems hardware	0	0	0	0	0
15 Information systems software	0	280	0	1,790	2,070
16 Data transmission systems	0	0	10	1,780	1,790
17 Processing signals	0	0	0	0	0
18 Optical/acoustical/x-ray systems	130	650	0	0	780
19 Transportation equipment	0	0	0	0	0
20 Transportation/traffic systems	400	390	0	30	820
21 Building/infrastructure	0	120	120	10	250
22 Managing environment/safety/health	20	690	10	20	740
23 Producing/distribution energy/water	0	170	50	10	230
24 Economics and management	1,630	290	0	3,980	5,900
25 Use of information systems	500	0	0	0	500
26 Leisure/tourism/art	670	60	0	380	1,110
27 Medical	430	5,710	80	0	6,220
28 Alpha/language	300	180	0	0	480
29 Gamma/social	250	230	0	0	480
Total	4,550	9,430	2,630	8,000	

Source: Estimate SEO.

presence of the harbour and Schiphol Airport. At a distance, the kind of knowledge in the Amsterdam Region would seem to follow from the heritage of the region, characterised by trade, transport and finance. These clusters are still strong in Amsterdam, and presumably they triggered the supply of knowledge for economics, management, information, data, tourism, art and culture. Moreover, these kinds of knowledge have a strong bias towards the service sector, and not manufacturing industries.

The service sector is a very large provider with its foundations in economics and management, information software and data transmission systems. To a large extent, this supply is found in the knowledge-intensive services. It concerns very specific services which are supplied and exchanged in the market.

Export as a percentage of turnover in the Amsterdam Region is also lower than the national average. Also SMEs have a higher percentage project market there. Manufacturing industry has less self-specifying firms (firms that know the global market, have the clients and define the product). The percentage of suppliers is the same as the national average. In Amsterdam Region there are far more industrial services than the national figure. In sum, small and medium-sized industrial firms in the region are dominated by suppliers and industries that operate in uncertain project markets. The region lacks (larger) self-specifying industrial companies, acting as leaders in industrial clusters by maintaining export markets and acting as 'importers' of information on potential innovative needs.

However, from the policy-maker's point of view, to what extent is this situation alarming? Actually, it is not. The presence of SMEs operating in uncertain project markets and industrial services is not specific to the Amsterdam Region. It should be regarded as a common feature of metropolitan areas (Hoover and Vernon, 1959; Richardson, 1973). Spatial clustering results in cheaper subcontracting (Scott, 1983). Components in the production process that have a high degree of uncertainty tend to be outsourced. Scott (1983) asserted that uncertain linkages tend to cluster spatially, and that, on the contrary, certain linkages tend to disperse spatially. Transaction cost economics offers a conceptual framework for this assertion. The importance of Scott (1983) is the implication for innovation and spatial factors. In common economic geography, innovation is supposed to depend positively on spatial clustering; the incubator hypothesis or spatial spill-over (positive external effects). However, one can also assert that innovation is positively related to linkages which are certain, frequent and predictable. The consequence of this assertion is that one will find more innovation in firms that have more linkages with distant clients. That is exactly what empirical evidence shows: export and innovation are positively related. How should we interpret this in the light of the incubator hypothesis? Possibly both factors counterbalance each other. That is, the disadvantage of uncertainty in spatial clusters is counterbalanced by spatial spill-over, and the lack of spatial spill-over in linkages with clients in export countries is counterbalanced by the certainty of the linkage.

Following Scott (1983), it is crucial to measure uncertainty. Interviews with entrepreneurs in the Amsterdam Region revealed that entrepreneurs in SMEs used the concept of project and series market. These concepts refer to the degree of regular demand by clients. Clients are divided into those two categories. A frequent, predictable client belongs to the series market, an unregular, unexpected client belongs to the project market. The importance of the split between series and project markets is that in the first type innovation is more likely. This higher chance follows from more intense and regular contact with the client, in which information is transferred. Moreover, nearby customers tend to be more uncertain.

Some General Evidence on the Knowledge Base in the Amsterdam Metropolitan Region (AMR)

These characteristics apply in particular to SMEs. It should be stressed that the Amsterdam Region has an abundance of smaller SMEs, and a handful of very large multinationals. The region lacks larger, medium-sized firms. Examples of Dutch multinationals that have establishments in the Amsterdam Region are: Hoogovens (steel mills, recently merged with British Steel), Royal Dutch Shell Laboratories, Akzo Nobel Chemicals, Philips Electronics. Those are not headquarters. The case of Philips Electronics is curious. Business-like head office functions are established in Amsterdam, in the proximity of the banks, business services, Schiphol Airport and last but not least an international metropolitan culture. However, technological development functions, the virtue of Philips Electronics, are still established in Eindhoven, a medium-sized city in the south-east of the Netherlands. Moreover, Philips Electronics is now investing in a technological campus there to develop its innovative potential.

To conclude, the Amsterdam Region is not a centre of many innovative manufacturing industries. The south-east of the country accommodates in absolute terms most of the innovative manufacturing firms in the Netherlands. Within the Randstad it is the Green Heart and the edge of Rotterdam where innovative firms tend to concentrate. There are many multinational headquarters in the region of Amsterdam where manufacturing predominates. The advantage of the agglomeration for innovation does not occur on the demand side, but occurs on the supply side of the firm. A first general look on the supply side is focused on the knowledge base of the Amsterdam Region. This knowledge base mostly consists of knowledge that favours service activities that have traditionally established themselves in Amsterdam.

Survey Results

Characteristics of the Sample

In total, 226 manufacturing firms were approached for the survey. These were 13 from the BRITE award list and 213 firms from a local database of firms in the Amsterdam Metropolitan Region. From these 213 firms 20 appeared as innovative firms and responded positively. This seems like a very low response rate but we have to bear in mind that only the innovative firms were considered. A majority (69 per cent) of the firms were private, national Dutch firms. The remaining firms were private multinationals. Most of the firms (69 per cent) were either micro firms or small. All the firms that responded were manufacturing firms. The chemicals, machinery and medical and surgical equipment and instruments were the sectors with the highest proportion of responses.

Location Factors

The innovative industrial companies in the Amsterdam Region were asked to rate the importance of twenty-six locational variables. These have been aggregated to transportation infrastructure, the knowledge environment, training and information, production factors, local knowledge, supply factors, demand factors and technical and professional labour (see Table 4.7). Of the general themes that are considered, the production factors are the most important, together with technical and professional labour. This observation indicates that this is the scarcest factor among innovative industrial firms in the Amsterdam Metropolitan Region. Further on, among the transport variables, access to the national road network is regarded as the most important transport mode. If the specific factors are considered, it is clear that *skilled personnel* and the *opportunity to acquire experts* are the most crucial.

Other results show that it is only partly true to suggest that supply-side factors explain the agglomeration effects of the Amsterdam Region. Most of the firms said that their most important contacts for innovation had been their clients. Suppliers rank second (see Table 4.8). This accords with the demand-pull hypothesis. However, the proximity of linkages with

Table 4.7. Sample characteristics/number of firms

Type of organisation		Size of firm	$	Sector	
private national firm	18	micro	6	22 printing/publishing	1
private multinational firm	8	small	12	23 oil/coal	1
public enterprise	–	medium	2	24 chemicals	4
other	–	large	6	25 plastics	
				26 glass/brick/building materials	2
				27 basic steel	1
				29 machinery	6
				31 other electronic devices	1
				32 audio, video, telecom	
				33 medical and surgical instruments	6
				35 other transport	2
				36 furniture/other industry	2
				37 recycling	

Walter J.J. Manshanden and Jan G. Lambooy

Table 4.8. The importance of locational factors to innovation

	mean
Transportation infrastructure	
low levels of traffic congestion	2.9
good access to Amsterdam	2.9
good rail connections	2.5
good access to national road network	3.3
good access to major airport	3.0
General and specialised business knowledge and information	
access to private general business services	2.5
access to private specialised business services	2.7
proximity of collaborators	3.0
proximity of business services	2.2
proximity of sources of information	2.4
Finance, training, knowledge and information	
access to financial capital	2.3
local public business support services	2.4
contributions from TECs	2.2
contributions from business links	1.1
contributions from universities	2.5
Factors of production	
availability of skilled manual labour	4.0
availability of suitable premises	3.4
cost of premises	3.3
Local industrial knowledge and experience	
presence of ex-colleagues	1.6
presence of friends	1.4
Supply factors	
cost of labour	3.0
proximity of suppliers	2.6
Demand factors	
proximity of customers	2.3
proximity of competitors	1.3
Technical and professional labour	
availability of professional experts to recruit	3.7

Note: Mean score where 1 = not important to 5 = very important.
Source: BRITE survey.

clients and suppliers is not regarded as especially important. One of the surprising findings is that proximity of clients, the most powerful incentive for innovation, is not of any great importance. However, as expected for innovative firms, export markets are more important and therefore relationships with international customers matter most in terms of innovation.

An interesting finding is the difference in importance of suppliers, comitors and clients with regards to spatial scope. If these three groups are

Table 4.9. The importance of contact networks related to innovation

Type of contact network	mean
learning	2.2
business	2.1
collaborators	2.5
friends	2.0
Important external sources of knowledge and information	
competitors	2.3
suppliers	3.0
customers	4.0

Note: Mean score where 1 = not important to 5 = very important.
Source: BRITE survey.

compared, it is clear that suppliers are mostly located in close proximity and clients at a distance (see Table 4.9). Clients tend to be located in the rest of the country and in the European Union, whereas suppliers are relatively more localised and regionalised. The result is, that within the 100 km range, suppliers dominate, and beyond that limit there are more linkages with clients. Further on, the USA appears to be an important source of supply for innovative firms whereas customers are more spatially dispersed in global terms. The different spatial scope between suppliers and clients of innovative firms is something that demands further research and, moreover, an economic explanation, as well as some elaboration on the specific role of the US economy. Competitors are mostly located in the rest of the European Union or the United States.

With regard to cooperation, the client also shows up as the most important actor (see Table 4.10). Competitors and non-profit organisations both have a very low score whereas other firms in the group, other companies and universities have an average or neutral score. This

Table 4.10. The geography of linkages

	Suppliers	Customers	Competitors
international			
Europe	24	32	32
USA	19	9	24
Japan	4	7	9
other Pacific Rim	2	0	0
global	1	10	9
national			
101 km Netherlands	17	28	15
regional 50–100 km	15	7	4
local (<50 km)	17	7	6
	100%	100%	100%

Source: BRITE survey.

confirms again that the demand side is the most important force in directing the innovation process. A qualitative example of one of the firms from the survey is illustrative of the spatial–industrial pattern of the Netherlands, where there is a limited knowledge base for innovation in manufacturing firms in the Amsterdam Region. The firm had agreements with Philips, the Polytechnic in Delft and a higher technical school in Haarlem. For the knowledge base of their product innovations, these firms depend on organisations in Eindhoven and Delft.

A number of the firms originated as manufacturing firms but are now specialising in design and conceptualisation. Such 'conceptual' firms should not necessarily be viewed as manufacturing firms, but as engineering firms. In any event such firms underscore the fact that they do not depend on suppliers in the region. They do not rely on their suppliers as an incentive for innovation as much as on their clients and competitors, both of which act on a global scale (see Table 4.11).

If the importance of information sources is regarded, it turns out that technical experts are regarded as the most important source. Clients are second, followed by designers and R&D experts and academics. Business services are regarded as unimportant factors.

Own capital is regarded as the most important source of financing (see Table 4.12). Bank loans or funding from other firms are regarded as unimportant. It is striking that public awards and subsidies are regarded as more important than bank loans or contributions from other companies. However, it has to be stressed that awards as funding are useless, because

Table 4.11. The importance of collaborators to innovation

Collaborator	mean
commercial research suppliers	
suppliers	3.0
government research establishments	1.9
research associations	2.3
consultancy services	2.2
non-commercial research providers	
universities or other HEIs	2.3
private non-profit organisations	1.6
clients, customers or competitors	
competitors	2.0
clients or customers	3.8
other firms within the group	
other firms within the group	2.8
other firms	3.5

Note: Mean score where 1 = not important to 5 = very important.
Source: BRITE survey.

Table 4.12. Importance of financial sources to innovation

Source	mean
bank debt	1.4
bank loan	1.3
loan government	1.2
venture capital	1.8
own money	1.3
public awards/subsidy	2.7
EC subsidy/awards	2.4
joint venture/partnerships	1.9
own capital	3.4
funds group firms	1.9
funds other companies	1.0

Note: Mean score where 1 = not important to 5 = very important.
Source: BRITE survey.

they tend to be given when the innovation is already there. The conclusion from financing is that individual entrepreneurs should have the opportunity to build up their own capital by saving and working, without being hindered by too strict a tax legislation. In the end, entrepreneurs take risks, when they know that they can take risks, and they provide their own best support.

Conclusion

If the relation between agglomeration and innovation in manufacturing industries is studied, one does not find a clear-cut picture. In the first instance, the conclusions depend on the spatial level. At the national level, a positive relationship between agglomeration and innovation is found (Brouwer, 1999). On the level of the Randstad, however, a negative relationship is found. In other words, the innovative firms tend to be located in the less urban areas of the Randstad. Such conclusions result from the somewhat complicated and spread-out nature of the urban system in the Netherlands. This leads to the conclusion that manufacturing firms in the suburban and less dense parts of the Randstad reap the benefits of agglomeration advantages, and not necessarily in the large cities themselves.

That explains why in the Amsterdam Region, a dense and urbanised region, there is not that much innovative manufacturing activity. In the Amsterdam Region, the heritage of the Golden Age is reflected in the present economic structure and the knowledge base. It is based on trade, transport, finance and insurance and specialised business services. This favours the development of a knowledge base comprising economics and management, information, data transmission (telecommunication), and urban consumer markets favouring medical sciences, life sciences, tourism, leisure and art. Modern manufacturing activities or high-tech activities are particularly under-represented in the Amsterdam Region. The role of the Amsterdam Region in organising the information and knowledge resources available may well be played in relation to other parts of the Dutch economy.

This implies that the concentration of manufacturing industries, and especially innovative manufacturing industries, is low in absolute and relative terms. As much as there is manufacturing industry, it is dominated by food processing, printing and publishing, metal processing and machines, chemicals (pharmaceuticals/paint) and oil. Absolutely, innovative manufacturing activity is concentrated in the south-east of the Netherlands, but with regards to innovation, agglomeration economies do occur. In other words, there are more innovative manufacturing firms in the south-east, but the chance that an industrial firm is innovative is larger in a more urban area like the Randstad.

The fact that Philips Electronics moved only its headquarters to Amsterdam supports this view. However, it has to be stressed that only those head office functions came to Amsterdam that fit the economic structure of the city: finance, law, design, culture. The technical laboratories of Philips Electronics remain in Eindhoven, and the multinational is even investing heavily in a technological campus in Eindhoven, and not in the Amsterdam Region.

The results of this international comparison among innovative industrial firms in the Amsterdam Region confirmed several other findings. This concerns the importance of the demand side of the firm and the importance of exports; in other words, agglomeration factors do not occur on the demand side of the firm. This research project indicates that agglomeration economies apply especially to supply factors of innovative firms. Not only does this project show that supply originates from a smaller spatial scope than clients or competitors, supply factors on the labour market (skilled technical personnel) are perceived as the most important factor for innovation. However, we have to bear in mind that this may be interpreted as the *scarcest* factor. Other typical supply factors appeared to be as important, such as motorways, accessibility and own capital.

Nevertheless, there is evidence that the incubator hypothesis is correct. It does not apply to the relationship with the client, but more to the supply factors of the firm. A lesson to policy-makers might be that it is quite clear what the components of a favourable climate are, in which innovative entrepreneurial spirits can thrive. In the first place, they should have the opportunity to dispose of their of own capital. Next, skilled personnel and technical experts should be easy to find. Then, space should be abundant, motorways accessible and the cost of space low.

Notes

1. with thanks to L. Endendÿk.
2. ... and the National Institute for Nuclear Physics and High Energy Physics...
3. ... on innovation in manufacturing industries...

References

Brouwer, E. (1999) 'Into innovation: determinants and indicators', PhD thesis, University of Amsterdam, Faculty of Economics, Utrecht, Elinkwijk.

Brouwer, E., Budil-Nadvornikova, H. and Kleinknecht, A.H. (1999) 'Are urban agglomerations a better breeding place for product innovations? An analysis of new product announcements', *Regional Studies*, 33, 6, 541–9.

Budil-Nadvornikova, H. and Kleinknecht, A.H. (1993) *De Regional Spreiding van Productinnovaties in Nederland*, Amsterdam: Stichting voor Economisch Onderzoek.

Hilpert, U. (1992) *Archipelago Europe – Islands of Innovation: Synthesis Report*, vol. 18, Prospective Dossier No. 1, 'Science, Technology and Economic Cohesion in the Community', Brussels, FAS, CEC, Science, Research and Development, DG/XII/411/92.

Hoover, E.M. and Vernon, R. (1959) *Anatomy of a Metropolis*, New York, Double Day.

Knight, R.V. (1986) 'The advanced industrial metropolis; a new type of world city', in *The Future of the Metropolis*, Berlin and New York, Walter de Gruyter & Co., pp. 391–436.

Lambooy, J.G. (1997) 'Knowledge production, organisation and agglomeration economies', *Geojournal* 41, 4, 293–300.

Lambooy, J.G., Huigsloot, P.C.M. and van de Lustgraaf, R.E. (1982) *Greep op de Stad?*, Den Haag, Staatsuitgeverij/Wetenschappelijke Raad voor het Regeringsbeleid.

Manshanden, W.J.J. (1996) 'Zakelijke diensten en regionaal-economische ontwik-keling; de economie van nabijheid', thesis, University of Amsterdam, Utrecht, Elinkwijk.

Manshanden, W.J.J. (1998) *Supply and Demand of Knowledge in Noord-Holland: Methodology, Results, Conclusions*, Amsterdam, Stichting voor Economisch Onderzoek.

Ministerie van Economische Zaken en Ministerie van Onderwijs en Wetenschap-pen (1979) *Innovatie: Het Overheidsbeleid Inzake Technologische Vernieuwing in de Nederlandse Samenleving*, Den Haag, Staatsuitgeverij.

Pirenne, H. (1925) *Medieval Cities: Their Origins and Revival of Trade*, Princeton, NJ, Princeton University Press.

Poot, A.P., Brouwer, N.M., Ouwersloot, J. and Rietveld, P. (1997) *Innovatie in de Regio: Provinciale Innovatieprofielen*, Den Haag, SDU.

Richardson, H.W. (1973) *The Economics of Urban Size*, Westmead, Takefield Limited.

Scott, A.J. (1983) 'Industrial organization and the logic of intra-metropolitan loca-tion: theoretical considerations', *Economic Geography*, 59, 233–50.

Vegt, C. van der and Manshanden, W. (1996) *Steden en Stadsgewesten: Econo-mische Ontwikkelingen 1970–2015*, Amsterdam, Stichting voor Economisch Onderzoek der Universiteit van Amsterdam.

Vegt, C. van der, Manshanden, W. and Muskens, J. (1999) *Amsterdamse Economische Verkenningen: Voorjaar 1999. Ontwikkelingen in de Regio Amsterdam*, Amsterdam, Stichting voor Economisch Onderzoek der Univer-siteit van Amsterdam.

CHAPTER 5

Paris: Urban Area, Technopolitan Spaces and Innovative Firms: The Dynamics of Innovation[1]

5 Paris

Urban Area, Technopolitan Spaces and Innovative Firms: The Dynamics of Innovation

Jeanine Cohen, Elisabeth Decoster and Muriel Tabariés

Major Characteristics of the Paris Metropolitan Region

Though not as large as London, New York or Tokyo, Paris is undoubtedly acknowledged to be one of the few global cities whose influence extends well beyond their national borders (Llewelyn-Davies *et al.* (1996)). As far as innovation is concerned, Paris is one of the prominent islands of 'Archipelago Europe' identified by Hilpert (1992) in his work for the FAST/Monitor programme of the European Communities Commission. As the capital city of France for more than one thousand years, Paris is the site of one of the most ancient universities of the world. The city has often distinguished itself by its innovating capabilities, and by a strong centralising and polarising power.

Already regarded as a first rank city with 814,000 inhabitants at the time of the first population census in 1831, it had more than 2,000,000 at the 1881 census, and was to reach 2,888,000 in 1911. Within its 'communal' boundaries, it was to keep, more or less, this maximum size till 1954, when it began to decline significantly, falling to 2,116,000 in 1999, while its suburbs as a whole went on growing. As a result, in 1999, the Parisian 'urban area', which, though quite comparable, does not exactly coincide with that of the 'Ile-de-France Region' (with some 11 million inhabitants), housed 10,561,000 people, 9,481,000 of whom are located in the agglomeration that is the 'urban pole' of this urban area, whereas more than 1 million are in the suburban ring.

The division of activities and jobs between the Ile-de-France Region and Metropolitan France as a whole shows that this demographic concentration reflects a socio-functional hierarchy within the national space economy (Cohen, 1985, 1989; GSP-Strates, 1989). In this hierarchy, the Paris Metropole Region presents some strong concentrations:

- Concentration of tertiary ruling activities in the realms of:
  - government and administration: State central services;
  - finance: Stock Exchange, holdings, insurances, banks and their auxiliaries.

  As far as the last four activities are concerned the respective shares of their French staff located in the Ile-de-France Region are 77, 56, 45 and 74 per cent. To put it another way, if one compares these percentages to the mean weight of the Ile-de-France Region, that accounts for 21.9 per cent of all French jobs (all activities together), and if one expresses this percentage as an index of 100, the respective Ile-de-France location indexes for these four activities are 352, 253, 207 and 336.

- Concentration of industry 'tertiary' functions of:
  - Firms' headquarters, that is to say, of strategic senior executives jobs in management (with an index of 156 in the Ile-de-France Region) and in marketing (an index of 130);
  - Production creation and design (an index of 120). This concentration may exist directly in tertiary industries: such is the case of R&D (in which 50 per cent of the national jobs of marketed services are located in the Ile-de-France Region, i.e. an index of 230, and even 53 per cent of the non-marketed services, with an index of 244). But it still is also remarkable in highly qualified secondary industries, such as electronics, aerospace, power production and dispatching, para-chemistry and pharmaceuticals, as well as newspaper printing and publishing.

- Importance of highly specialised SMEs, namely consultancy, mainly delivered to the enterprises, of whom 55 per cent of the national staff are located in the Ile-de-France Region, and that are therefore, as well as R&D services, far more 'francilian' than average.

- Significant presence of transports and telecommunications mostly their engineers (transports) and professionals (telecommunications). This importance is particularly thrown into relief by air transport, where 86 per cent of the national staff are registered in the Ile-de-France Region (see Figure 5.1).

The history of the Paris development is therefore the one of a polarising centre, creative and redistributive, integrating the main strategic functions, namely, the link to the global scale and to innovation.

Description of the Region and its Location

The physical development of Paris was limited until the eighteenth century by the lack of water system and transport. After that period, the acceleration of its industrial development and the attraction of new immigrant

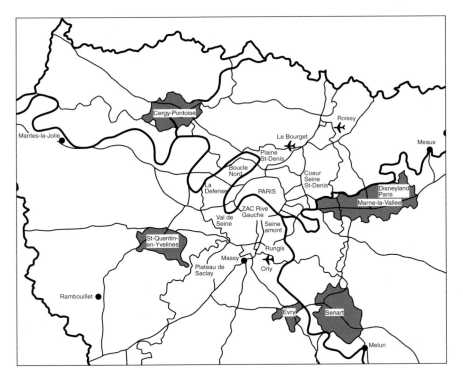

Figure 5.1. Ile-de-France *département*

workers led the government to undertake a vigorous reshaping of the urban fabric, and during the Napoleon III Second Empire (1852–1870), the alterations made by Baron Haussmann resulted in the destruction of old dense wards of the town, to bring a hygienic water supply, sewage systems and rubbish treatment, to build great new institutions, such as stations and railways linking Paris to its suburbs and to the other cities, and new avenues.

At the end of the nineteenth century, the building of a metropolitan railway network was decided and undertaken to serve Paris. The first line opened in 1900, eight others by 1913 and three more in the 1930s. In addition, at that time, some of its closest suburbs benefited from extensions of the existing lines. As early as the period before the First World War, travel to work daily commuting developed, and could increasingly rely on this metropolitan railway network, as well as the national one, run by the SNCF (*Société nationale des chemins de fers français*). These railway networks, in essence, allowed workers to keep their jobs in Paris, while for housing they moved more and more to its suburbs. They were attracted there by better, larger and cheaper houses than in Paris, where housing had become rare, tiny, uncomfortable and expensive. A. Faure (1986) called this move 'the green dream'.

159

Jeanine Cohen *et al.*

Periodically overcrowded, the urban transport network was enhanced several times after the Second World War. The metropolitan railway network, previously run by two companies, merged with buses in a unique public corporation, the RATP (*Régie autonome des transports parisiens*, 1948–49). From 1961 on (first opening 1969), it was supplemented by a large-gauge, high-speed, regional network. In the meantime, President De Gaulle launched a spatial restructuring of the Ile-de-France Region. He created a special authority for this region (the *District*); internal reorganisation, with the design of eight new *départements* out of the original three. A new urban development plan, the 'Design and urbanism guiding outline' (*Schéma directeur d'aménagement et d'urbanisme*, SDAU) was produced. This outline, elaborated in 1965, was first revised in 1969, then revised again and finally approved in 1976 (since that time, it has been replaced by a second one in 1994).

In this guiding outline, the building of 'new towns' beyond the remote outskirts, some 30 km from Paris, drew its inspiration from the British model of the Abercrombie Plan for London, though the Green Belt is not as strictly preserved and the distance from the centre not as large as in the London model. They were built during a period of periurban growth (Berger *et al.*, 1980; Beaucire, 1991). This was started by the building of high-rise estates in the outer ring (in Massy, to the south of Paris, and in Sarcelles, to the north), then by diversified buildings (collective or detached, rental or for home ownership) (Sallez, 1995), then by the fancy for home ownership of detached houses, giving way to the building of numbers of 'new villages'.

The increase in the length of the time spent in commuting to work, and even the isolation of this population, prompted the authorities to accelerate the urban transport network enhancement. The RATP and SNCF networks were interconnected in 1975. Since then, intra-metropolitan transports of every kind have not paused in their integrating and networking (train, underground, regional express network, light automatic vehicles, buses, tramways, shuttles, local and private lines), nor in their interconnecting with the intercities and international networks, in a few inter-modal nodes, such as 'Roissy-2', with planes and high-speed trains, or Massy, with high-speed trains, along with motorways. This provides Paris with one of the best integrated public transport systems in Europe.

The metropolitan space displays a notable internal division (Cohen, 1988), that stems from strong legacies, on the one hand, and from new trends, on the other (Cohen, 1992). These may be summarised as:

1   a central business district is still identifiable in the centre-west of the agglomeration, even though it has been subject to successive shifts towards the west. At present, the more concentrated build-up of jobs, matching the even more concentrated build-up of managerial jobs, are

in the Paris 8th *arrondissement* and, above all, in the La Defense area, located in the 'communes' of Puteaux and Courbevoie (Hauts-de-Seine *département*);

2 the inner suburbs, quite recently very industrial, still show traces of this specificity and frequently remain under-equipped in services, compared to their surrounding areas;

3 the outer suburbs, far less dense and far more extended, are very diverse. They include areas that remain under the influence of the ancient little cities, their respective former centres of attraction, and opposing blue-collar suburbs to technopolitan suburbs (Ibbou *et al.*, 1998);

4 to this radial-concentric differentiation must be added a north-east–south-west asymmetry.

At the transitional period between the twentieth and twenty-first centuries, this asymmetry gives way to a new and more complex system than the previous division between, on the one hand, the western and south-western suburbs, based on capital equipment goods and large premises inherited from metallurgy (cars, aerospace, electrical industries), and, on the other, the northern, eastern and south-eastern neighbourhoods of Paris, along with the close inner suburbs, where were to be found numbers of small premises, often sub-contractors, as well as intermediate goods industries, basic metalwork and mechanical industries (Duong, 1983).

From the mid-1980s, the divide separates, inside Paris *intra-muros*, the CBD (Central Business District), to the west, on the one hand, and a services area, from where the secondary industries withdrew strongly, to the north, east and even to the south and centre, on the other. In the suburbs, this divide continues between, on the one hand, to the north and mainly to the east, an area strongly dedicated to transport, that overlaps, mainly to the north, a continuing manufacturing area, and, on the other, to the west and to the south, the more or less recent CBD extensions of La Defense, Neuilly-sur-Seine, Saint-Cloud, etc., prolonged by a vast periurban arc, where jobs are more qualified than in the north-east, including far more executives and professional workers (Tabard and Chateau, 1989; Tabariés, 1997), and where the R&D function is more represented (Cohen, 1990a, 1997).

In addition, from the 1960s to 2000, the regional space has been reorganising. The centre of Paris is losing its density in jobs, the administrative centres of the new *départements*[1] made up of the inner suburbs, recently very blue-collar, are progressively becoming second-rate centres, endowed with services such as those of the government (prefectures, decentralized services of the various ministries, related establishments, such as the universities), the semi-public social institutions (social security offices, pension funds) or such as the institutions in charge of the local economic development (Chambers of Commerce and industry). In the outer suburbs, this multipolarity, organised into a hierarchy, has developed even more clearly, with, in addition, a notable and apparently spontaneous development of business services (Cohen, 1993, 1994).

Population Size and Structure

While the size of the *de facto* Greater Paris kept on growing, the boundaries and definitions of this extended agglomeration had to be altered several times, in order to take these changes into account. These changes may be summarised as:

- 1900: 4 million inhabitants (the urban unit is the agglomeration, defined by the continuity of the developed sites: it stands out in sharp contrast to its rural environment).

- 1954: 6.4 million (the capital urban area comprises not only the central agglomeration, but also its emerging suburban area).

- 1990: 9.3 million (along with the central agglomeration, several surrounding, less important, agglomerations, and an extended background of periurban *communes* are to be aggregated in the industrial or urban population area: *zone de peuplement industriel ou urbain*, or Z.P.I.U.).

- 1999: 10.6 million (in the urban area). In the latest definition, one takes more and more into account the growing importance of daily commuting that links continuous central spaces with peripheral developed sites, which are more and more discontinuous and remote.

Though the residential agglomeration is still noticeably more extended than the jobs agglomeration,[2] the jobs tend more and more to follow the residents (Cohen, 1991, 1994). The exception to this up to now has been the majority of the headquarters clerks, commerce and some services jobs of the central business district and the historical centre.

Thus, the spatial differentiation according to the jobs functions and qualifications (cf. Cohen, in Simmie, 1997, p. 52) follows in great part the socio-spatial differentiation of the dwelling places (in addition to Tabard and Chateau, 1989 and Tabariés, 1997 already mentioned, see Brun and Rhein, 1994; Ramaux *et al.*, 2000). The reinforcement of this difference must be considered when interpreting the results of the most recent observations about commuting. This has led to the establishment, at the agglomeration periphery, of more auto-centred jobs basins, whose virtual boundaries are less easily crossed than in the past (Beckouche *et al.*, 1998; Berger and Saint-Gérand, 1999; Berger *et al.*, 1998) and to the acceptability of the average travel to work time in the Ile-de-France Region (INSEE, 1999), that stems in part from the transfers and/or the creation of jobs in the outer metropolitan area.

The Paris Economy: Achievements and Poorer Performance of the Capital

Paris and the Ile-de-France Region contrast sharply with the rest of France by the manifest superiority of a good many economic indexes. These include the following:

- Whereas the Ile-de-France Region houses 18.8 per cent of the resident population of Metropolitan France, it contains 21.9 per cent of its jobs, and the activity rate of the francilian population is higher than the Metropolitan French one (INSEE, 1990 Population census).

- Its contribution to the Gross Domestic Product of France is 27.8 per cent (INSEE, Regional counts, 1996).

- It includes the vast majority of firms' headquarters.

- On the Paris Bourse, 376 companies are listed on the official stock market register in 1997, and 304 on the second market.

But this is not a catalogue of the undisputed merits of one of the 'regions that win' (Benko and Lipietz, 1992). This gain, indeed, is won from the important changes entailing overwhelming job shedding that were suffered during the period of jobs crisis. This is deepening and involves major economic restructuring. Thus, there were 459 companies on the official stock market register in 1994. However, 83 of them are therefore missing three years later. Only the second market registered newcomers. Unemployment is taking its time to go down and may suffer new waves again. By 1998 it was 10.7 per cent of the active francilian population.

Traditional jobs areas are the most affected. New jobs in fact go on to locate beyond the francilian boundaries, that is to say they do not completely die out. But these departures are only poorly offset by emerging jobs in the central area of Paris and a high proportion of its inner suburbs and the region has recently undergone slight job decreases from 4.976 m in 1992 to 4.958 m in 1997.

Characteristic Firms and Premises

The marketed services are the strongest contingent among the francilian jobs (28.3 per cent), followed by the non-marketed services (19.4) and commerce (12.2). Among the remaining two-fifths are then to be found transport and telecommunications (8.3), capital equipment goods industries (7.8), construction-civil and agricultural engineering (6.6) and the

Table 5.1. Job structures of the francilian economic activities, 1990: production and services functions

Activity (*U* code *niveau 15A*) Jobs (among which most francilian branches: in *T* code, *niveau 40*)	1. Production				
	Jobs, of which* (%),	Eng.	Pro.	Exc.	S.W.
U01 Agric. sylvic. fishing	89.1	1.3	1.0	2.2	3.0
02 Agr. and food industries	47.5	6.7	3.5	6.9	50.1
03 Energy prod. and distrib.	55.2	34.0	17.0	22.7	20.3
04 Intermediary goods industries	66.8	15.0	8.0	8.5	38.7
05 Capital equipment goods industries	70.7	27.2	23.3	5.7	31.6
(T15A) Professional electricals	69.3	37.2	25.6	4.7	23.3
(T17) Aerospace, ships and arms	75.1	27.1	30.7	5.7	31.6
06 Consumption goods industries	46.7	9.2	7.0	6.8	44.5
(T12) Parachemists, pharmaceut.	38.2	20.8	15.4	9.9	25.7
(T22) Printing and publishing	60.1	20.0	15.2	7.6	35.8
07 Construction	73.4	7.1	4.5	9.4	55.9
08 Commerce	21.9	16.3	11.5	7.9	35.1
(T26) Non-food wholesale	30.9	26.1	17.1	8.4	25.8
09 Transports, telecomm.	29.5	15.7	13.9	9.3	38.5
(T31) Transports	36.1	17.5	8.4	8.3	41.1
(T32) Telecoms, post	13.7	3.8	47.4	15.4	24.6
10 Marketed services	23.4	24.1	14.5	4.9	28.6
(T33) Marketed services mainly to the entr.	27.8	44.4	24.7	2.5	12.8
11 Real estate rental and leasing (= T35)	19.3	20.8	15.4	9.9	25.7
12 Insurance (= T36)	7.5	48.2	29.8	4.8	7.2
13 Financial institutions (= T37)	6.3	53.2	26.4	2.3	7.2
14 Non-marketed services (= T38)	10.3	3.5	20.1	8.2	41.3
Total	30.9	17.2	13.2	7.4	37.2
(thousands)	1,566				

Notes: * Eng = Engineers; Pro. = Professionals; Exc. = Executives; S.W. = Skilled workers; UnW = Unskilled workers; Farm. = Farmers and others; CSH = Craftsmen, shopkeepers and enterprises heads; ESP = Executives and Superior intellectual professions; InP = Intermediary professions; Clk = Clerks.
Source: INSEE, RGP – Active population in the workplace.

consumption goods industries (5.8 per cent). The other sectors of the 'level 15' activities code bring less jobs (see Table 5.1).

However, some of them, by their very concentration in the capital region, and, more particularly, in the central Paris and La Defense area, are absolutely characteristic of the Parisian metropole. This is the case with financial activities, insurance companies and banks, including seven out of the ten largest premises of Paris *intra-muros* (the three others being the R.A.T.P., Radio-France and the department store Galeries Lafayette (INSEE, Bridge file, 1997).

UnW.	Farm.	2. Services Jobs, of which*: (%)	CSH.	ESP.	InP.	Clk.	3. Diverse	4. Total (%)
33.6	58.9	10.9	10.3	15.1	18.2	56.4		0.4
32.8		52.5	24.7	14.4	17.2	43.7		1.4
6.0		44.8	1.0	19.0	42.3	37.7		1.3
29.8		33.2	13.2	17.4	31.6	37.8		3.2
4.9		29.3	6.0	21.3	31.6	37.8		7.8
9.2		30.7	6.2	24.3	28.7	40.8		T15: 3.6
4.9		24.9	1.4	19.1	31.7	47.8		1.0
32.5		53.3	14.2	31.0	28.4	26.3		5.8
28.2		61.8	2.2	32.7	41.3	23.8		1.4
21.4								2.2
23.1		26.6	51.6	8.2	11.4	28.8		6.6
29.2		78.1	18.1	15.6	20.6	45.7		12.2
22.6		69.1	10.5	24.2	28.3	37.0		4.9
22.6		70.5	7.4	11.0	24.1	57.5		8.2
24.7		63.9	11.7	8.7	21.3	58.3		5.7
8.8		86.3	0.2	14.4	29.4	56.0		2.5
27.9		76.6	9.1	23.3	23.9	43.6		28.4
15.6		72.2	8.0	29.8	21.4	40.8		12.3
28.2		80.7	3.5	14.2	12.2	70.1		0.4
10.0		92.5	1.4	24.0	30.8	43.8		1.3
10.9		93.7	0.6	27.5	18.0	53.9		3.6
26.9		89.7	0.1	24.4	27.8	47.7		19.4
24.3	0.7	68.9	8.7	21.3	24.6	45.4		100
		3,498					12	5,076

Complexes, such as the set of activities that gather in and near the big airport platforms of Orly, and, even more, of Roissy-en-France, are themselves particularly characteristic of the Parisian metropole. These include air transport, transport auxiliaries, services, even aeronautic industry. Nine out of ten of the biggest premises of the Val d'Oise, five out of ten of the Val-de-Marne and three of the Seine-Saint-Denis *département*s are part of these complexes.

Among the most strongly represented sectors, only a few branches are responsible for these ranks. Among marketed services, it is the case of services mainly delivered to the enterprises, that themselves account for 12.3 per cent of the francilian jobs. Their presence in the Ile-de-France Region is well above the French average (with an index of 176). Food wholesale commerce (4.9 per cent of the francilian jobs, with an index of 141), as well as some industries, such as aerospace, arms, parachemicals, pharmaceuticals, newspaper printing and publishing, and above all electricals and professional electronics (3.6 per cent of the francilian jobs, with an index of 159) are also among those branches that are characteristic of the Ile-de-France Region, both by their size and by their concentration.

The car industry, especially if one considers its factories, is no longer part of these characteristic Parisian sectors. However, its headquarters and functional head establishments remain in the Ile-de-France Region, more precisely in the Hauts-de-Seine *département* for the headquarters and R&D (Renault, Peugeot S.A. and P.S.A.-Citroën), in the Yvelines and Essonne *département*s for R&D. Those are the preferred locations for other sectors, such as R&D and engineering, as well as high-tech industries (electronics: IBM-France, Alcatel, Thomson, Bull; aerospace: Aérospatiale, S.N.E.C.M.A., Dassault-Aviation). And it is interesting to note that, in several cases, such as P.S.A.-Citroën in Vélizy-Villacoublay or Renault in Lardy, the setting-up of research premises was deliberately chosen for this area, that was remote from their existing premises, separating the two functions.

Innovation in the Paris Economy

Paris, its Growth and Innovation: Industrial Dynamics, 1950–2000

The fact that the Paris agglomeration has been the main focus of French industrial development for two centuries is in very significant correlation with its important size. Indeed, the accelerated growth of this very size translates into a rapid rise of cumulative processes that led to spatial consequences. These are spacing out and decentralisation as answers to polarisation excesses, and geographic segmentation of production, according to a socio-functional hierarchy.

Until the turning point in the 1950s, the Parisian transformative industry developed swiftly so that in 1954 its staff in the Parisian agglomeration (with its suburban area), i.e. 1,240,000 jobs, was seven times as strong as the Lille-Roubaix conurbation staff, eight times the Lyons agglomeration staff, and seventeen times the fourth ranked agglomeration according to this criterion, the Marseilles agglomeration (after INSEE Population census, active population in the workplace). This industrial development was initiated by an *inventeur*s milieu, that was formed in Paris over a long period, thanks to the presence of business and political milieux, as well as

Table 5.2. Proportion of socio-professional categories and groups related to R&D in France, in the Seine *département* and in Paris, 1954

SPC or SPG/total staff, in %	France	Seine dépmt	Paris aggl. + SA	Paris *intra muros*
socio-professional categories:				
engineers, private sector	0.4	1.1	–	1.3
professionals, private sector	1.0	2.3	–	2.0
socio-professional groups:				
professions, senior executives	2.9	6.5	6.3	–
middle ranking executives	5.9	10.6	10.6	–

Source: INSEE, Population census 1954, Active population at the place of work.

the scientific, technical and professional milieux of the universities, schools and institutions. This was combined with the proximity of a vast potential clientele. The proportion of the private sector engineers among the local jobs was highest in Paris *intra-muros*, with an index of 300, compared with a particularly poor national average (see Table 5.2).

Industrial development relied mainly upon chemical or physical processes aiming to produce material or new goods. Among these increasingly capital equipment goods (such as trains, cars, planes, machines and electrical devices). The jobs boom in metallurgy, a very Parisian sector, during the period stretching from 1906 to 1968, compared well with a decline of numbers in other industries, such as textiles and garments.

Because they are strong consumers of space and heavy equipment, and also cause damage to the environment, secondary industry factories and warehouses have been pushed out of the urban centre. This process has been accelerated by increasing service needs and the means to finance them. This has allowed the development of a heterogeneous tertiary sector (Hautreux and Rochefort, 1965), the leading segment of which successfully competed with those secondary industries for the central locations that were vital for it.

The result has been polarising dynamics with multiplying effects and the redistribution of secondary industry outside Paris. These decentralisations mostly dispersed manufacturing jobs (Lipietz, 1977). They also, in some cases, have sown the seeds of new high technology activities embedding, developing and aggregating in new territories (see, for instance, Grégoris and Jalabert, 1997; Bernardy, 1997; Rousier, 1997). These new clusters emerged mostly in some of the decentralisation areas of industries such as electronics or aerospace, where the arrival of new scientific and technical jobs, even originally mixed with far more numerous Taylorised jobs, could initiate an innovating dynamic, in those territories where it was helped by a local innovative milieu.

Jeanine Cohen *et al.*

After the 1950s, some pioneer industries left Paris and its inner suburbs to settle in the outer metropolitan area, e.g. Renault cars at Flins-sur-Seine in 1952. These moves were seldom pure and simple transfers. They were mostly decided following a need for expansion that usually stemmed from development and therefore, frequently, concerned wealthy enterprises. Half of the jobs created by the industrial decentralisations were brought by only 4 per cent of the decentralising enterprises, and a quarter by only ten of them. These were Renault, Thomson-CSF, the S.N.I.A.S., S.A.V.I.E.M., Citroën, La Radiotechnique, D.B.A., Creusot-Loire, Honeywell-Bull and Kleber-Colombes (Ferniot, 1976).

These enterprises were very powerful and could bring many jobs locally. As a result, meeting their new demands, some local actors, such as representatives, wishing to attract these jobs to their constituencies, developed direct agreements with the companies to supply an industrial estate or specific aids in some cases. The multi-premises enterprises in this way built up a network, where each site could be specialised to a segment of their production, thus optimising their respective specificities (Aydalot, 1976).

The correlation between the agglomeration size and the socio-functional division of labour perpetuates, and even becomes more marked, as the major part of the manual workers find themselves in the middle or the little cities, or even in the country. In contrast, the Parisian metropolitan area concentrates the executives and professionals as shown in Table 5.3.

At the same time R&D functions grew in a great portion of the productive spaces of the Parisian agglomeration. In particular, they developed

Table 5.3. Jobs and urbanisation levels of the communes, profile of each urban unit bracket, 1982

(%)	Execu-tives	Profes-sionals	Clerks	Skill. Workers	Unsk.	Far-mers	Craft, Shopk.
Paris agglomeration	14	22	34	15	9	0	6
U.U. 200 000-2 million	10	21	30	19	14	1	7
U.U. 100–199,999	8	20	29	21	15	1	6
U.U. 50–99,999	8	19	29	20	17	1	7
U.U. 20–49,999	7	19	29	19	18	2	8
U.U. 10–19,999	6	17	25	20	21	2	9
U.U. 5–9,999	6	16	22	20	23	5	10
Urban units < 5,000	5	14	20	19	24	6	11
Rural communes	3	10	13	13	19	31	12

Note; * Executives; Professionals; Clerks; Skilled workers; Unskilled workers; Farmers; Craftsmen, shopkeepers, heads of enterprises.
Source: INSEE, Population census, Active population at the place of work; Extract from Ch. Balley, J. Cohen, P. Lenormand, N. Mathieu (1991*) L'ancrage territorial de l'emploi en milieu rural*, Paris, UP1-CNRS, URA 142 Strates, Report for the A.N.P.E. under the aegis of P.I.R.T.T.E.M.-C.N.R.S.

more and more to the south-west of Paris and its inner suburbs, scattered more and more towards the Saclay Plateau and the new towns of Evry, to the south, and Saint-Quentin-en-Yvelines, to the south-west (Guieysse, 1983; Peyrache, 1984; Cohen, 1985; Decoster and Tabariés, 1986).

The metropolitan employment structure is now comprised of the design (and more broadly, R&D), commercial and managerial functions of the peri-productive activities, delivering services mainly to the enterprises (finance, holdings, consultancy, inter-industrial commerce, transport and telecommunications), along with the industries hiring high rates of senior executives, engineers and professionals (GSP-Strates, 1989). The secondary industries, in which the management functions are particularly concentrated in the Ile-de-France Region, are energy, pharmaceuticals, computers, industrial equipment, electronics, aerospace and newspaper publishing.

In the 1990s, the area that is both specialising in design and R&D functions and strikingly concentrating those activities is the innovative area of the south–south-western outer metropolitan arc of Paris. This area, sometimes dubbed 'Paris-Sud' or 'technopole Ile-de-France Sud' (centred on *La Cité scientifique* of the Saclay Plateau) and what we call the francilian technopolitan area, contains most of those industries with the exception of energy. In addition, it also contains medical, precision and optical instruments, as well as the physical and natural sciences R&D, computing consultancy, software realisations, data processing, data banks and other consultancy services.

New Clusters
A Less Agglomerated Territorial System

The new industrial spaces characterised by R&D functions are located across a large area. This extends from the western and south-western inner suburbs of Paris, close to La Defense business centre, to the outer metropolitan arc as far as Evry, the Saclay Plateau and Saint-Quentin-en-Yvelines, via Vélizy-Villacoublay. Some additional patches appear as an extension of this outer metropolitan arc, at Réau and Moissy-Cramayel in the Seine-et-Marne *département* to the south-east, and at Les Mureaux as well as Cergy-Pontoise to the north-west.

The existence of territorial determinants to R&D development is manifest (Cohen, 1988, 1990a, 1990b). The factors that explain the technopolitan locations are deliberate enterprise strategies. They aim to develop their R&D and to get close to the scientific University of Orsay and to the GRE laboratories. As a result, the large groups of electronic industries built their research centres in the Essonne *département*, at Orsay, Palaiseau, Nozay, La Ville-du-Bois or Marcoussis, from the end of the 1960s.

The geographical position of these new clusters is well spaced out, not to say loose. This accords with observations on Hertfordshire, in the London Metropolitan Region (Simmie, 1997). This geography is less related to the need for close proximity, e.g. to allow swift face-to-face exchanges with the customers, the suppliers or the competitors, than it is related to the local presence of innovative milieux (see the works of the GREMI, namely Aydalot, 1986; Maillat *et al.*, 1993). This presence is the focus of spatial dynamics of a new kind, illustrating the strategies of localised development. In the period 1970–80, primacy in location factors passes to the development of a territory by a population able and qualified to meet the requirements and new characteristics of innovation, the new conditions of production and its organisation (Scott and Storper, 1986; Salais and Storper, 1993; Veltz, 1996).

Firms' Relations to Innovation: Several Types of Territorial Milieux

In the case of the Paris Metropolitan Region several types of production organisation and of relations to innovation co-exist (Decoster and Tabariés, 1993). The following types may be found:

1 The 'metropolitan milieu': this consists of the relations of the big firms and of the high technology firms whose logistics are extraterritorial, of the high level R&D centres, and of innovation consultancy activities, that are closely linked to the superior tertiary sector and to the decision functions of Paris. It therefore comprises a set of high-level services, highly polarised in the central business district, from Paris-West to La Defense. The dominant mode of innovation is the research in and advancement of technological innovations.

2 'Micro-milieux': these are high technology sectors gathered around great public and private research centres and SMEs. They are at diverse stages of development. They are highly concentrated in the southern periurban area. They collect there and renew the specialisations and activities of the high technology industry of the Parisian inner suburbs that are expanding. They are also to be found emerging in the other inner suburbs, near the research laboratories of the big firms. The activities that these micro-milieux are comprised of are rather orientated towards technological creation.

3 Finally, there exists what can be dubbed a 'diffuse industrial milieu'. This has poor internal cohesion as well as low spatial polarisation. It tries hard, by means of technology transfers, to access innovation, with the help of some institutions such as the regional centres for innovation and technology transfer (CRITT). The predominant activities are those of exploitation and technological development.

The metropolitan milieu is strongly linked with the national level in a country as centralised as France because the regulation level of scientific and technologic activities is the nation. The micro-milieux and the diffuse industrial milieux function at the regional–local scale. This is the level at which complex interactions (linked to the informal, to the tacit) take place. This also involves training, recruitment and interdisciplinarity.

A Micro-milieu in *La Cité scientifique*: The 'Photonic' Pole

The francilian technopolitan area is characterised by several micro-milieux that are already formed or emerging. They are defined by the presence and the importance of research actors, of R&D activities of the big firms and of high technology SMEs. The subsystems are relatively homogeneous. They gather together SMEs that are alike in respect of their profile, their technological trajectory and the nature of their markets.

These SMEs develop advanced and very specific uses of technologies, in protected or captive markets, and they therefore have a very particular productive and entrepreneurial logic. This relies on very high quality for limited production runs or for custom-made products. They do not rely on price competition through mass production, consequently, they are less capable of exploring new areas of economic activities. The whole micro-milieu tends to live in a closed world, with technological performance as their common purpose. The spread from 'competitivity poles' (Aglietta and Boyer, 1983) maintains the local dynamic of the micro-milieux and reinforces the homogeneity of the innovation system. In a way, this is a specifically local and very structuring high technology production circuit.

These micro-milieux are, more or less, spatially polarised. They stem from the networks generated on technological, economic and spatial bases. They are strongly structured by socio-professional networks, and not by institutional networks. The applied research centres created to implement large national programmes (Atomic Energy Commissariat: *Commissariat à l'énergie atomique*, CEA; National Centre of Telecommunications Studies: *Centre national d'études des télécommunications*, CNET; National Centre of Spatial Studies: *Centre national d'études spatiales*, CNES, particularly the Centre of Nuclear Studies of the CEA CCEN-CEA), have strongly structured these local production and innovation systems. They have contributed to the establishment of dense networks between the productive and scientific fabrics.

Organisational proximity and spatial proximity sometimes coincide, as in the micro-milieu of instrumentation and 'photonics' (Decoster and Tabariés, 1993). This is a mixture of electronics, computing and optics. A technological pole of these activities has been formed in *La Cité scientifique* and its surroundings. Scientific and industrial specialisations match one another. There is an important and ancient spatial concentration of training institutions, of specialised research teams, of instrumentation and optics enterprises, as well as enterprises using opto-electronics. They all have a very high technological level.

This concentration generated economic and technological relations that are highly developed in *La Cité scientifique*. Spatial proximity constitutes an essential factor of synergies. The local labour market, the training and professional trajectories of the individuals play an essential part in making up this socio-professional community.

In this pole, two actors are particularly important for the development:

1 university research centres that develop a strategy of technological con-tinuity, stretching from fundamental research to technology transfer;

2 instrumentation SMEs, that play a very important part in the diffusion of innovative technologies towards new sectors. Their technological know-how allows them to link up fundamental research and industry, as well as to play a driving role in collaboration and technology trans-fer.

This kind of micro-milieu is fragile. It depends both on the leading big firms' decisions, and on state decisions in the realm of research and defence. However, stabilising elements stem from the critical mass of locally created competences, know-how, and also from learning and from cooperation practices developed in the networks that are specific to the local milieu. Thanks to this critical mass, an association, Optics Valley, has just been created, allowing the big firms locally represented (Thomson, Alcatel) to support local development in optics (Decoster and Tabariés, 2000).

Research Networks in *La Cité scientifique*

Two broad kinds of techno-economic logic are at the root of the networks allowing the milieux to collaborate and be structured, one around the Saclay Centre of Nuclear Studies CEN-CEA and the other, more complex, around the higher education and research centres (Decoster and Tabariés, 2000). They coincide with two kinds of R&D valorisation: putting to work either the outcomes, or the scientific competences. Roughly, the first kind comprises externalisation dynamics, such as patents, enterprise cre-ation and technology transfer, for example, the CEA. In the second kind, cooperation and competences creation, that are the main strengths of the francilian teams of fundamental research, prevail.

The cooperation dynamics are twofold:

1 The excellence valorisation of the competences is related to precisely targeted technologies and industrial policies, that aim to reinforce and open the innovation networks to high technological level enterprises.

Increasing the density of the networks must increase the technological creation abilities of the local milieu. The priority of the technopole is not, in this case, to diffuse its dynamism to the whole production fabric, local or national, but to allow focused technological advances to be made.

2   The opposite of this excellence strategy, a technological continuity strategy, is developed in the more professional engineering schools (agriculture-agronomy, optics), the actions of whose teams are inspired by a broader vision of valorisation, and show the point of combining its two kinds. Such a strategy aims to completely change the technological system and culture, and, more globally, to rethink the whole scientific and technical diffusion chain. It may well be the way to solve the apparent contradiction between the research excellence policies and the local development policies. Like the action of the CRITTs, it allows links to be established between non-technopolitan and technopolitan partners (SMEs as well as research-training centres), and contributes to making the whole regional economic fabric benefit from the spin-offs and externalities of the technopole. It diffuses the learning effects created among *La Cité scientifique*, the habits and a cooperation culture, to an industrial milieu which is segmented and far less organised.

The Role of Public Actors

Confronted since 1973 with the persisting jobs crisis, the national government presented in 1982 administrative decentralisation acts, that were voted in and implemented from 1982 to 1984. These new policies devolved to territorial bodies substantial rights and the means to organise their own economic development. Despite the extension or legal recognition of their rights, the local actors did not undertake much more direct economic interventions for all that, but rather used them to enhance public services dedicated to the economy. They focused on increasing human competences (development of research training, help in the employment of high competences by the enterprises), assistance in the rejuvenation of the industrial fabric, and interregional and international agreements.

These technopolitan policies are at the crossroads of several public policies. It is in the realm of technological policies that new initiatives of some territorial bodies may be observed. For instance, regional councils, general councils of the *départements* and local communities contribute to financing some research equipment, even research consumables, or provide grants. Regions try hard to become places where scientific and technological policies are promoted. Some 30 per cent of the research and technology credits of the regional council budgets are dedicated to

supporting technology transfer bodies operations or collaborative programmes between research laboratories and enterprises.

This classical kind of intervention, that has been developed in the rest of
France for several years, was instituted later in the Ile-de-France Region,
due to the better initial endowment of the capital-region in research activities. During the 1980s, the Ile-de-France Region did not change very much
its poor involvement in economic and technological development policies.
These have been developed only in recent years. In contrast, the intervention of the *départements* in technological policies has been considerable. Although this was not one of their responsibilities, they seized the
opportunity provided by the regional power vacuum in this area.

During the period 1980–90, the Essonne *département* general council
was the most active body. It established itself as one of the key actors in
the bringing together of research and local industry. It is the only territorial body that sought to carry out a global innovation policy. It promoted
competences and technological resources developed from the technological
resources in its area. Its policies were not really new compared to those
that other French regions had been carrying out for a long time. It aimed
to reposition research, taking into account criteria such as the competitiveness of the local industrial fabric and the development of future strategic
sectors with the elaboration of its technological policies. Whereas the
regional policies of help to technology remained on the fringes of the
higher education system, the Essonne General Council was the only body
to develop local policies relying on the universities.

The national government, responding to the demands of some local
actors, attempted to organise the capacities of the southern Ile-de-France
area into a technopolitan form. It created the association *La Cité scientifique* in 1988. At the end of the 1980s, the local territorial bodies,
regions, *départements* and communes took hold of the project and put
new life into it. They were actively involved in initiatives aimed at innovation promotion and research–industry cooperation. The Essonne General
Council created a special service for research, education and technology
transfer. It attempted to bring logistical aid to local actors' involvement in
cooperative programmes. It provided support to enterprises that wished to
develop cooperation agreements and joint-ventures with foreign firms
(from Germany and Britain, up to now); it organised regular arrangement
of meetings between industrialists and researchers on technological topics.
More particularly they focused on materials and lasers. These are two
fields that are highly represented in the *département* and likely to have
spin-offs for the local economy. The most original features of these policies
were the creation of institutes. These were granted new premises and gathered academic teams, particularly in the realm of plant biotechnology
(*Institut de biotechnologie des plantes*, IBP).

In contrast to these positive policies, no large-scale answers were provided to the need for local venture-capital. There is evidence, from some examples in other French regions, that local powers can become involved in this issue that is so essential to local development (be it as initiators or as financial partners for the more risky projects). The lack of involvement of the territorial bodies in local venture-capital 'micro-organisms' in the francilian technopole has constituted a regional deficiency, which is just being tackled at present.

The obligation made by the national government to the fifteen *communes* of the Saclay Plateau to cooperate in order to define their own strategic urban plan accelerated the public awareness of the technopolitan idea. The development of three initiatives *La Cité scientifique*, the Intercommunal district of the Saclay Plateau (*District intercommunal du plateau de Saclay*, DIPS) and the initiative of the General Council of the Essonne *département*, reinforced the idea.

Despite this, a lack of organisation and coordination is still a problem for this milieu, in which the diverse initiatives do not always converge. Although the local name persists, the association *La Cité scientifique* disbanded in 1995. This was an expression of failure at the collective level. The Essonne *département*'s General Council has now restarted these dynamics, channelling them towards a selective support to two privileged domains, genomics and optics.

Innovative Firms in the Francilian Technopolitan Area: Survey Results

Characteristics of the Sample

Using the same questionnaire as that administered in Amsterdam, London, Milan and Stuttgart, the survey on innovative firms of the francilian technopolitan area of Paris-Sud drew mainly on the list of the awards of the BRITE European programme financing pre-competitive collaborative and cooperative research in industrial and material technologies, and, in a smaller number of cases, on a local database, the directory of firms of the innovative francilian district of the Saclay Plateau (*La Cité scientifique* de Paris-Sud), in the south–south-west of the Parisian urban area.

In France, among the 543 BRITE projects carried out in firms' premises located on the national territory, 299, i.e. 55 per cent, were located in the Ile-de-France Region. Of these 219 were based in three (out of eight) *départements* of the south and west of the region. These were the Hauts-de-Seine *département* in the inner suburbs, the Yvelines and Essonne *départements* in the outer suburbs. This confirms our previous work, that demonstrated both a specialisation of the Hauts-de-Seine *département* in the function of industrial direction, including R&D (Cohen, 1990b) and the emergence and development of new technopolitan areas in the south–south-western arc of the outer metropolitan area (Decoster and Tabariés, 1993). An update (Cohen, 1998) and a survey on the present location of the most characteristic branches of the new technopolitan productive system (Cohen *et al.*, 2000) confirm that the positions of the most dynamic and innovative industrial zones of the Parisian urban area are still concentrated in the south-west, with its two components of above average industrial direction, to the west, and of above average, even exclusive, R&D, to the south and south-west.

The location by *commune*s of the research projects is consistent with this geography. By comparison with a great number of projects located in the Hauts-de-Seine *département*, in La Defense area and in *commune*s next to the industrial central business district (Suresnes, Rueil-Malmaison, Saint-Cloud, Nanterre, La Garenne–Colombes, Boulogne–Billancourt), it presents an almost equal number of projects located in the south–south-western outer metropolitan arc of Paris, in *commune*s that were mostly still rural. The vast majority of these projects are located in only three *commune*s, Orsay, Vélizy-Villacoublay and Marcoussis. But these *commune*s are not contiguous, and the twenty other *commune*s where the other projects are located in the francilian technopolitan area form a kind of stretched chain. The main area of this chain, that covers seventy-three *commune*s, of which there are forty-seven in the northern part of the Essonne *département*, nineteen in the south-eastern part of the Yvelines *département*, five in the south-eastern part of the Hauts-de-Seine *département* and two on the western borders of the Val-de-Marne *département*, is the most specifically technopolitan area in the Ile-de-France Region. It is dedicated to R&D, without much association with business direction functions (management, marketing), contrary to the major part of the Hauts-de-Seine *département*. That is why we chose to focus on these new clusters of the East-Yvelines, North-Essonne and of the neighbouring communes of the Hauts-de-Seine and Val-de-Marne *départements*.

Several different projects were being carried out simultaneously by several parts of the same firm. These even involved several teams in the same location or the same researcher. Apart from one very big firm, the research centre of its group, itself one of the mainsprings of the French electronic research, where the two most recent studies were carried out in manifestly different domains, we administered only one questionnaire by firm. This focused on its most recent innovation that had won a BRITE award. Due to this limitation, the number of questionnaires that we could administer to this database was reduced in size.

The sample size was therefore increased by interviewing some innovative firms extracted from a local database. According to the technopolitan core location of *La Cité scientifique* and to our aim to question the notions of clusters and proximity, we chose these other innovative firms in

Table 5.4. Sample composition

Type of organisation	
Private national firm	55
Private multinational firm	30
Public enterprise	9
Other	6
Total N = 100%	33
Size of firm	
Micro < 20 employees	24
Small 21 to 250	27
Medium 251 to 1000	15
Large >1000	34
Total N = 100%	33
Industrial sector	
Chemical products less pharmaceuticals	1
Television, radio and communication equipment	3
Medical, precision and optical instruments, watches and clocks	6
Aerospace	4
Electricity, gas and water supply	1
Construction	3
Software consultancy and supply	2
R&D on natural sciences	10
Services mainly to the enterprises	3

Source: BRITE/local innovative firms' survey.

the 1998 economic directory of the Saclay Plateau District, covering the fifteen communes of *La Cité scientifique*. As a result they are close neighbours to the Nuclear Studies Centre, the scientific University of Paris-XI-Orsay, the CNRS group of laboratories, the *Ecole polytechnique* and to numerous other scientific and technical establishments.

Thirty-three interviews have been completed, twenty-five of which concern firms of the francilian technopolitan area benefiting from a BRITE (or THERMIE) European award. Eight others were innovative firms of the core of this area, not helped by this programme. Table 5.4 shows the resulting composition of the sample.

Half of the thirty-three enterprises are French and private, whereas a bit less than a third are private multinationals, and less than 10 per cent are public. The remaining 10 per cent comprise associations for developing commercial interests (*groupements d'intérêts économiques*, GIE). They gather partners with diverse status.

A third of the firms (eleven) have more than 1,000 salaried employees. This is a proportion that is well above what these firms represent in the Ile-de-France Region. This shows evidence of the firm capacity needed to secure European funding. It also shows their importance for innovation production.

Although not in proportion to the area as a whole, an even higher number (thirteen) has less than fifty salaried employees. This reflects the differences between the two subgroups of the survey. Whereas, in the BRITE database, the big firms are clearly more present than the SMEs, the opposite situation prevails in the Saclay Plateau district directory. All the firms of the district are registered there, and the vast majority of them are small firms, according to the classical French size pyramid. Due to this, the local database firms that we contacted were mostly SMEs. A lot of them, that were not innovative, were discarded.

The range of branches of economic activity represented is relatively limited. Out of the thirty-three:

- 10 belong to R&D (7 BRITE, 3 DIPS);

- 6 belong to medical, precision, and optical instruments, watches, clocks (5 BRITE, 1 DIPS);

- 4 (all BRITE) are aerospace builders;

- 3 belong to the television, radio and communications equipment (1 BRITE, 2 DIPS);

- 3 belong to construction (3 BRITE);

- 3 belong to services mainly delivered to enterprises (3 BRITE);

- 2 are in computing machinery (1 BRITE, 1 DIPS);

- chemical products are represented by a firm from the DIPS directory;

- electric power production and distribution by a firm from the BRITE database.

Local Clusters, Linkages and Networks

The questions aimed at discovering the importance for these technopolitan innovative firms of their networks made a distinction between two kinds of contacts, labour and production networks (learning, business networks, collaborators, friends), on the one hand, and external sources of knowledge and information, on the other hand (Table 5.5).

Among the labour and production networks, it emerged that business networks (customers, suppliers, competitors or business services) were the most important. Their mean score on a scale ranging from 1 (not important) to 5 (very important) is 3.24. But the external collaborators are also important (2.88). They are significantly ahead of the friends or ex-colleagues (1.64) and of the institutions in charge of learning (education, formation and information), that scored only 1.15.

As far as the external sources of knowledge and information are con-

Table 5.5. Linkages and networks

Contact networks	Importance for innovation Mean scores*
Type of network	
Learning	1.15
(education, training or information)	
Business	3.24
(customers, suppliers, competitors or business services)	
Collaborators	2.88
(external organisations)	
Friends	1.64
Important external sources of knowledge and information	
Academics	2.63
Experts from other parts of the group	2.13
Suppliers	2.16
Customers	2.91

Note: * 1 = not important to 5 = very important.
Source: BRITE/local innovative firms' survey.

cerned, the answers confirm the decisive importance of the usual business partners for the innovative firms. Out of twenty categories of potential providers that were listed in the questionnaire, only four emerged as significant. Customers (2.91) as well as universities and other higher education establishments (HEIs) researchers (2.63) are the most important. These are followed by suppliers (2.16) and the other experts of the group (2.13). With the exceptions of the lawyers (1.75) and the competitors (1.72), the others are not very important.

The strong importance of business networks does not necessarily entail the importance of close geographic proximity (Table 5.6). The diverse locations (by level: regional, national, international, or by part of the world) were scored on a scale from 1 to 4, depending on the proportion (1–25 per cent, 26–50 per cent, 51–75 per cent or 76–100 per cent) of the innovative firms' partners that they contained. Table 5.6 shows that whereas, for the suppliers, France as a whole is rated 46, with merely 8 for the local suppliers and 15 for the other regional suppliers, compared with 23 for the other national suppliers, the other countries are rated 79, with Europe less France scoring 51 points, the USA 18 and Japan 10. As to the clients, the need for proximity is even weaker. Local clients are shown to be no less important than local suppliers (8), but the other regional clients are merely rated 5. However, the importance of the rest of France is higher (57). International clients are the most important, with a total of 98 points. Europe is still ahead (45), but the importance of USA (20) and Japan (14) is higher for the clients than it was for the suppliers, and some other parts of the world without suppliers are not without clients: the Pacific Rim is rated 6 and the rest of the world 13.

Table 5.6. Geography of linkages

Locations	Suppliers	Customers	Competitors
	Sum of scores*	Sum of scores	Sum of scores
International			
Europe	51	45	39
USA	18	20	51
Japan	10	14	17
Other Pacific Rim	0	6	0
World-wide	0	13	0
National			
101 km to France	23	57	18
Regional/local			
Regional 51 to 100 km	15	5	8
Local < 51 km	8	8	15

Note: * Sum of scores = total score for all firms by quartile. Where 0 = no links to the specified location to 4 = 76–100 per cent links to the location.
Source: BRITE/local innovative firms' survey.

The competitors' geography displays the prominence of the USA (51), followed by France as a whole (41) and the rest of Europe (39). As competitors, the Japanese firms (17) are well behind, but their score nevertheless is higher than those that they reach as clients and as suppliers.

It is interesting to note that the local presence of competitors (15), the local clustering of which, in this francilian technopolitan area, is precisely our main present concern, is more important than the local presence of suppliers or customers. The relationship is the reverse in what the questionnaire dubbed the 'rest of the region'. This covers broadly the Ile-de-France Region minus its technopolitan area and the south-western Parisian basin. This is consistent with the intra-regional division of production functions (with the south-western outer metropolitan arc specialising in R&D) that we pointed out above.

Turning to external collaborators for innovation, their detailed scores on a scale from 1 not important to 5 very important, point out once more the importance of customers for the innovative firms. They are rated the best mean score (3.16), whereas the suppliers are only ranked fourth (with 2.28) and almost all the other external collaborators (associations, services, competitors) are rated 1 to 1.5 (see Table 5.7).

Ranked second and third, with respectively 2.53 and 2.47, the academics from universities or other HEIs, on the one hand, and from the government research establishments (GREs), on the other, appear to be important for the innovative firms that they are likely to go on attracting. The GREs are even more important for the Saclay Plateau innovative firms, since their own mean scores, if one ignores the BRITE firms, would

Table 5.7. Importance of collaborators

Collaborators	Mean scores*
Other firms of the group	2.03
Competitors	1.44
Customers	3.16
Suppliers	2.28
Other firms	1.94
Universities or other HEIs	2.53
GREs	2.47
Private non-profit organisations	1.03
Research associations	1.22
Consultancy services	1.19
Other services	1.03

Note: * 1 = not important to 5 = very important.
Source: BRITE/local innovative firms' survey.

be 3.71, ahead of the customers (3.43), the suppliers (2.14) and people from universities or other HEIs (2).

For the whole number of interviewed firms, the intermediary scores of the other firms of the group (2.03) and other enterprises (1.94) support the feeling that they need contacts, emulation with the other innovative firms, even a kind of monitoring. Besides, these intermediary scores are also observed for the subgroup of the Saclay Plateau innovative SMEs. The only difference is that business services replace the 'other firms of the group', that rarely exist in their cases because of their small size. So they are rated the lowest score, 1, whereas the business services and the other enterprises each score 1.71.

Location Factors of the Francilian Technopolitan Firms

Thus, we have shown that the milieux of production and scientific and technical activities are important for the technopolitan innovative firms. But beyond this importance of a technopolitan fabric, there is, moreover, some evidence that urbanisation effects, external to the firm but internal to the urban region, the Paris Metropolitan Region as a whole, prove, some of them at least, to be important location factors of these firms (see Table 5.8).

Certainly, the first of them (with a mean score of 3.77), the availability of professional experts to recruit, is a factor that, inside the Paris Metropolitan Region, highly concerns the technopolitan area. The area concentrates numbers of engineers *grandes écoles* as well as scientific and technical universities that train such experts. The importance of collaborators' proximity (2.84), as well as the contributions of universities and

Jeanine Cohen *et al.*

Table 5.8. Importance of reasons for the location of innovative firms in the Paris Metropolitan Region

Urbanisation effects, external to the firm but internal to the urban region	Mean scores*
Availability of professional experts to recruit	3.77
Access to major airport	3.74
Good access to Paris	3.1
Proximity of collaborators	2.84
Good access to national road network	2.84
Contribution from universities or HEIs	2.77
Good rail connections	2.61
Availability of suitable premises	2.28
Cost of premises	2.1
Proximity of customers	2.1
Proximity of business services	2.1
Proximity of sources of information	2.1
Presence of ex-colleagues	2.1
Access to financial capital	2
Cost of labour	1.9
Local public business support services	1.87
Access to private general business services	1.84
Access to private specialised business services	1.74
Access to skilled manual labour	1.68
Proximity of suppliers	1.68
Other	1.58
Low level of traffic congestion	1.47
Contribution from TECs	1.42
Presence of friends	1.42
Contribution from business links	1.35
Proximity of competitors	1.32

Note: * 1 = not important to 5 = very important.
Source: BRITE/local innovative firms' survey.

other HEIs (2.77) back up this factor and its links with the technopolitan area. In a way, the fact that the lowest score, 1.32, goes to the competitors is itself consistent with this need of the innovative firms to draw without too much competition on a local breeding ground of experts that are rare and lacking elsewhere. But these schools and universities are generally considered to belong to the Paris Metropolitan Region, where the vast majority of them have their origins. The Orsay Scientific University, dubbed 'University of Paris-South' (*Université de Paris-Sud*) is officially the university of Paris-XI, for instance. In some cases, e.g. the *Ecole polytechnique*, this francilian location is exclusive at the national scale and related to the capital function of Paris.

The score of access to a major airport, that just ranks second with 3.74, leaves little doubt of the importance of the Paris metropole as a whole for

Table 5.9. Professional and technical expertise

Professional expertise	Worked directly on innovation Sum of scores*	Staff holding higher qualification Sum of scores	Recruited within 50 km Sum of scores
Technology	115	122	68
Finance	6	17	12
Marketing	12	39	15
Training or recruitment	4	10	6
Production process	18	40	23

Note: * Sum of scores = total score for all firms by quartile. Where 0 = none to 4 = 76–100 per cent.
Source: BRITE/local innovative firms' survey.

the innovative firms of the francilian technopolitan area. This is backed up by the score of the access to Paris (3.1). The importance of transport networks also extends to the road network (2.84) and the rail network (2.61).

The fact that people who worked on innovation, mainly experts in technology and very highly qualified (see Table 5.9), were not usually recruited within 50 km, shows that the labour market for these high-level experts may be vast, at the national, even international scale. But another reason explains the lower total score of this factor. It is that the specific research to produce the innovation is mostly a development and/or a by-product of previous work by researchers earlier. It is the case, in particular, of the research financed by the BRITE awards, that frequently allow a doctoral student to have his or her research supervised and financed. The carrying out of this research is therefore rarely the occasion for the firm to recruit permanent staff (at this stage, at least).

This staff is strongly attached to the quality of local life (see Table 5.10). The attraction of a good lifestyle environment received almost everyone's approval, with a mean score of 4. In fact, the notion 'encompasses all the others', as several interviewees answered. The other four proposed factors all received high scores. The proximity of good schools for the children (3.54) and good housing (3.5) is rated higher than the proxim-

Table 5.10. Importance of local requirements for human capital

Local requirements	Mean scores*
Availability of good housing	3.5
Proximity of good schools	3.54
Proximity of good leisure facilities	2.74
Proximity of good public services, e.g. hospitals	2.74
Good environment	4.0

Note: *1 = not important to 5 = very important.
Source: BRITE/local innovative firms' survey.

Jeanine Cohen *et al.*

ity of good leisure equipment or of good public services, e.g. hospitals, that were each scored 2.74.

The Innovative Firms and the World Markets

The questions concerning the geographic or sectoral framework of innovation, on the one hand, and the effect of its production on exports, on the other, finally enable us to put innovation back in the context of world markets (see Table 5.11).

In response to the question whether the innovation was new to the world (in which case, the innovator is an 'absolute innovator') or only to France, to the sector or to the firm (the innovator is then a 'relative innovator'), almost two-thirds of the firms (64 per cent) answered that they were absolute innovators, whereas slightly more than a third thought they were not. The two firms' subgroups are present in both categories, the non-BRITE Saclay Plateau SMEs by halves, and the BRITE firms more in the category of absolute innovators (a little more than two-thirds) than in the category of relative innovators (a little less than one-third).

Nevertheless, when asked what was the proportion of innovation exported, more than half the firms (52 per cent of the absolute innovators and 58 per cent of the relative innovators) could not answer. One firm refused explicitly this information. Mostly, the reason presented was that it was 'too early to answer', either because the innovation was not yet on the market, or because the figure was not known yet. Finally, in other cases, the product was not exported separate, and/or it was part of a broad deal with the customers. In these cases it was impossible to determine its specific contribution to exports. It must be pointed out that the absolute innovators who made this kind of response were big industrial groups, e.g. construction groups that sell integrated civil engineering. As to the firms who could answer (48 per cent of the absolute innovators and 42 per cent of the relative innovators), it may be seen that the absolute innovations

Table 5.11. Innovation and exports

Total Exports	Innovation novelty New to the world Leaders (%)	New to France, sector or firm Followers (%)	(%)
Too early to know	52	58	55
1 to 20%	0	17	6
21 to 40%	0	8	3
41 to 50%	5	0	3
51% or more	43	17	33
Total N = 100%	21	12	33

Source: BRITE/local innovative firms' survey.

lead to more exports (over 40 per cent for all the firms) than the relative innovations. Only 17 per cent of these firms export over 40 per cent of their total innovation sales, whereas 25 per cent export less, and even 17 per cent export less than 20 per cent of their total innovation sales.

Conclusion

Due to the main influence of European cooperation projects in our BRITE survey, the importance of local links could have been slightly underestimated for those innovative firms. But it really appears that the big firms, largely involved in the global economy, have not the same location strategy and do not look for the same externalities as the technopolitan innovative SMEs. These are looking for a technological atmosphere and SMEs information flow, that they find locally through their clients, the universities or the GRE laboratories, whereas the big firms have access to internal information and can afford higher technological risk in projects that may not be immediately marketable. The externalities expected by the big firms seem to be mostly generic, whereas those expected by the SMEs seem to be mostly specific.

But some common needs of all the innovative firms appear through a clear hierarchy of their location factors: they are mainly interested in a highly qualified labour market, good access to Paris, its major airports, the rail and road networks, the proximity of universities and the availability of land and premises as well as their costs.

Finally, it appears that, in the case of the Paris Metropolitan Region, the need for proximity of the technopolitan innovative firms is mainly comprised of the need to find large numbers of professional experts to recruit and of the decisive benefits of collaborations with the universities or other HEIs and with the GREs.

This does not mean that the innovative firms do not need strong links with the other usual partners. On the contrary, they need a very strong interactivity with their business partners, especially their customers, and, significantly too, their suppliers. Even the need for some suppliers' proximity remains especially high tech ones. This was the reason, for instance, of the settlement of IBM or Microsoft in the francilian area, respectively at Corbeil and at Les Ulis, with a mainly commercial purpose. Furthermore, some local innovative firms are also each other's suppliers or clients.

But the enhancement of transport and communications allows better networking between function-specialised areas. As a result, the past constraint of relatively close proximity of suppliers and customers can be considerably loosened, allowing the most innovative firms to target even the world market.

The role of public actors has been important, though not equally constant and efficient. The early sectoral policies and spatial planning

Jeanine Cohen *et al.*

[handwritten: planning]

operations of the national government, later in part relieved by local actors and their own policies, have helped the technopolitan area to develop and innovation to accelerate. The possibility for territorial representatives to channel, organise and partly offset the propensity of firms to delocalise is shown. Nevertheless, their 'nomadism' (Zimmerman, 1998), far from stopping, continues to be observed.

It is certain that the development of the innovative firms must be put in a dynamic context. From this viewpoint, the persistent distinct position of sectoral, functional and organisational subgroups in the chain of the francilian technopolitan area allows us to consider them the innovative 'clusters' of the Paris Metropole Region in 2000.

Notes

1. Picture © Ecole Polytechnique, Philippe Lavialle.
2. Nanterre for the Hauts-de-Seine *département* (92), Bobigny for the Seine-Saint-Denis (93) and Créteil for the Val-de-Marne, in the inner suburbs; in the outer suburbs, Melun still is the centre of the unchanged Seine-et-Marne *département*; Versailles, former administrative centre for the late, vast Seine-et-Oise *département*, is now the one of the Yvelines, whereas Evry has won this new function for the Essonne *département*, and Cergy for the Val d'Oise.
3. The translation of these different extensions is that, in the Ile-de-France Region, the number of occupied active residents is 4,862,608 (INSEE, 1990 census, 1/20 poll), whereas the jobs for the workplace rises to 5,075,974 (cf. Liagre *et al.*, 1995): the figures are not yet issued for the workplace in 1999. There were consequently some 200,000 active residents, residing outside but working inside the Ile-de-France Region, more than active residents residing inside but working outside this region. Despite this difference between the two numbers, their own internal respective ventilations by economic activities remains very close.

References

Aglietta, M. and Boyer, R. (1983) *Pôles de compétitivité, stratégie individuelle et politique macro-économique*, Paris, CEPREMAP.

Aydalot, Ph. (1976) *Dynamique spatiale et développement inégal*, Paris, Economica.

Aydalot, Ph. (ed.) (1986) *Milieux innovateurs en Europe*, Paris, GREMI.

Beaucire, F. (1991) 'L'évolution démographique et sociale de la couronne péri-urbaine d'Ile-de-France (1968–1982)', *Géographie Sociale*, 11, 57–64.

Beckouche, P., Damette, F., Vire, E. *et al.* (1998) *Géographie économique de la région parisienne*, Paris, DREIF-Communication.

Benko, G. and Lipietz, A. (1992) *Les régions qui gagnent*, Paris, Presses Universitaires de Paris.

Berger, M., Fruit, J.-P., Plet, F. and Robic, M.-C. (1980) 'Rurbanisation et analyse des espaces ruraux périurbains', *L'Espace Géographique*, 4, 303–13.

Berger, M. and Saint-Gérand, T. (1999) 'La Métropole s'étend et les pôles régionaux s'affirment', CNRS-UP-I, 8 and X, UMR LADYSS, supplement to '*4-pages*' *de l'Observatoire des rapports entre rural et urbain*, 2: 'Entre villes et campagnes, les mobilités des périurbains'.

Berger, M., Saint-Gérand, T. and Beaucire, F. (1998) *Les Ménages contre les aménageurs? Migrations résidentielles et navettes domicile-travail des périurbains en Ile-de-France*, Paris, Collections INED.

Bernardy, M. (1997) 'Centres de R&D et compétitivité des firmes: avantages spécifiques et effets réciproques, l'exemple de Grenoble', in J. Cohen, D. Hart and J. Simmie (eds), *Recherche et développement régional: Travaux franco-britanniques*, Paris, Publications de la Sorbonne, pp. 195–212.

Brun, J. and Rhein, C. (eds) (1994) *La ségrégation dans la ville*, Paris, L'Harmattan.

Bureau, M.-C., Moatty, F. and Valeyre, A. (1991) *Dossier d'étude du CEE*, 37, Paris, Centre d'Etude de l'Emploi.

Camagni, R. (ed.) (1991) *Innovation Networks*, London, Belhaven.

Cohen, J. (1985) 'Productifs et non productifs: Localisation de la production industrielle et géographie des emplois en région parisienne', thesis, University of Paris-I.

Cohen, J. (1988) 'Mutations de l'emploi en région parisienne', *Espace, Populations, Sociétés*, 3, 437–46.

Cohen, J. (1989) 'Paris et la province: vingt ans de mutation du système productif français', in A.-M. Lakota and C. Milelli (eds) *Ile-de-France, un nouveau territoire*, Montpellier and Paris, GIP RECLUS and La Documentation Française, pp. 9–25.

Cohen, J. (1990a) 'Emplois de haute technologie et technopoles: la Cité scientifique de Paris-Sud dans le contexte national et régional', in G. Jalabert and Ch. Thouzellier (eds) *Villes et technopoles*, Toulouse, Presses Universitaires du Mirail, pp. 181–90.

Cohen, J. (1990b) 'Les transformations de l'industrie et de la localisation des emplois dans l'agglomération parisienne', *Annales de Géographie*, 554, July–August, 385–405.

Cohen, J. (1991) 'Parigi, una metropoli multimilionaria tra periodi di declino e crescita', in *La città europea: il progetto metropolitano*, Bologne, Ente Autonomo per le Fiere di Bologna-G.E. Faenza Editrice, pp. 47–53.

Cohen, J. (1992) 'La division intra-régionale du travail en Ile-de-France: spécialisations fonctionnelles et qualification des emplois', in M. Berger and C. Rhein, *L'Ile-de-France et la recherche urbaine*, Paris, Géomedia (Séminaire DATAR-Plan Urbain), pp. 130–2.

Cohen, J. (1993) 'La nouvelle division intra-métropolitaine du travail dans le Grand Paris. Centralité et complémentarités fonctionnelles', in METT-Plan Urbain-DATAR-CGP along with the Agence d'Urbanisme de la Communauté Urbaine de Lyon, *Métropoles en déséquilibre?*, Paris, Economica, pp. 199–219.

Cohen, J. (1994) 'Emploi et extension urbaine: restructuration infra-régionale', *INSEE-Regards sur l'Ile-de-France*, 26, December, 12–14.

Cohen, J. (1997) 'R&D, market and planning in the Greater Paris: technopolitan spaces and the international restructuring of firms', in J. Simmie, *Innovation, Networks and Learning Regions?*, London, Jessica Kingsley Publishers, pp. 51–65.

Cohen, J. (1998) 'Fonctions et localisations', in Th. Saint-Julien (ed.) *Atlas de France, Vol. 9 Industries*, Montpellier and Paris, GIP-RECLUS and La Documentation Française, pp. 68–73.

Cohen, J. (1999) 'Recomposition et respiration du territoire', in V. Gollain and

A. Sallez (eds) *Emploi et territoire en Ile-de-France: prospective*, La Tour d'Aigues (F-Vaucluse), Editions de l'Aube, pp. 115–35.

Cohen, J., Decoster, E. and Tabariés, M. (2000) *Dynamiques spatiales de la Cité scientifique de Paris-Sud: Innovation, compétitivité, territoire*, Paris, Rapport pour le CNRS-SHS, Programme 'Les enjeux économiques de l'innovation'.

Decoster, E. and Tabariés, M. (1986) 'L'innovation dans un pôle scientifique et technologique, le cas de la Cité scientifique Ile-de-France sud', in Ph. Aydalot (ed.) *Milieux innovateurs en Europe*, Paris, GREMI, pp. 79–100.

Decoster, E. and Tabariés, M. (1993) 'Innovation, technopole and regional planning: the Ile-de-France sud technopole', in J. Simmie, J. Cohen and D. Hart (eds) *Technopole Planning in Britain, Ireland and France: The Planned Regional Acceleration of Innovation*, Working Paper No. 6, London, University College London, The Bartlett, Planning and Development Research Centre, pp. 83–101.

Decoster, E. and Tabariés, M. (2000) 'Enracinement et développement de micro-milieux innovateurs en Ile-de-France Sud: l'exemple des technologies optiques', paper presented to the Association des Sciences régionales de langue française Conference *Développement régional, économie du savoir, nouvelles technologies de l'information et de la communication*, Crans-Montana (Switzerland), 6–9 September.

Duong, Ph. (1983) 'Les mutations de l'emploi industriel en région Ile-de-France', thesis, University of Paris-I.

Estienne, P. (1978) *La France*, Paris, Masson, vol. 2, Chap. 4.

Faure, A. (1986) 'De l'urbain à l'urbain: du courant de peuplement parisien en banlieue (1880–1914)', in G. Burgel (ed.) *Villes en parallèle*, 15–16, 'Peuplements en banlieue', pp. 154–72.

Ferniot, B. (1976) *La décentralisation industrielle*, Paris, IAURIF.

Gordon, R. (1990) 'Systèmes de production, réseaux industriels et régions: les transformations dans l'organisation sociale et spatiale de l'innovation', *Revue d'Economie industrielle*, 51, pp. 304–39.

Grégoris, M.-T. and Jalabert, G. (1997) 'Technopole, développement local et récession économique: l'exemple de l'agglomération toulousaine', in J. Cohen, D. Hart and J. Simmie (eds) *Recherche et développement régional*, Paris, Publications de la Sorbonne, pp. 149–66.

GSP-Strates (P. Beckouche, J. Cohen, F. Damette, J.-Ch. Fischer and J. Scheibling) (1989) *Métropolisation et aires métropolitaines: internationalisation et enjeu urbain*, Paris, Survey for the Commissariat Général du Plan in the frame of the GIP 'Mutations économiques et urbanisation'.

Guieysse, J.-A. (1983) 'La recherche scientifique et technique dans l'industrie. Le cas de la région parisienne', thesis, University of Paris-I.

Hautreux, J. and Rochefort, M. (1965) 'Physionomie générale de l'armature urbaine Française', *Annales de Géographie*, 406, pp. 660–77.

Hilpert, U. (1992) *Archipelago Europe: Islands of Innovation*, FAST/Monitor FOP 242, vol. 18, Brussels, Commission of the European Communities.

Ibbou, S., Ramaux, C., Sainsaulieu, Y., Tabariés, M. and Tutin, C. (MATISSE-University of Paris-I) (1998) *Polarisation et ségrégation spatiales: systèmes d'emploi et systèmes d'habitat en Ile-de-France (1975–1990)*, Survey for the DATAR, Programme 'Ville et emploi', 3 vols.

INSEE (1954) Recensement de Population, Population active au lieu de travail.

INSEE (1990) Recensement de Population.

INSEE (1982) Recensement de Population.

INSEE – Ile-de-France (1996) Comptes régionaux.

INSEE – Ile-de-France (1999) 'Déplacements quotidiens: la périphérie toujours plus mobile', in 'A la page' No. 168, April, pp. 1–4.

Liagre, M.-O. et al. (1995) 'Les relations industrie–services', final report of the CRIES think tank on the productive system for the Ile-de-France Region, Montigny-le-Bretonneux and Paris, INSEE Direction Régionale de l'Ile-de-France and CCIP.

Lipietz, A. (1977) Le capital et son espace, Paris, Maspero.

Llewelyn-Davies, UCL Bartlett School of Planning and Comedia (1996) Four World Cities: A Comparative Study of London, Paris, New York and Tokyo, London, Survey for the Department of Environment and Government Office for London.

Maillat, D., Quevit, M. and Senn, L. (eds) (1993) Réseaux d'innovation et milieux innovateurs: un pari pour le développement régional, Neuchatel, EDES.

Perrin, J.-C. (1991) 'Réseaux d'innovation – milieux innovateurs: développement territorial', Revue d'Economie régionale et urbaine, 3–4, 343–74.

Peyrache, V. (1984) La localisation des établissements de haute technologie en Ile-de-France, Paris, University of Paris-I, DEA.

Pinchemel, Ph., Balley, Ch., Pumain, D. and Robic, M.-C. (1971) 'Croissance urbaine et apports migratoires', paper presented at the CNRS Conference Analyse interdisciplinaire de la croissance urbaine, Paris.

Ramaux, C., Sainsaulieu, Y., Tabariés, M. and Tutin, C. (2000) 'Polarisation spatiale et ségrégation sociale en Ile-de-France', in E. Perrin and N. Rousier (eds) Ville et emploi, Le territoire au cœur des nouvelles formes de travail, La Tour d'Aigues (F-Vaucluse), Editions de l'Aube.

Rousier, N. (1997) 'Internationalisation et développement des technopoles: Grenoble et les réseaux internationaux', in J. Cohen, D. Hart and J. Simmie (eds) Recherche et développement régional, Paris, Publications de la Sorbonne, pp. 167–81.

Rousseau, M.-P. and Prud'homme, R. (1992) Les bénéfices de la concentration parisienne, Report for the IAURIF, Creteil, University of Paris-XII, L'OEIL.

Rowe, F. and Veltz, P. (eds) (1991) Entreprises et territoires en réseaux, Paris, Presses de l'Ecole Nationale des Ponts-et-Chaussées.

Salais, R. and Storper, M. (1993) Les mondes de production, Enquête sur l'identité économique de la France, Paris, Editions de l'Ecole des Hautes Etudes en Sciences Sociales.

Sallez, A. (1995) 'Dynamique urbaine: une analyse qualitative et économétrique pour la France', Revue d'Economie Régionale et Urbaine, 5, 825–39.

Scott, A. and Storper, M. (1986) Production, Work and Territory, London, Allen and Unwin.

Simmie, J. (1997) Innovation, Networks and Learning Regions?, London, Jessica Kingsley Publishers.

Simmie, J. and Sennett, J. (1999) 'Innovative clusters: global or local linkages?', National Institute Economic Review, 170, 87–93.

Tabard, N. and Chateau, F. (1989) 'Les catégories professionnelles dans les villes d'Ile-de-France: proximités et distances', in A.-M. Lakota and C. Milelli (eds) L'Ile-de-France, un nouveau territoire, Paris, GIP-RECLUS and La Documentation Française, pp. 47–64.

Tabariés, M. (1997) 'Déséquilibres intra-régionaux en Ile-de-France', in

A. Martens and M. Vervaeke (eds) *Polarisation sociale des villes européennes*, Paris, Anthropos, pp. 173–90.

Veltz, P. (1994) 'Dynamique des systèmes productifs, territoires et villes', paper presented at the Conference IFRESI, Lille, CNRS-PIR Villes, 16–18 March.

Veltz, P. (1996) *Mondialisation, villes et territoires, l'économie d'archipel*, Paris, Presses Universitaires de Paris.

Zimmerman, J.-B. (1998) 'La prossimita nelle relazioni impresi-territori: nomadismo e ancoraggio territoriale', *L'industria*, 3, July–September.

CHAPTER 6

London: International Trading Metropolis

6 London

International Trading Metropolis

James Simmie and James Sennett

Major Characteristics of the London Metropolitan Region

Brief History and Major Characteristics of the London Region

London developed rapidly as a centre of world trade from about the seventeenth century onwards. As a result of its success, the population of the built-up area reached over half a million by 1700 and doubled again to 1 million by the time of the first census in 1801. Economic and population growth continued through the nineteenth century so that the population had already reached some 6.5 million by 1911.

Much of this growth was built upon national and international trading activities. Growing concentrations of specialised business services supported these external economic linkages. As a result, London has become one of the leading quartet of world cities (Simmie, 1994, Ch. 8). These cities, which include Paris, New York and Tokyo as well as London, are defined by their concentrations of business and other activities that are significant in world terms, and for their consequential co-ordination and control of global economic activity.

Table 6.1 shows the major functions of world cities. These are finance and commerce, communications, culture and knowledge. First rank cities contain significant concentrations of all three functions. Second rank cities, such as Amsterdam, are strong in two of them. Third rank cities, such as Milan, tend to be significant in global terms in one major function such as finance and commerce. London's dual roles as both the national capital and a world city have been the key influences on the structure and dynamics of its regional economy.

The London economy is particularly characterised by its national and international trading links. The City is home to 554 foreign banks and there are 526 major foreign companies listed on the London Stock

James Simmie and James Sennett

Table 6.1. World city functions

Rank	Function	City
First rank	All three major functions Finance and commerce; communications; culture and knowledge	London, Paris, New York, Tokyo
Second rank	Two major functions	
	Finance and commerce; culture and knowledge	Amsterdam, Hong Kong
	Finance and commerce; communications	Frankfurt
	Communications; culture and knowledge	Berlin, Rome, Madrid
Third rank	One major function	
	Finance and commerce	Zurich, Milan, Chicago
	Communications	Lisbon, Brussels, Bonn
	Culture and knowledge	Copenhagen

Notes: Finance and commerce = Banking, business, insurance, stock exchange; Communications = Transport, telecommunications, government; Culture and knowledge = Tourism, entertainment, exhibitions, science and education.
Source: London Planning Advisory Committee *et al.* (1991, p. 13).

Exchange (London Development Partnership, 1999a, pp. 47 and 51). It is highly dependent on importing products from both the national and international economies. In 1990, for example, London imported some £53.4m worth of products and services from the rest of the UK economy, and £13.3m from the rest of the world (Centre for Economics and Business Research, 1996, p. 23).

These high volumes of international trade are enabled by the development of key infrastructure systems such as air transport and telecommunications. High level economic and political decision-making tends to be conducted face-to-face between key personnel. This requires their movement often between different countries. Table 6.2 shows that by 1994

Table 6.2. International passengers through major world airport systems

Major world airport systems	International passengers 1994 millions	Change 1984–94 (%)
London	66.5	66
Paris	36.8	80
Tokyo	21.4	118
New York	20.7	17
Los Angeles	12.7	115
Chicago	6.2	68

Source: Llewelyn-Davies *et al.* (1998).

194

Table 6.3. World city communications costs

| World cities | Relative costs. London = 100 | |
	Telecommunications	Transport
London	100	100
New York	84.6	171.6
Paris	188.3	133.8
Tokyo	190.7	171.6
Frankfurt	265.8	142.7

Source: Corporation of London (1999) *Competitiveness of London's Financial and Business Services Sector*, London, Corporation of London, p. 16.

more international passengers passed through London's Heathrow Airport than any other world city airport.

In addition to the movement of people, international business is also dependent on the transmission of high volumes of information. The rapid development of advanced telecommunications has revolutionised the ways in which some of London's key sectors can do business. In addition, the privatisations and liberal regulatory regimes installed during the 1980s have also made London one of the cheapest world cities from which to operate. Table 6.3 shows the relative costs of both telecommunications and transport for London as compared with its major world city competitors. Apart from the notable exception of telecommunications in New York, the interaction costs of doing business from London are cheaper than elsewhere.

The history of London's development is therefore one of several centuries of economic and population growth driven by national and international trade. It has a very open economy characterised by the export of various types of financial and business services and the import of products and services. The scale and importance of this trade are such as to make London one of the four leading world cities in terms of its finance and commerce, communications, culture and knowledge. Advanced, lightly regulated, and comparatively cheap telecommunications and international passenger transport facilitate its trading linkages.

Description of the Region and its Location

Many of the international visitors to London do not venture much outside of the central area. Until around 1861 much the same could be said for most of London's own residents. The reason for this was the lack of transport. In terms of the daily routines of most residents the functional geographic extent of London, at this time, was a maximum of about one hour's walk from the centre.

The first underground railway was opened in 1863 and this began the transformation of the distances that workers could commute to the centre

Table 6.4. Commuting patterns into Greater London, 1991

Residence	Workplace Inner London (%)	Outer London (%)	Totals
Greater London	79	78	2,652,440
ROSE	19	17	602,070
Rest of UK	3	3	94,840
Total	1,809,380	1,539,970	3,349,350

Source: Government Office for London (1996) *London in the UK Economy: A Planning Perspective*, London, DoE, p. 39.

on a regular daily basis. The rapid expansion of mass transportation greatly increased the geographic boundaries of London's functional daily urban system. It also led to the massive suburbanisation of the inter-war period which was stopped around the extent that it had reached in 1938 by the post-war introduction of London's Metropolitan Green Belt.

The Green Belt did not stop the functional extension of London into the Home Counties and beyond. Table 6.4 shows that by 1991 there were over 600,000 regular commuters into Greater London from the rest of the South East (ROSE) and nearly 95,000 from even further than that. By the 1990s therefore the functional London region extended well beyond the boundaries of Greater London into the ROSE (Mogridge and Parr, 1997). It is now a large complex region with numerous economic sub-areas, none of which correspond to the existing administrative boundaries (Hall, P., 1989, p. 8).

Figure 6.1 shows the functional ring structure of the London Region in the context of the Greater South East Region. At its core is a multifunctional central business district consisting mainly of the City of London, Westminster and parts of other inner London boroughs. This area is roughly bounded by the main line railway stations and the circle line tube. This area is sometimes referred to as the Central Statistical Area (CSA, e.g. Llewelyn-Davies *et al.*, 1998). Surrounding this central employment core is a ring consisting of the remaining inner London boroughs. These boroughs composed the rest of the now defunct Inner London Education Authority (ILEA). They are sharply polarised between the richer boroughs to the West and some of the poorest districts in the United Kingdom to the East.

Beyond this ring are the rest of London's boroughs. These comprise outer London. The two rings together made up the now abolished Greater London Council administrative area. The system of governance for this area is a complex mélange of separate boroughs, advisory councils, the Government Office for London and, soon, the London Regional Development Agency.

Beyond the M25 is a further ring composed of what are known as the Home Counties. These make up the Outer Metropolitan Area (OMA)

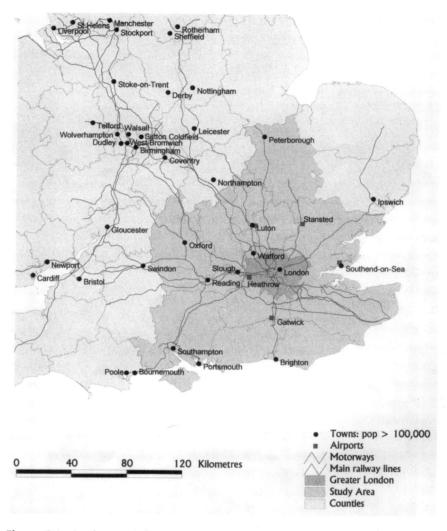

Figure 6.1. Study area infrastructure map.

which is functionally part of the London Metropolitan Region. Despite the administrative balkanisation of this total area into separate boroughs and counties, the economic, social and communication ties between them are so strong as to constitute a single but highly complex daily urban system (Champion *et al.*, 1987).

Beyond the OMA is a further more loosely integrated ring of London oriented counties making up the rest of the old South East Region (ROSE). Beyond this again is a further ring of counties, which are also functionally connected to London. All the rings together make up the

Greater South East (GSE) shown in Figure 6.1. This total area was divided into three separate government offices by the Thatcher administration. These are the Government Office for London (GOL), the Government Office for the South East (GOSE), and the Government Office for the East (GOE). The Blair administration has added a further set of regional development agencies covering these same administrative areas. They are the South East England Development Agency (SEEDA), and the East of England Development Agency (EEDA). After the election of London's new mayor in 2000, the London Development Agency (LDA) was also established.

The geographic area that functions as the integrated London region is therefore composed of a complex set of rings spreading out from the urban core. This area extends well out into the GSE as defined in Figure 6.1.

Population Size and Structure

Up until the middle of the nineteenth century most of London's then 2 million population was crowded within about one hour's walk of the centre. The coming of mass public transport allowed people to spread out into the growing suburbs. By the 1960s the total population of Greater London had reached some 8 million. Nevertheless, decline had already set in from the centre outwards by the beginning of the century. By the 1970s the populations of both inner and outer London were falling. The net results of these declines were that the total population of Greater London had fallen to 6.7 million by 1981. After 1983, partly as a result of new house building in the old Docklands area, the population began to increase slowly so that by 1996 it had reached 7 million.

Table 6.5 shows the population for each of London's rings during the early 1990s. It demonstrates a classic metropolitan structure of high density living in the centre falling away with distance from the inner area. There is a very distinctive break between Greater London as a whole and the OMA/ROSE. This dramatic fall in density is partly a reflection of the restrictions on urban development imposed by the Metropolitan Green Belt.

Table 6.5 also shows that in terms of total numbers, the Greater South East Region contained just under 17 million residents. Of these, about 5.5 million live in the OMA with a further 4.9 million in the ROSE. The remainder live within the boundaries of Greater London.

These populations are highly polarised both spatially and socially. Some 37 per cent of the resident population of Greater London are in professional, managerial and technical occupations compared with an average for the UK as a whole of 30 per cent (Foy *et al.*, 1999, p. 62). At the same time eighteen of London's mostly eastern and inner area boroughs are among the fifty most deprived districts in Britain (ibid., p. 69). Around three-quarters of all

Table 6.5. London's rings

Areas Definitions	Area sq. km	Population 000s	Density per sq. km	Jobs 000s	Density per sq. km
Central area					
Central statistical area	27	170	6,296	1,020	37,778
Inner area (rest of)					
Inner London Boroughs ex. CSA	294	2,173	7,591	805	2,738
Remainder of the urban area					
Outer Boroughs of Gr. London	1,257	4,050	3,221	1,430	1,137
Outer Metropolitan Area					
Home Counties (OMA)	9,651	5,511	571	2,235	232
Remainder of South East Region					
Rest of South East (ROSE)	15,996	4,889	306	1,726	108
Total Region					
South East including Gr. London	27,224	16,793	617	7,215	265

Source: Llewelyn-Davies *et al.* (1998, p. 20).

unemployed black people in Britain live in Greater London (Government Statistical Service *et al.*, 1998, p. 59) Meanwhile, the so-called 'Golden Belt' of counties running from Dorset to Suffolk at the western extremities of the South East are the main concentrations of both predicted population growth (Hall, 1989, p. 88) and innovation, as will be shown later.

The London Economy

London and the South East are the main engine of the UK economy. Table 6.6 shows that together they are responsible for around one-third of Britain's entire gross domestic product (GDP). Greater London's GDP per head is the highest in the UK. It is almost 25 per cent higher than the UK average (Government Statistical Service *et al.*, 1998, p. 49). GDP per head is even higher for commuters from ROSE than it is for the residents of Greater London.

Table 6.6. Trends in gross domestic product for London

Areas	GDP in £m @ 1990 prices			
	1983	1993	% change	% of GB in 1993
Inner London	39,614	43,088	9	9.1
Outer London	29,857	35,045	17	7
Rest of the South East	66,048	87,108	32	18.3
Rest of Great Britain	248,481	310,759	20	65
Great Britain Totals	384,000	476,000	24	100

Source: Llewelyn-Davies *et al.* (1998, p. 26).

A key feature of the agglomeration economies of the region is that there are some 238,000 businesses registered for VAT in Greater London alone. This represents about 15 per cent of the UK total. The area also accounts for around a quarter of all businesses in the UK which have a turnover of £5m or more (ibid., p. 49). These uniquely large numbers and diversity of firms in Greater London make it a particularly diverse and complex economy. They are also significant in the unique agglomeration economies found in the region.

All this does not, however, mean that London is immune to economic crises. During the 1980s there was an unprecedented boom in employment in the South East. Over one million jobs were created, half of them in financial and business services. This left London particularly exposed to the crisis in these sectors which followed the 1987 Stock Market crash in New York. The resulting recession saw the loss of 800,000 jobs during the early 1990s (Centre for Economics and Business Research, 1996; Gordon, 1999). A further boom followed this from 1993–97 mainly in sectors such as business services, employment agencies, distribution and catering. Many of these jobs were female and/or part-time.

Table 6.7 shows the structure and geographic distribution of employment across the London Region in 1995. It shows that in terms of employment, the London economy is highly specialised both sectorally and spatially. As far as sectors are concerned, banking, finance and insurance (23 per cent), public administration, education and health (22 per cent) and distribution, hotels and restaurants (21 per cent) account for two-thirds of total jobs in the region. Manufacturing (11 per cent) and construction (10 per cent) account for a further fifth of the total. In general terms, therefore, the regional economy is highly specialised in both marketed and public services. Overall, manufacturing provides a relatively small but significant and productive proportion of total employment.

Table 6.7 shows that employment in the region is also specialised in spatial terms. Inner London, for example, contains disproportionate concentrations of jobs in banking, finance and insurance, and other services. Outer London, on the other hand, is the base for a very high proportion of construction workers. The OMA contains concentrations of employment in energy and water, manufacturing, together with public administration, education and health. ROSE also contains disproportionate numbers of workers in manufacturing, and public administration and health. Collectively, these figures illustrate a fairly classic metropolitan spatial division of labour. High value added marketed services requiring limited space are concentrated in and around the urban core. Moving away from the core more land-hungry manufacturing activities are to be found. Public services are distributed across space roughly in proportion to the population numbers.

Within this general spatial division of specialised labour, six sub-regional

Table 6.7. Employment structure, London Region, 1995

Areas	Sectors (SIC 92)									
	Agri-culture	Energy Fishing	Manufact. Water	Construct.	Distribut. Hotels Restaurant	Transport Communi-cations	Banking Finance Insurance	Pub admin. Education Health	Other Services	Totals
		1 (%)	2 (%)	3 (%)	4 (%)	5 (%)	6 (%)	7 (%)	8 (%)	9 (%)
Inner London	1	21	14	5	21	26	38	23	36	24
Outer London	2	14	17	76	21	25	17	18	19	24
OMA	74	51	48	14	44	38	34	42	34	38
ROSE	23	14	21	5	14	11	11	17	11	14
Total South East Total N = 100%	57,745	51,184	901,027	775,721	1,673,541	527,534	1,833,063	1,706,836	384,821	7,911,472

Source: Census of Employment, NOMIS.

economies have been identified within the London Region. Within Greater London itself, Buck *et al.* (1997) have identified three distinctive spatially identifiable specialised areas. These are:

1   The CSA extending from White City in the west to Canary Wharf in the east. This area contains specialised, advanced and internationally oriented services. These demonstrate a strong competitive performance.

2   The Heathrow economy to the West contains a dynamic combination of specialisations including both those that are directly airport-related and others that have more in common with the western crescent of ROSE.

3   On the other side of Greater London is outer East London. This contains many former industrial areas. It has therefore been subject to dramatic structural change. The local workforce tends to be relatively unskilled.

Outside Greater London but within the ROSE, Banks *et al.* (1997) have identified a further three specialised sub-regional economies. These include:

1   The advanced economies to the west and south. They specialise mainly in producer services and information technology. They benefit from a highly qualified workforce, good airport access and strong economic prospects. They are constrained by tight land use planning restrictions, which are squeezing more routine functions out of the area as a result of land and property cost pressures.

2   To the east and south of the ROSE there is the coastal belt. This mainly borders the Channel and Thames Estuary. These areas have specialised in the past in shipping, tourism and retirement resorts. Much of the first two has either been restructured or lost entirely to foreign competition.

3   Finally there are the restructuring industrial economies. These include older industries such as motor cars, port and defence functions. These have been subject to major job losses since the 1980s. Some of the areas most affected by such losses have been places like the Medway towns, Oxford/Banbury, Southampton and Portsmouth.

The spatial economy of the London Metropolitan Region is therefore a large, diverse and highly complex mixture of both success and failure. By and large, those areas which have specialised in internationally competitive activities like financial and business services, air transport or information technology have prospered. Those that started with older industries such as docking, defence services and car making have failed to remain competitive. As a result, these industries and areas have been subjected to major restructuring processes.

Innovation in the London Economy

Innovative Sectors in the LMR

The rate of innovation in the south-east has been considerably higher than that for any other region in the UK since at least the 1940s. Harris (1988), for example, using a database of significant innovations held at the Science Policy Research Unit (SPRU), University of Sussex, calculated that the level of innovation in the SE was one-third higher than the UK average between 1945–83. Some of this may be accounted for by the above average levels of key inputs to innovation in the region. These include professional staff such as scientists, engineers and designers in higher proportions than the UK average (Llewelyn-Davies et al., 1997, p. 51), and business enterprise R&D at around twice the UK average (Foy et al., 1999, p. 59).

The effort devoted to innovation in the LMR is reflected in the levels of outputs of innovations. Table 6.8 shows a comparison of the most innovative sectors in the UK as identified in the 1997 Community Innovation Survey (CIS), and the proportions of those firms located in the LMR. For the purposes of this analysis the most innovative sectors are defined as those in which more than half of the firms interviewed reported the introduction of an innovation during the survey period.

Top of the list in Table 6.8 is chemicals and chemical products. This is the sector which includes pharmaceuticals. Some 83 per cent of firms in this sector reported introducing innovations between 1994–96. Over a third of them were located in the LMR. The LMR also contains high proportions of all the firms in other innovative sectors. These include insurance and pensions, radio, TV and communications equipment (32 per cent), office accounting and computing machinery (49 per cent), medical precision and optical instruments (51 per cent), electrical machinery (29 per cent), machinery (24 per cent), rubber and plastic products (25 per cent), computer and related services, other transport equipment (21 per cent), and food products and beverages (21 per cent). Thus the LMR not only specialises in some of the most innovative manufacturing and service activities in the UK, it also contains between a fifth to a half of all the UK firms operating in those sectors. This has important implications for the agglomeration economies of the region that will be addressed later.

Not only is innovation in certain key sectors heavily concentrated in the LMR as a whole, but also it tends to be concentrated still more in some parts of the region rather than others. Table 6.9 shows that innovation in manufacturing is especially concentrated in an arc of the Home Counties and ROSE stretching from Cambridgeshire, Bedfordshire and Hertfordshire in the north, through Buckinghamshire, Oxfordshire and Berkshire in the west, to Wiltshire, Hampshire and Surrey in the south. In all these counties some 60 per cent to 80 per cent of all manufacturing firms reported introducing innovations in the mid-1990s. Only a small minority

Table 6.8. Innovative sectors in the London Metropolitan Region

Sectors	NACE code	Innovative firms UK 1 (%)	Proportion of innovative firms in London Region 2 (%)
Chemicals & chemical products	24	83	34
Insurance & pensions	66	78	na
Radio, TV & comms equip	32	77	32
Office, accounting & computing	30	76	49
Medical, precision & opt instrs	33	75	51
Electrical machinery	31	72	29
Leather products & footwear	19	68	17
Machinery n.e.c.	29	64	24
Rubber & plastic products	25	64	25
Computer & related activities	72	63	na
Other transport equipment	35	63	21
Motor vehicles	34	61	9
Post & telecommunications	64	60	na
Financial intermediation	65–67	58	na
Food products & beverages	15	58	21
Non-metallic mineral products	26	54	10
Basic metals	27	54	12
Textiles	17	54	7
Research & development	73	51	na
Publishing, printing & rec media	22	38	40
Furniture	36	46	33

Notes: 1 Sectors in which >50 per cent of firms introduced new technological products and processes between 1994–96; 2 Proportion of total UK firms in sector located in the LMR.
Source: CIS (forthcoming).

of the remaining counties in Britain can match these rates of innovation output.

Table 6.9 also shows that the Greater London appears rather like the hole in a doughnut as far as manufacturing innovation is concerned. Only around half the firms there reported the introduction of an innovation during 1994–96. Table 6.10, however, suggests that there may be some compensation for Greater London's relatively poor performance in manufacturing innovation as a result of the concentration of innovative service sectors such as financial intermediation (LQ 2.27) and auxiliary financial intermediation (LQ 2.73). Employment in these two sectors is more than twice the national average in Greater London.

Table 6.10 shows location quotients (LQs) for employment in the most innovative service sectors identified by the CIS. Table 6.11 shows a similar analysis for manufacturing employment. Both tables show that, in terms of employment, there is further sectoral specialisation within counties in dif-

Table 6.9. Counties with over 50 per cent of manufacturing firms introducing new technological products and processes in the period between 1994–96

Rank:	County	Percentage
1	Berkshire	80.6
2	Buckinghamshire	76.0
3	Warwickshire	73.7
4	Bedfordshire	73.3
5	Cambridgeshire	72.7
6	Oxfordshire	70.6
7	Wiltshire	70.0
8	Surrey	68.2
9	Grampian	67.9
10=	Durham	66.7
10=	Cheshire	66.7
12	Hampshire	63.8
13	Hertfordshire	63.0
14=	West Yorkshire	62.5
14=	Lincolnshire	62.5
14=	Lothian	62.5
17	Devon	61.9
18	Northants	60.0
19	Humberside	57.9
20	South Yorkshire	57.8
21	Essex	57.5
22	Derbyshire	57.4
23	Kent	54.8
24	Greater Manchester	53.1
25	Cleveland	52.9
26	Hereford and Worcester	51.7
27=	London	51.0
27=	Strathclyde	51.0
29	North Yorkshire	50.0

Note: Counties where number of responses from the survey is >15.
Source: CIS 2, Eurostat.

ferent types of innovation. This indicates the co-location of different types of innovative firms in particular counties. Frequently these counties turn out to be located in the western arc.

Table 6.10 shows that employment in research and development services is concentrated in the western arc with particularly high LQs in Berkshire (5.79), Hertfordshire (4.13), Oxfordshire (3.61) and Cambridgeshire (4.96). The western arc features again with respect to computer and related activities with the highest LQ (4.06) in Berkshire.

Table 6.11 also shows that there are some noteworthy concentrations of innovative manufacturing sectors in the western arc counties. These include office machinery and computers in Berkshire (3.06),

Table 6.10. Location Quotients for most innovative service sectors in the London Metropolitan Region, 1996

Sector Service sectors	NACE Code	Counties Beds	Berks	Bucks	East Suss.	Essex	Hants	Herts	Kent	Ox	Surrey	W. Suss.	Cambs	Gtr. Lond.
Water transport	61	0.04	0.43	0.10	1.10	0.81	3.3	0.18	10.35	0.12	0.58	0.10	0.03	1.26
Post and telecommunications	64	0.94	1.72	1.04	1.07	0.86	0.93	1.31	0.98	0.92	1.09	0.85	1.16	1.43
Financial intermediation	65	0.54	0.79	1.08	1.40	0.95	0.87	0.66	0.72	0.61	0.77	1.12	0.64	2.27
Insurance and pensions	66	0.30	1.42	1.09	1.13	1.02	1.29	1.05	1.37	0.30	2.16	1.94	1.98	1.41
Financial intermediation auxiliary	67	0.64	0.76	0.47	0.83	0.79	0.80	0.91	0.95	0.38	1.60	1.10	1.44	2.73
Computer and related activities	72	1.58	4.06	2.68	1.01	1.23	1.96	2.06	0.59	1.30	2.82	1.00	1.49	1.46
Research and Development	73	2.96	5.79	1.31	0.27	2.62	0.63	4.13	1.03	3.61	3.03	0.39	4.96	0.94

Notes: Location Quotients: a value of 1.00 would occur if the county had the same proportion of employees for each sector out of total employment to that of Great Britain as a whole.

Most innovative sectors = 50 per cent or more of firms in the UK introducing new technological products and processes between 1994 and 1996 from the CIS survey combined with Butchart's (1987) definition of high-tech industries.

Source: Annual Employment Survey, NOMIS.

Table 6.11. Location Quotients for most innovative manufacturing sectors in the London Metropolitan Region, 1996

Sector Manufacturing sectors	NACE Code	Counties Beds	Berks	Bucks	East Suss.	Essex	Hants	Herts	Kent	Ox	Surrey	W. Suss.	Cambs	Gtr. Lond.
Food products and beverages	15	0.53	1.18	0.77	0.51	0.60	0.38	0.37	0.51	0.68	0.18	0.42	1.22	0.37
Tobacco products	16	0	0	3.12	0	0	3.82	0	0	0	3.90	0	0	0
Leather products and footwear	19	0.16	0.05	0.39	0.09	0.46	0.07	0.17	0.58	0.11	0.09	0.42	0.67	0.48
Chemicals and chemical products	24	0.84	0.95	0.70	0.52	0.67	0.88	1.37	1.06	0.53	0.58	1.73	0.90	0.53
Rubber and plastic products	25	1.38	0.46	1.05	0.79	0.90	0.77	0.97	0.96	1.04	0.63	0.60	1.16	0.30
Other non-metallic products	26	0.95	0.46	0.28	0.67	0.80	0.41	0.35	0.92	0.35	0.40	0.60	0.96	0.21
Fabricated metal products	28	1.28	0.65	0.89	0.52	0.88	0.78	0.84	0.66	0.51	0.56	0.78	0.60	0.31
Machinery and equipment	29	1.96	0.81	1.23	0.62	1.04	1.36	0.97	0.67	0.70	0.57	1.00	1.97	0.21
Office machinery and computers	30	1.10	3.06	2.02	1.08	1.93	2.37	2.83	0.41	1.23	1.37	0.69	2.40	0.52
Electrical machinery/apparatus	31	1.70	0.61	1.02	1.25	1.26	1.31	1.15	0.84	1.11	0.64	1.05	0.63	0.40
Radio/t.v. communications equip.	32	0.76	1.70	1.94	0.88	1.93	1.68	1.28	0.64	0.23	1.25	1.21	1.55	0.31
Medical precision instruments	33	2.32	1.10	2.05	1.28	1.71	2.38	1.65	1.90	1.53	1.27	2.65	1.67	0.44
Motor vehicles, trailers	34	4.18	0.51	0.33	0.06	0.90	0.85	0.25	0.30	2.31	0.46	0.13	1.08	0.36
Other transport equipment	35	0.48	0.33	0.68	0.26	0.36	2.58	0.45	0.19	0.35	0.75	1.06	0.85	0.11

Notes: Location Quotients: a value of 1.00 would occur if the county had the same proportion of employees for each sector out of total employment to that of Great Britain as a whole.

Most innovative sectors = 50 per cent or more of firms in the UK introducing new technological products and processes between 1994 and 1996 from the CIS survey combined with Butchart's (1987) definition of high-tech industries.

Source: Annual Employment Survey, NOMIS.

Buckinghamshire (2.02), Hampshire (2.37), Hertfordshire (2.83) and Cambridgeshire (2.40). Medical precision instruments is another important innovative sector in the LMR. This is particularly concentrated in Bedfordshire (2.32), Buckinghamshire (2.05), Hampshire (2.38) and West Sussex (2.65).

Despite these geographic concentrations of employment in innovative sectors, it should be noted that the western arc covers a very large area. Table 6.5 showed that the total area of the OMA and ROSE taken together is around 25,000 sq. km. The western arc probably includes at least half of this total. Many of the specialised employment concentrations are not even located in contiguous counties. This raises questions about the time proximity barriers that follow spatial separation and mitigate against the maintenance of strong regular linkages between them. This issue will be raised again below.

Innovation and Clustering in the LMR

Interest in the identification of spatial concentrations of co-located innovative firms has been inspired by the work of Michael Porter (1990). It has been taken up by the new RDAs in their innovation strategies particularly by the East of England Development Agency (1999) and the Government Office for the South East (1998). Porter has argued that 'Nations succeed not in isolated industries ... but in clusters of industries connected through vertical and horizontal relationships' (1990).

One of the key issues raised by this assertion is the importance and significance of intra-cluster linkages and networks. As the concept of clusters has been developed, these connections have received increasing emphasis. Waits (1997), for example, argues that 'regional economic performance (quality jobs, wealth creation) is the product of a "portfolio" of competitive, export-oriented, technology driven industry clusters and is dependent on collaborative actions between industries and public institutions to lay the foundations that support industry competitivenes'. In this view, clusters may be initiated either by market actions such as in the most famous of them all in Silicon Valley, or by public intervention such as in the software clusters of Austin, Texas. They are also dynamic in that any given cluster may be emerging, where inter-firm linkages are being established; expanding where linkages have achieved critical mass and represent a region's current specialisations; or transforming, in which case mature segments may be in decline and the seeds of new clusters may be being formed.

Cooke also argues that fully functioning clusters have formal sector support infrastructure. Accordingly he defines clusters as 'Geographically proximate firms in vertical and horizontal relationships, involving a localised enterprise support infrastructure with a shared developmental vision for business growth, based on competition and cooperation in a specific market field' (Cooke, 1999).

While the evidence presented in Tables 6.10 and 6.11 shows that there are spatial concentrations of co-located innovative firms in certain sectors in some counties, there is little empirical evidence on how far these may constitute functioning local clusters. Despite the general enthusiasm shown particularly by both GOSE (1998) and EEDA (1999) for encouraging cluster development as a basis of their new regional innovation strategies, there is also a lack of evidence on precisely what their contributions to innovation might be. These are some of the key issues addressed by the research reported here.

The defining characteristics of an established cluster are its horizontal and vertical linkages. These include intra-cluster organisation and production networks along with external linkages to other firms and customers. Much of the literature and policy analyses have tended to focus on the question of intra-cluster organisation. To some extent this is because of both researchers' and governmental institutions' natural interest and focus on their own areas and responsibilities.

This interest in the identification and encouragement of local clusters has, not surprisingly, discovered some at least 'emerging' clusters with sufficient internal linkages to have formed formal associations and therefore to meet Cooke's (1999) requirement of having a formal local representative organisation. Cooke himself has identified clusters of marine construction in Southampton, biotechnology and motor sport in Oxfordshire, biotechnology and ICT in Cambridge, motor sport in Guildford, and financial services and new media in London. The GOSE has identified representative sector support associations such as Southern Bioscience, Wired Sussex, Farnborough Aerospace Consortium, Electronics Action Group, Oxfordshire Motorsport Forum and Southern Medical. Interestingly, however, GOSE also comments that 'all these organisations are relatively new' (GOSE, 1998, p. 9). They are also all market-driven and self-organising clusters. In the Eastern region EEDA has also identified clusters of life sciences, information and communications technology, electronics and research centres (EEDA, 1999, p. 2). No evidence is offered on whether or not these groupings are formally associated in any way.

While it is possible to identify spatial concentrations of innovative sectors in the LMR, some of which are formally associated clusters, it is not yet clear either if most of the concentrations are moving in this direction or if they are, whether this will contribute significantly to the innovative performance of individual firms. Much of the debate on these issues focuses on the relative importance of intra-cluster networks and linkages compared with other regional agglomeration economies on the one hand and international trade on the other (see e.g. Hart and Simmie, 1997; Simmie, 1998a, 1998b).

Some General Evidence on Clustering in the LMR

There are a number of factors in the LMR which either do not encourage the development of networked clusters with strong internal linkages or which may enable innovation more than such clustering behaviour. First, a number of studies have suggested that local production networks can only be found among a minority of firms in the LMR. Hart and Simmie (1997) showed that only a small minority of innovative firms in Hertfordshire regarded local networks as making significant contributions to their innovations. A survey undertaken in 1999 by CM International on behalf of the Eastern Region's Innovation and Technology Counsellors also highlighted 'a relative paucity of networking among firms' (quoted in EEDA, 1999, p. 22). Finally, a study by Gordon (1996b) of locationally sensitive businesses in London, Reading and Swindon, found that R&D activities (i.e. those most likely to be directly involved in innovation) did not value highly the presence of the kinds of actors that would be expected to be involved in local cluster networks. Thus the availability of general (3 per cent) or specialised (4 per cent) services, or the proximity of suppliers (7 per cent) and competitors (8 per cent), all of whom might be expected to be networked in strong clusters, were not rated as important for R&D activities.

Second, the South East is a dynamic and changing region. Some of this change mitigates against the development of stable local clusters. Table 6.12 shows that the LMR's specialised sub-sectors have been subject to both employment change and movement during the 1990s. It might be expected that successful clusters would be marked by geographic stability and employment growth. Such conditions are most likely to be found in column two which lists those sectors that have experienced both employment growth and geographic concentration.

Among the more innovative sectors identified by the CIS, Table 6.12 shows that radio and TV services are one of the few to experience both growth and concentration in inner and outer London. Post and telecommunications is another sector that has experienced the same phenomena in outer London. Two sectors stand out in this category in the ROSE. They are medical appliances and pharmaceuticals.

Table 6.12 also shows that most other innovative sectors have been experiencing either employment loss, decentralisation or have been in competition with faster employment growth outside the region. Taken together, these experiences do not suggest that innovation in the LMR is generally associated with stable and growing clusters.

Third, the economy of the LMR is also marked by some characteristics which may both aid innovation and mitigate against the development of stable clusters. One of these is the high rate of new business formation. Foy et al. (1999) show VAT registrations in 1966 as a percentage of the total stock of businesses in the three regions which contain the LMR.

Table 6.12. London and ROSE specialised sub-sectors

Area	Employment growth Faster growth elsewhere	Growth and concentration	Employment loss and decentralisation	Loss but retention
Inner London	Business services Commission agents Dealing real estate Insurance support Advertising Accounting Professional services	Banking support Extraction Legal services Estate agents Film prod/dist Banking Radio/TV services Professional associations	Wholesale dist. Post and telecomms Print and publishing	Scheduled road/rail Railways
Outer London		Business services Retail distribution Cleaning services Estate agents Misc. transport Air transport Radio and TV Post and telecomms Canteens Household distribution Dispensing chemists Police	Misc. foods Suppl. air services Motor parts	Wholesale dist. Mixed retail Scheduled road/rail Research and development General construction
ROSE	Private nursing Air transport	Retail Wholesale machinery Supporting air servs. Wholesale chemicals Medical appliances Wholesale other Pharmaceuticals	Office machinery National defence Pulp, paper, board Electric equipment Research and development Optical instruments	Soap/toilet preparation Telecomms equipment Sea transport Supporting sea services

Source: Government Office for London (1996, pp. 23–5).

While the UK average is 10.5, the figure for London is 13.9, for the South East 11.3, and for Eastern 10.3. The three-year survival rate for London is lower than the UK average while the survival rate is slightly higher than average in the ROSE (ibid., p. 57). These constantly high rates of new business formation probably facilitate innovation but involve streams of new firms at the start of network formation. The lower survival rate of new firms in London also means the probable death of any local networking that they may have been involved in.

Finally, much of the LMR's success as an innovative city region is based on its internationally oriented economy. Llewelyn-Davies *et al.* (1997) rightly point out that 'The key engines of growth in the region are the "export" sectors – those bringing net wealth into the region.' This echoes the classic distinction between basic (exporting) and non-basic (mainly local) industries. Innovative exporters are highly likely to value external and international networks and linkages above local connections (Simmie, 1998a, 1998b). This also tends to emphasise the importance of demand pull, as opposed to technology push arguments concerning the major stimulants of innovation The strong export orientation of most innovative firms provides strong incentives to establish regular (series) markets with their national and international customers. The general evidence cited so far indicates that these seem to take precedence in the LMR over more local cluster networks and linkages.

The general evidence presented here should not be taken as the basis of an argument that innovative firms do not have local networks. It is readily agreed that it is in the nature of economic activity that firms are generally connected to their local economies in numerous ways. Some of these will include linkages to general business services such as banks and accountants. Others will consist of the use of office suppliers and motor car servicing facilities. The main question addressed here, however, is how significant are these local general linkages for innovation? Second, over and above these types of external networks, what other types of linkages and urban assets make major contributions to stimulating and enabling firms to become successful and competitive innovators? These questions are addressed in the following analysis of a survey of innovative firms in the LMR.

Survey Results

Characteristics of the Sample

As with the other European cities, the sample frame adopted for the empirical part of the study was the lists of firms that had won the common European award for Basic Research for Industrial Technologies for Europe (BRITE). This award provided support to industry for pre-competitive collaborative research in materials, design and manufacturing technologies.

The aims of the programme were to stimulate technological innovation through the incorporation of new technologies and scientific and techno-logical collaboration.

During the course of the programme up to 1999, the date of the inter-views, firms located in the South East region had won some fifty-six awards. Most were located in the LMR. Some firms had won more than one award but were only interviewed with respect to their most recent award. Telephone interviews were conducted with all the surviving indi-vidual award-winning firms. This yielded a total sample of thirty-three firms. Table 6.13 shows the nature and composition of the sample.

Table 6.13. Composition of the BRITE sample

Type of organisation	(%)
Private national firm	52
Private multinational firm	39
Public enterprise	6
Other	3
Total N = 100%	33
Size of firm	
Micro <20 employees	30
Small 21 to 250	37
Medium 251 to 1000	18
Large >1000 employees	12
No information	3
Total N = 100%	33
	Numbers
Industrial sector	
Chemical products less pharmaceuticals	1
Rubber and plastic products	1
Non-metallic mineral products	1
Machinery not elsewhere classified	2
Electrical machinery	2
Medical, precision and optical instruments, watches & clocks	1
Motor vehicles	2
Pharmaceuticals	1
Basic metals ferrous	1
Insulated wire and cable	1
Electronic components including semiconductors	2
Medical and surgical equipment	4
Instruments and appliances for measuring, checking	4
Aerospace	1
Software consultancy and supply	4
R&D on natural sciences and engineering	2
No information	3
Total	33

Source: BRITE firms survey.

From Table 6.13 it may be seen that a majority (51 per cent) of the firms were private, national, UK firms. A significant proportion (39 per cent) were multinational companies. Small proportions were either public enterprises or other types of organisation. Most of the firms were micro (30 per cent) or small (37 per cent) in terms of their total numbers of employees. There were smaller proportions of medium-sized firms (18 per cent) and a small, but significant element of large companies (12 per cent).

The firms came from a select collection of manufacturing and service sectors. Prominent among the manufacturing sectors were medical and surgical equipment, and instruments and appliances for measuring and checking with four firms apiece. Services were represented by software consultancy and supply (4), and R&D on natural sciences and engineering with two firms. Taken together, they form a reasonably representative set of examples of the most innovative sectors in the UK as identified by the CIS.

Significance of Local Clusters, Linkages and Networks

Turning first to the question of the relative importance of local clusters for innovation in the LMR, all the definitions cited above are agreed that the first defining characteristics of an established cluster are its horizontal and vertical linkages. These include intra-cluster organisation and production networks along with external linkages to other firms and customers. The geographic extent of these linkages must also be reasonably local and significant over and above the normal run-of-the-mill networks that all firms have simply by virtue of being in business.

The survey of BRITE award-winning firms shows that they do indeed use external linkages and networks to assist them in the development of specific innovation projects. Table 6.14 shows that both business networks and other collaborating organisations played important parts in their innovations. The mean score on a scale from not important 1 to very important 5, for business networks which included customers, suppliers, competitors and business services was 3.56. Similarly, for collaborators which include mainly both public and private research and development organisations, such as government research establishments or research associations, the mean score was 3.61. Other characteristically local networks such as those including local universities, training organisations (1.81), friends or ex-colleagues (1.9) were given much lower scores for their contributions to innovation.

Table 6.14 also shows that one of the main uses of business networks and linkages was to acquire important elements of external knowledge and information. Suppliers scored 2.38, while customers were rated as slightly more important at 2.94. Apart from academics (2.68), these were the two highest scores from a list of some twenty potential sources which included

Table 6.14. Linkages and networks

Contact networks Type of network	Importance for innovation Mean score 1 not important to 5 very important
Learning	1.81
(education, training or information)	
Business	3.56
(customers, suppliers, competitors or business services)	
Collaborators	3.61
(external organisations)	
Friends	1.9
(friends or ex-colleagues)	
Important external sources of knowledge and information	
Suppliers	2.38
Customers	2.94

Source: BRITE firms survey.

a whole raft of general business service providers and specialised consultants.

While these figures support one of the basic tenets of functioning clusters, namely the significance of external networks and linkages, the data on the geography of these connections tell a somewhat different story. In the BRITE survey firms were asked to specify the locations of their vertical linkages in terms of their suppliers and customers. They were also asked to identify the locations of potential horizontal linkages in terms of where their main competitors were located. In order to simplify these responses they were divided into quartiles and scored 0 for no linkages to a particular location up to 4 for more than 76 per cent links to the identified area. These scores were then summed for the entire sample. The higher the resulting scores, the greater were the linkages with the area identified. Lower total scores signify fewer linkages with the location specified. The results of this analysis are shown in Table 6.15.

In respect of vertical linkages between the firms and either their suppliers or their customers, the strongest links are shown to be national followed by European, and in the case of customers, in the USA. National suppliers and customers located more than 101 km from the innovating firms scored totals of 56 and 55 respectively. European suppliers scored 40 and customers 48. These figures compare with 32 or less for suppliers and customers located less than 100 km for the innovating firm.

The potential for horizontal linkages with firms in the same sector as the BRITE award-winners was limited by their international dispersion. Assuming that firms working in the same fields are also likely to be competitors, Table 6.15 shows that there is a greater tendency for them to be located in Europe (51) or the USA (59) than in the UK (34) or locally (23). Thus potential horizontal linkages with competitors are limited by their

James Simmie and James Sennett

Table 6.15. Geography of linkages

Locations	Suppliers Sum of scores	Customers Sum of scores	Competitors Sum of scores
International			
Europe	40	48	51
USA	25	36	59
Japan	23	30	33
Other Pacific Rim	18	20	19
Worldwide	21	30	31
National			
101 km to UK	56	55	34
Regional/local			
Regional 51 to 100 km	32	30	23
Local <50 km	32	25	23

Notes: Sum of scores = total score for all firms by quartile. Where 0 = no links to the specified location to 4 = 76–100% links to the location.
Source: BRITE firms survey.

generally smaller numbers within the LMR than in other advanced national economies such as Europe, the USA and Japan.

Within these broad geographical patterns, a factor analysis of the types of external collaborative inputs to the BRITE innovations revealed that they fell into four main groups. These were commercial research suppliers, non-commercial research providers, clients, customers and competitors, and other firms. Table 6.16 shows the mean scores ranging from 1 not important to 5 very important for the various collaborators in these groups. Top scorers are clients or customers (3.33) that Table 6.15 has

Table 6.16. Importance of collaborators

Component	Supplier	Mean score
Group 1	Commercial research suppliers	
	Suppliers	2.42
	Government research establishments	1.97
	Research associations	2.2
	Consultancy services	1.61
Group 2	Non-commercial research providers	
	Universities or other HEIs	2.58
	Private non-profit organisations	1.33
Group 3	Clients, customers or competitors	
	Competitors	1.57
	Clients or customers	3.33
Group 4	Other firms within the group	
	Other firms within the group	2.3

Note: Mean score where 1 = not important to 5 = very important.
Source: BRITE firms survey.

already shown are not likely to be located within the LMR. Universities or other higher education establishments (HEIs) are next with 2.58. As collaboration with such institutions was a condition of winning a BRITE award, this figure should be interpreted as rather low, considering all firms presumably had to have such a partner!

Suppliers recorded the third highest score (2.42) for the perceived importance of their contributions to innovation. Again, Table 6.15 has already shown that they are more likely to be located nationally or even in Europe than within the LMR. Taken together, group 1 and 3 show the significance of vertical linkages for innovating firms. These often extend outside the LMR. The most important linkages among them are with clients or customers.

It may be concluded from this discussion that there is not much evidence to support the hypothesis that clusters based on local linkages and networks play key roles in innovation in the LMR. Although business and collaborator contact networks are important for innovation, only a minority of their linkages are geographically confined within the LMR. They are more likely to be national or European in their extent rather than local. This is even more likely to be the case with respect to competitors. Finally, the perceived importance of most external collaborators is not great. Only clients or customers score particularly highly with respect to their importance to the BRITE award-winning firms.

Reasons for the Innovative Success of the LMR

Given the above doubts about the significance of clustering as a basis for the undoubted innovative success of the LMR, what other factors that characterise the region could be responsible for this success? In order to investigate this issue firms were asked to rank the importance to innovation in the LMR of a wide range of possible contributions. A factor analysis of their replies revealed that they regarded a number of traditional agglomeration economies as significant. These could be classified into Hoover's (1937, 1948) classic distinction between urbanisation and localisation economies. To these may be added both internal and globalisation economies (Simmie and Sennett, 1999).

Urbanisation economies, and their dynamic counterpart – innovative milieu effects – consist in the main of economic effects that arise outside the firm but within the urban region. Five such groups were identified by the BRITE firms as contributing in different degrees to their innovations. These were transportation infrastructure; general and specialised business knowledge and information; finance, training, knowledge and information; factors of production; and technical and professional labour. The more detailed elements making up these main components were rated by the firms for their importance to innovation. This was done on a scale ranging

Table 6.17. Importance of reasons for the location of innovative firms in the London Metropolitan Region

Urbanisation effects, external to the firm but internal to the urban region		Mean scores
Group 1	Transportation infrastructure	
	Low levels of traffic congestion	2.27
	Good access to London	2.61
	Good rail connections	2.39
	Good access to national road network	2.9
	Good access to major airport	3.27
Group 2	General and specialised business knowledge and information	
	Access to private general business services	1.57
	Access to private specialised business services	1.6
	Proximity of collaborators	2.1
	Proximity of business services	1.5
	Proximity of sources of information	1.7
Group 3	Finance, training, knowledge and information	
	Access to financial capital	1.97
	Local public business support services	1.62
	Contributions from TECs	1.27
	Contributions from Business LINKS	1.43
	Contributions from universities	2.42
Group 4	Factors of production	
	Availability of skilled manual labour	2.33
	Availability of suitable premises	3.29
	Cost of premises	3.35
Group 8	Technical and professional labour	
	Availability of professional experts to recruit	3.77
Localisation reasons, external to the firm but internal to the industry		
Group 5	Local industrial knowledge and experience	
	Presence of ex-colleagues	1.65
	Presence of friends	1.4
Group 6	Supply factors	
	Cost of labour	2.39
	Proximity of suppliers	1.93
Group 7	Demand factors	
	Proximity of customers	1.6
	Proximity of competitors	1.23

Note: Mean scores of importance to innovation. 1 = not important to 5 = very important.
Source: BRITE firms survey.

from not important 1, to very important 5. The resulting mean scores are shown in Table 6.17.

It may be seen from Table 6.17 that the factor rated most important by the firms was the availability of professional experts to recruit (3.77). High-quality, usually highly qualified labour, is a crucial requirement for innovation. Without the knowledge and experience possessed by such workers, innovation, particularly high-technology innovation, simply cannot take place. So one of the key reasons why the LMR is the most innovative region in the UK is the concentration of highly competent professional and technical workers in its local labour markets. Much of the region's innovative success hangs on the availability of such workers and this issue will be taken up again later in the chapter.

Other factors of production that were of some importance to firms included land and labour in the form of skilled manual labour (2.33), and suitable premises (3.29) at reasonable cost (3.35). Premises and their cost may be regarded as important by firms more because of the difficulties associated with acquiring them than because of their direct contribution to innovation. The Metropolitan Green Belt (MGB) severely restricts the availability of land and buildings in the south-east. It contributes to increasing their price and therefore adds to the costs of production in the region. It may well be an important factor in the decentralisation of innovative firms to the outer parts of the western ROSE.

Table 6.17 also shows that firms rated good transportation infrastructure as quite important in their choice of location. In particular, good access to a major airport (3.27) was rated as an important locational consideration by innovative firms. This is a significant finding in the context of the international networks and linkages used by firms as demonstrated by Table 6.15. Heathrow Airport is renowned for the number of business destinations served (Table 6.2) and is a critical piece of infrastructure enabling firms to maintain linkages with their important international suppliers, customers and to monitor what their main competitors are doing. Access to Heathrow is geographically skewed to the west of London for both road and public transport. Road access within one hour extends well beyond Newbury to the west and barely reaches the centre of London in the east (Llewelyn-Davies, 1997, Map 17, p. 79). This again favours location in the western arc for firms that are dependent on regular international networks and linkages.

No other factors were rated as important as professional labour, the availability and cost of premises, and good access to a major airport. These represent the major urbanisation effects for innovative firms in the LMR.

In addition to urbanisation economies, three components connected with localisation economies emerged from the factor analysis of all locational considerations. Localisation economies are generally external to the firm but internal to the industry. If strong industrial clustering was an important requirement for innovative firms in the LMR, it might be expected that individual factors associated with such arrangements would be rated highly. This is not the case.

The localisation components that emerged from the factor analysis included supply and demand factors that would be expected to be important if strong local vertical linkages were significant contributors to innovation. They also included local industrial knowledge and experience which could be expected to form the basis of a cluster or new industrial district atmosphere where such a phenomenon existed and was perceived by firms to make important contributions to innovation.

In fact, Table 6.17 shows that proximity to both customers (1.6) and suppliers (1.93) is not rated as important by the BRITE firms. The same may be said about the presence of friends (1.4) and ex-colleagues (1.65). This would seem to reinforce the findings shown in Table 6.15 which suggested the greater importance of national and international networks and linkages as compared with those within the LMR.

Given the importance attached by firms to the availability of professional and technical labour in the development of innovations, a closer analysis was conducted of their use, qualifications and recruitment. Firms were asked to say what proportions of different kinds of people were employed in the development of their innovations. Their responses were divided into quartiles and scored from 0 = none to 4 = 76 to 100 per cent. The higher the sum of these scores, the higher the proportions of particular types of labour were employed, possessed higher qualifications or were recruited locally. Table 6.18 shows the results of these analyses.

The two types of labour most frequently employed on the development of innovations technologists (96) and those involved in production processes (51). The technologists (100) were the most likely to hold higher formal qualifications such as degrees or higher diplomas. Where recruitment was required to work on the new innovation projects, technologists (69) were also the most likely to have been recruited from within 50 km.

Local recruitment was not a strong feature of firm behaviour for two main reasons. The first was their already significant internal resources of graduates and R&D employees. The second was their ability to recruit the

Table 6.18. Professional and technical expertise

Professional expertise	Worked directly on innovation Sum of scores	Staff holding higher qualification Sum of scores	Recruited within 50 km Sum of scores
Technology	96	100	69
Finance	26	42	54
Marketing	40	45	49
Management	35	46	50
Training or recruitment	23	37	47
Production processes	51	48	48

Note: Sum of scores = total score for all firms by quartile. Where 0 = none to 4 = 76 to 100%.
Source: BRITE firms survey.

Table 6.19. Importance of local requirements for human capital

Local requirements	1 not important to 5 very important
Availability of good housing	3.58
Proximity of good schools	3.53
Proximity of good leisure facilities	3.06
Proximity of good public services, e.g. hospitals	3.03
Good environment	3.85

Note: Mean score for importance.
Source: BRITE firms survey.

necessary highly qualified staff over a wide area. This recruitment area extended over much of the south and into international labour markets. It was marked by highly qualified individuals spiralling up their chosen career paths. In order to achieve their career goals they often had to move over significant distances.

Where career advancement is frequently accompanied by residential mobility, the ability to attract and recruit professional and technical labour to innovation projects is partly dependent on their personal quality of life requirements. This was reflected in the survey findings by the high scores recorded for the local requirements of such highly paid workers. These factors are important to insure the presence, retention or recruitment of these crucial human resources. Table 6.19 shows that relatively high scores were recorded for all the major quality of life requirements investigated. These included the availability of good housing (3.58), the proximity of good schools (3.53), the proximity of good leisure facilities (3.06), the proximity of good public services (3.03), and a generally good environment (3.85). Residential mobility is an important way of satisfying these requirements. Highly paid professional and technical workers in constantly changing labour markets are likely to have several chances to achieve them in the context of longer distance movements for career reasons. The ROSE, in particular, provides multiple opportunities for the achievement of these quality of life requirements.

A final reason for the relative success of the LMR, in terms of the high rates of innovation found there, is its major function as an international hub or gateway city. Table 6.15 has already shown the importance of international linkages to innovative firms. Table 6.17 showed the significance of good access to a major airport in facilitating these networks and linkages. Table 6.2 demonstrated the predominance of London Heathrow among other major international hub airports. All this adds up to the position of the LMR as the UK's major gateway or frontier city. More so than any of the old coastal port frontiers, the LMR is now the most significant international gateway to the UK. The flows of people, experience, ideas, and international best practice through the LMR on a daily basis provide

Table 6.20. Innovation and exports.

Exports	Innovation novelty		
	New to the world Leaders (%)	New to UK, sector or firm Followers (%)	Total (%)
Not on market as yet	44	62	50
1 to 20%	0	0	0
21 to 40%	4	0	3
41 to 60%	17	13	16
61 to 80%	9	13	9
More than 81%	26	12	22
Total N = 100%	23	8	31

Source: BRITE firms survey.

critical leading edge inputs to innovation there. They also provide the networks and linkages to international clients and customers who are also such an important part of the demand pulls for innovation.

Exports of innovations new to the world are an important manifestation of the outward-looking and international trading role of the LMR. BRITE awards are given to develop inventions which have already been the subject of some R&D and are regarded as promising commercial innovations. The awards are given before the inventions are brought to market. At the time of interviewing, therefore, some of the projects had not quite arrived in their respective markets. Table 6.20 shows that this amounted to 50 per cent of the total sample. Despite this all projects were catagorised according to their degree of novelty. This ranged from 'new to the world' through 'new to the UK, sector, or firm'. Those firms producing innovations new to the world are regarded as 'leaders' in their fields. Those developing innovations in the UK, their sector or their firm for the first time are regarded as 'followers'.

Table 6.20 shows that leaders (26 per cent) were twice as likely as followers (12 per cent) to be exporting more than 81 per cent of their innovation. Overall, among those innovations that had been brought to market, 50 per cent of firms were exporting more than a fifth of their total output. The exporting potential and requirements of leaders of innovation in the LMR are considerable. The dual characteristics of leading edge innovation, new to the world, and their consequential competitiveness in advanced international markets, are a special feature of innovative activity in the LMR. The region's accessibility to new people and ideas from around the world plays an important role in both the inputs to these innovations and their export outputs.

Conclusion

Looked at from the point of view of the space economy of the LMR, the key components of innovation are the internal characteristics of the firms, the local sectoral linkages and support systems within particular industries, the nature and scale of the region's urban assets, and its connections with and competitiveness in advanced international markets. First, as far as internal characteristics of firms is concerned, research in the Cambridge region has shown that 90 per cent of firms rated sources of innovation within the firm as dominant within their innovative activities (Keeble *et al.*, 1999). In particular, the individual entrepreneur's inclination to innovate and the ways in which key internal human resources are organised are very significant factors driving innovation (Vaessen and Wever, 1993; Vaessen and Keeble, 1995).

The survey of BRITE firms reported in this chapter confirms the significance of both the inclination of different types of firms to innovate and the importance of their internal organisation and resources in determining their capability to innovate. The strong combinations of these characteristics among the award-winning firms contributed to the high proportion of firms who appeared to be producing highly novel and world-beating innovations. Leading firms with innovations new to the world made up 74 per cent of the those interviewed.

Second, localisation economies, as first identified by Hoover (1937, 1948), consist of economies which are external to the firm but internal to the industry or sector. Marshall (1952) argued that one of the main reasons for the spatial concentration of industries is the fact that market success depends on specialisation and the development of effective industrial organisation. The benefits of localised specialisation include increases in the quality and specialisation of the labour force and the increased use of highly specialised machinery. Taken together the 'concentration of firms in close geographical proximity allows all to enjoy the benefits of large-scale production and of technical and organisational innovations which are beyond the scope of (most) individual firms (Keeble and Wilkinson, 1999). The empirical evidence gathered so far indicates that such intra-sectoral relationships are in the minority in the LMR.

There is no doubt that a number of highly specialised and innovative industrial sectors have many firms co-located in various parts of the LMR. Despite this, there is not much evidence that this leads to these sectors developing functioning sectoral organisation on a local or regional basis. Where such evidence exists, it is often a phenomenon that develops after individual firms have made their innovation and locational decisions on an individual and independent basis.

Various factors mitigate against the development of locally organised industry sectors or clusters in the LMR. These include the sheer size of the urban region which extends over some 25,000 sq. km; the lack of empirical evidence of locally confined networking; changes in both the structure of the labour force and its location; high birth and death rates among new firms; and the international orientation of most innovative firms. While, on the one hand, there is evidence from the survey of the importance of vertical business and collaborator networks, on the other hand these turn out to be more often based on national and international linkages than local networks. The survey also highlights the limits to local horizontal linkages with many possible connections being national or international rather than confined within the LMR. In general, local linkages of all types were not rated as particularly important by respondents to the survey.

Third, urbanisation economies consist of external economies available to all firms irrespective of sector. They are therefore external to both the firm and industry but largely confined or internal to the urban region. The main dynamic characteristics of urbanisation economies are that:

Firms and other actors will change who and what they buy from and sell to, simply in response to current advantage and their very specific requirements. The system is without any particular observable organisation or inter-agent loyalty, and simply functions as an ecology of activities benefiting from proximity, and developing emergent forms of specialisation – possibly including distinct forms of economic culture.

(Gordon and McCann, 1998)

This may be defined as a 'pick and mix' space economy.

The possibilities for discontinuity and breakdown of static frameworks required by product innovation are greatest in core metropolitan regions such as London. The sheer numbers and densities of other relevant firms provide endless opportunities for discontinuities and new recombinations of factor inputs to innovation on an irregular 'pick and mix' basis. Some 15 per cent of all UK businesses are located in Greater London alone. Around a third of all the most innovative firms in the UK are located in the LMR. The most innovative sectors are also over-represented in the LMR. Somewhere between a fifth to a third of all the firms in the most innovative sectors are concentrated in the urban region. Many of them are to be found in the 'golden arc' running from Cambridgeshire around the west of Greater London as far as Surrey.

The main urbanisation economies that firms rated as important to their innovations were the availability of professional and technical expertise, skilled labour and premises, and access to a major international hub airport. Professional and technical labour provides the major key to innovation in the LMR. For the firms interviewed, this was particularly true with respect to technologists and production workers. Without these two groups innovation could not take place. Although the concentration of such highly qualified and skilled groups is an important feature of the LMR in general, their recruitment to particular innovation projects often took place over quite long distances. Such recruitment patterns seem to reflect moves made by career spiralists as they improve their employment with each successive geographic move.

The attraction and retention of such key labour are important reasons why firms tended to rate quality of life features as making significant contributions to their innovative capabilities. The ability to offer highly paid key staff the kinds of homes, schools, public services, leisure facilities and environments that they want is an important external advantage to firms located in the western arc of the OMA and ROSE.

Finally, since Hoover's original work (1937, 1948) major economic changes have taken place. One of the most important of these, particularly since the 1970s and accelerating during the 1990s (Veltz, 1993; Gordon, 1996), is the globalisation of the world economy. This has involved, among other phenomena, internationalisation, growing instability in product markets, more intense competition, and greater emphasis on competition based on quality and variety rather than price. These changes place a competitive premium on economies which may accrue locally but which may be gathered from around the advanced economies.

At first sight, globalisation would appear to reduce the incentives for firms to invest time and resources in purely local clusters. Instead, they clearly need to be competitive in international markets. This requires capabilities for fast changing business strategies, flexibility, and constant recombinations of specialised suppliers and other business partners. Globalisation and changing products have also reduced the importance of traditional localised factors of production. All these factors seem to emphasise the importance of 'weak ties' (Granovetter, 1973) which are multiple, open-ended, changing, and link both national producers and international customers.

In the context of globalisation, inputs to innovation are unlikely to be locally confined. In studies of innovation in SMEs in the Cambridge region (Keeble *et al.*, 1999), and in this survey of BRITE firms in the LMR, firms used both national and international inputs to their innovations. These included research collaborations and professional staff recruitment. Both of these key inputs to innovation were more often sought at the UK national and even international level than within the local urban region.

The markets for innovation are mostly found among the more advanced G7 economies or those rich in natural resources such as oil. Demand pulls are one of the most significant elements of the whole process. Without the possibility of selling innovations the main incentive for engaging in the activity at all would be missing. A key feature of globalisation is the growing significance of international markets. Innovative and competitive firms sell much, and sometimes all, of their outputs into other national markets. In the BRITE survey this was particularly true of the innovations that were described by firms as being new to the world. Linkages with clients and customers in these foreign markets are therefore crucial to the commercial success of innovative new products and services.

The LMR, with its long history of international trade, functions as a major gateway and frontier with international customers and suppliers. Heathrow Airport serving multiple business destinations is a key infrastructural asset facilitating such contacts. Through it flow streams of people carrying with them ideas and knowledge of international best practice. The communication of this experience is best accomplished with face-to-face meetings. These are especially important in the initial stages of the development of innovations.

To sum up, the evidence presented here shows that the LMR is the key innovative region in the UK. This success rests on a unique combination of the internal characteristics of the firms found there: the concentration and co-location of numerous innovative sectors and firms in the urban region; the availability of highly qualified professional and technical labour; and a long and continuing tradition of competitive international trade. The international orientation of the firms in the urban region rather than their local linkages is a key source of inputs to innovation and the identification of the export markets into which many of them are sold.

References

Banks, N., Gordon, I.R. and Gudgin, G. (1997) *South East Economy Review: Summary Report*, Guildford, Government Office for the South East.

Business Link Hampshire (1999) *Assistance for Small Businesses with Innovative Ideas*, Portsmouth, Hampshire Innovation Service.

Buck, N., Crookston, M., Gordon, I.R. and Hall, P. (1997) *A Socio-economic Assessment of London*, London, Association of London Government.

Centre for Economics and Business Research (1996) *London's Contribution to the UK Economy*, London, London Chamber of Commerce.

Champion, A.G., Green, A.E., Owen, D.W., Ellin, D.J. and Coombes, M.G. (1987) *Changing Places*, London, Edward Arnold.

Cooke, P. (1999) 'The networked economy', presentation delivered at ESRC workshop on networks and clusters, December, School of Public Policy, University of Bristol.

East of England Development Agency (1999) *Innovation and Technology Strategy*, Cambridge, EEDA.

Foy, S., Walton, F. and Campbell, M. (1999) *The State of the UK Regions: A Regional Profile*, Leeds, Policy Research Institute, Leeds Metropolitan University.

Gordon, I.R. (1996a) *Out-movers from the Thames Valley: Report of a Study for TVEP*, University of Reading, CaSAER.

Gordon, I.R. (1996b) 'Territorial competition and locational advantage in the London Region', paper presented to the American Association of Geographers annual conference, Charlotte, NC.

Gordon, I.R. (1999) *The People: Where Will They Work? London and the South East*, Reading, Department of Geography, University of Reading.

Gordon, I.R. and McCann, P. (1998) 'Industrial clusters, agglomeration and/or social networks?', paper presented at the Regional Science Association British and Irish Section conference, York.

Government Office for Eastern Region (1998) *Innovate for Success: The Eastern Region Innovative Initiative*, Cambridge, GOE.

Government Office for London (1996) *London in the UK Economy: A Planning Perspective*, London, Department of the Environment.

Government Office for London (1997) *The London Innovation Strategy: Consultation Draft*, London, GOL.

Government Office for the South East (1998) *Developing a Regional Innovation Strategy for the South East: A Report on the Conclusions of the Ashdown Park Workshop*, 1–2 July, Guildford, GOSE.

Government Statistical Service *et al.* (1998) *Focus on London 98*, London, Government Statistical Service, GOL and LRC.

Granovetter, M. (1973) 'The strength of weak ties', *American Journal of Sociology*, 78, 1360–80.

Granovetter, M. (1985) 'Economic action and social structure: the problem of embeddedness', *American Journal of Sociology*, 91, 481–510.

Hall, P. (1977) *The World Cities*, London, Weidenfeld and Nicolson.

Hall, P. (1989) *London 2001*, London, Unwin Hyman.

Hart, D. and Simmie, J.M. (1997) 'Innovation, competition and the structure of local production networks: initial findings from the Hertfordshire project', *Local Economy*, November, 235–46.

Hoover, E.M. (1937) *Location Theory and the Shoe and Leather Industries*, Cambridge, MA, Harvard University Press.

Hoover, E.M. (1948) *The Location of Economic Activity*, New York, McGraw-Hill.

Keeble, D., Lawson, C., Moore, B. and Wilkinson, F. (1999) 'Collective learning processes, networking and "institutional thickness" in the Cambridge Region', *Regional Studies*, special issue: regional networking, collective learning and innovation in high technology SMEs in Europe, 33, 4, 319–32.

Keeble, D. and Wilkinson, F. (1999) 'Collective learning and knowledge development in the evolution of regional clusters of high technology SMEs in Europe', *Regional Studies*, special issue: regional networking, collective learning and innovation in high technology SMEs in Europe, 33, 4, 295–303.

King, A.D. (1991) *Global Cities: Post-Imperialism and the Internationalization of London*, London, Routledge.

Llewelyn-Davies *et al.* (1997) *South East Economy Research Study: Summary Report*, Guildford, Government Office for the South East.

Llewelyn-Davies *et al.* (1998) *Four World Cities: A Comparative Study of London, Paris, New York, and Tokyo*, London, Llewelyn-Davies.

London Chamber of Commerce (1996) *London's Contribution to the UK Economy*, London, London Chamber of Commerce and Industry.

London Development Partnership (1999a) *Competitiveness of London's Financial and Business Services Sector*, London, Corporation of London.

London Development Partnership (1999b) *London the Knowledge Capital: An Innovation and Knowledge Transfer Strategy for London*, London, London Development Partnership and Government Office for London.

London Planning Advisory Committee *et al.* (1991) *London: World City Moving into the 21st Century*, London, HMSO.

Marshall, A. (1952) *Principles of Economics*, London, Macmillan.

McCann, P. (1995) 'Rethinking the economics of location and agglomeration', *Urban Studies*, 32, 3, 563–79.

Mogridge, M. and Parr, J.B. (1997) 'Metropolis or Region: on the development and structure of London', *Regional Studies*, 31, 2, 97–115.

Porter, M.E. (1990) *The Competitive Advantage of Nations*, London, Macmillan.

Simmie, J.M. (ed.) (1994) *Planning London*, London, UCL Press.

Simmie, J.M. (ed.) (1996) *Innovation, Networks and Learning Regions?*, London, Jessica Kingsley.

Simmie, J.M. (1998a) 'Innovate or stagnate: economic planning choices for local production nodes in the global economy', *Planning Practice and Research*, 13, 1, 35–51.

Simmie, J.M. (1998b) 'Reasons for the development of "Islands of innovation": evidence from Hertfordshire', *Urban Studies*, 35, 8, 1261–89.

Simmie, J.M. and Hart, D. (1999) 'Innovation projects and local production networks: a case study of Hertfordshire', *European Planning Studies*, 7, 4, 445–62.

Simmie, J.M. and Sennett, J. (1999) 'Innovative clusters: global or local linkages?', *National Institute Economic Review*, 4, 170, October, 87–98.

Sternberg, R. (1996) 'Reasons for the genesis of high-tech regions – theoretical explanation and empirical evidence', *Geoforum*, 27, 2, 205–23.

Storper, M. (1995) 'The resurgence of regional economies, ten years later: the region as a nexus of untraded interdependencies', *European Urban and Regional Studies*, 2, 3, 191–221.

Vaessen, P.M.M. and Keeble, D. (1995) 'Growth-oriented SMEs in unfavourable regional environments', *Regional Studies*, 29, 489–505.

Vaessen, P.M.M. and Wever, E. (1993) 'Spatial responsiveness of small firms', *Tijdschrift voor Economische en Sociale Geographie*, 84, 119–31.

Veltz, P. (1993) 'L'économie des villes, entre la montée du global et le retour du local', Territoires et Sociétés (mimeo).

Waits, M.J. (1997) 'The state of cluster-based economic development in Arizona', paper presented to the International Society of Optical Engineering, Phoenix, Arizona State University.

CHAPTER 7

Conclusions: Innovative Cities in Europe

7 Conclusions

Innovative Cities in Europe

Peter Wood

Introduction

The essence of innovativeness is difficult to distil in a city such as London. It arises out of myriad processes of entrepreneurial, technical and market invention and risk-taking, many of which are of only passing influence or have no significant outcome. Innovativeness depends on the social characteristics of the population as well as economic organisation. Such localised influences, however, actually often inhibit novelty. A legacy of past success may be a good indicator of adaptability but it may also lay a dead hand on change as the rest of the world moves on. Large cities tend to attract inventive individuals and support them in developing ideas. Opportunities for collaboration may be greater than elsewhere, but so is intensity of competition, and many more projects may fail than succeed.

Above all, urban innovativeness requires responsiveness to wider conditions outside the local area. This no longer means simply a national market for particular goods or services, perhaps also developing some exports. Today, innovation must seek to succeed in international markets, and enhance complex production processes and products. These require knowledge of the diverse and interlinked technologies and management skills that, for example, sustain modern information exchange and computation, communications systems, media production processes, transportation logistics, global financial markets, international tourism, environmental quality, community health care, or consumer services. The resources of experience, contact networks, risk-taking ability, and capital required to lead developments in these markets are often beyond the scope even of major companies, so that they depend on sustained outside collaboration, including often state support.

Like all regions, therefore, cities are innovative to the extent that they enable local strengths to respond to complex, often global-scale opportunities. This requires organisational responses that can combine the power of corporate capital and the opportunism of small business; manufacturing technology and service expertise; entrepreneurial forms of freedom and

Peter Wood

effective public regulation and support; new ideas encouraged by a stable established institutional and physical infrastructure; and a capacity for trial and error through support for risk-taking. Innovativeness certainly requires an educated and experienced workforce. But it must also be flexible and not over-specialised. Urban scale itself supports diversity, not just by broadening local economic options but also by encouraging new connections. As in the past, therefore, the innovativeness of modern cities depends on their status as centres of exchange, especially of information and expertise in an increasingly information-dominated world. The benefits are felt beyond cities themselves. In recent decades their global role has also made a growing contribution to national economies.

The future of cities in the age of globalisation and instant telecommunications is today a common preoccupation (Castells, 1989; Sassen, 1994; Brotchie *et al.*, 1995; Graham and Marvin, 1996). This book, based on five case studies of European cities, has focused specifically on the context they provide for manufacturing innovation. The cases obviously differ in many important ways, but the peculiarities of each has also enabled salient points of comparison to be drawn between them. This concluding chapter attempts to do this, summarising key findings and examining what the cases suggest about the essence of urban innovativeness at the end of the twentieth century. How do the distinctive mechanisms of urban exchange benefit cities today? We argue that the answer to this question depends on the type of city being considered. Also, that urban experience suggests significant modification of the prevailing orthodoxy on industrial districts and regional innovative milieux. In particular, the relationships between local development and the globalising economy are strongly influenced by the form taken by both national innovation systems and national urban systems.

For cities in Europe, local 'milieux' or localisational economies are more important in some innovation and urban contexts than others. Such locally organised models, found among our cases in Germany (Stuttgart) and Italy (Milan), apply less to internationally orientated metropolitan cities that dominate national urban systems, such as London, Paris, and even Amsterdam. This is especially the case in the UK where an organisationally and technically more diffuse national innovation system has prevailed in the past than in some other European countries. In general, dominant metropolitan cities tend to have service-dominated cores, with manufacturing innovation spread to the outer areas of their functional hinterlands. Economic inter-relationships supporting innovation are not particularly localised, but extend across the metropolitan region, involving service and manufacturing functions in complex, overlapping, global market-orientated networks. These characterise the greater south-east region of England, the Paris basin, and much of the Netherlands.

The spectrum of European urban innovativeness is thus influenced by two associated characteristics of local economic variation. The first is broadly organisational and sectoral, with highly organised, industrially based and institutionally supported innovation systems contrasted with 'pick and mix' systems that are weakly organised, contingent on often unplanned opportunities, service-led and primarily market responsive. This spectrum corresponds closely with the scale and organisation of the national urban system, running from devolved systems of medium–small cities to those dominated by internationally orientated metropolises. Individual cities may, of course, combine various elements of variation. Any local model may succeed, subject to periodic crises and challenges of adaptation. Generally it appears that some formerly successful specialised medium-sized industrial cities have had to reappraise their success during the 1990s, while metropolitan cities have enjoyed a revival as a basis for globally orientated innovation. Some new local economic clusters have emerged, even within metropolitan areas, although they often appear to be based more on labour availability, market developments, property conditions or, increasingly, policies that consciously combine these, than on spontaneous local associations of firms in the same industry (see Castells and Hall, 1994a on the special phenomenon of planned 'technopoles', and Braczyk *et al.*, 1998, on the role of regional governance in promoting innovation). In any event, they must be responsive to international market shifts, and require sustained innovation-orientation to survive.

National Economies and Urban Systems

The earlier chapters demonstrate most clearly that the innovativeness of each case study city strongly reflects national experience of economic innovativeness, and also their positions in the wider urban system. The dominant characteristics of these national systems, as reflected in the material presented earlier, may be summarised thus.

The German Model: Stuttgart

The Stuttgart case, within Baden-Würrtemburg, has for long been regarded as a model of high quality, manufacturing-orientated technical innovativeness, supporting the success of German engineering, automobile and electrical production. As elsewhere in Germany, faith in this traditional model, based on regional clusters of institutionally and technologically related firms, was shaken by the 1990s' recession and the consequent need to adapt to new technologies and forms of organisation and intensified market competition, including that from Eastern Europe.

Stuttgart is a medium-sized industrial city (2 million people) within a generally multi-nodal German urban system, including many other medium-sized and smaller cities. Its innovative manufacturing strengths have depended on:

- the technical efficiency of manufacturing;

- integrated industrial clusters based on vehicles, mechanical/electrical engineering and electronics;

- dominant large firms in vehicles-related production, with a strong medium-sized firm segment in engineering;

- institutional networks of relationships between firms and political actors;

- strong export orientation and a consequent vulnerability to global competition.

The survey reported in Chapter 2 also shows that innovation by firms in the city is characteristically:

- orientated to long-term product innovation, by both large and medium-sized firms;

- strongly directed to specialist, often producer customer requirements;

- highly specialised, based on in-house staff technical capability;

- supported mainly from retained profits;

- based on firms' own technical resources, rather than looking outside for collaboration;

- little dependent for technical development capability on outside bodies, even universities and research labs.

Regional non-commercial institutions generally offer indirect rather than direct support for innovation. For example, universities and research institutes provide occupational and research training and education, supported by close liaison with large firms. For small–medium enterprises, technical and commercial guidance is provided through decentralised information networks, based on semi-public intermediary agencies. Perhaps most important are stable employer–employee relationships. The 'untraded interdependencies' supporting flexible and efficient coordination of innovation have in the past particularly depended on Stuttgart-based networks of integration and learning, including firms, institutions and political actors.

This system obviously retains many strengths, including the quality of the workforce and industrial relations, a strong medium-sized firm sector, a high reputation for technical quality, and a self-sufficient orientation to long-term investment. On the other hand, the Stuttgart system underwent a period of crisis in the early 1990s, exposing some of its weaknesses. In particular, these included:

- the rigidities of the inherited institutional relations;

- slowness in recognising the shift from investment goods to the growing impacts on innovation of service, information and market knowledge inputs;

- the need for organisational as well as technological innovations, with institutional changes required at both firm and regional levels.

In short, the speed of knowledge exchange reduced the value of the city's accumulated technical experience and knowledge. Institutions were slow to overcome functional, political and, perhaps most important, cognitive inertia. Not only was there a need to develop new sectors, such as micro-electronics, information technology, new materials and biotechnology, but also to direct attention more towards organisational and service innovations.

Characteristically, a region-wide institutional approach has been adopted to support new economic associations including, for example, a service/media cluster, to augment traditionally technology-based innovative associations. The technical academy has also been broadened to include social scientists. Realisation of the changing situation has thus brought an active response. It remains to be seen how effectively traditional strengths can be successfully adapted to exploit the leading elements of modern economic growth.

The Italian Model: Milan

Milan is the most important industrial city of Italy, with a population of 4 million, and 1.8 million jobs. Chapter 3 emphasises the strong influence of its history of industrialisation over the past 150 years, through various phases of development. In recent decades, there has been a tendency for new industrial areas to develop away from the old industrial districts, and for the centre to become increasingly service-dominated, as in London and Paris. The city nevertheless retains a high degree of dominance in the Italian industrial system. Evidence is presented for the concentration there of national and regional high-technology industries, including computer, information technology, precision instruments, computer services and research and development activities. Among the factors that favour Milan's continuing success are its transport and other infrastructure; the availability of various high quality factor inputs, including skilled labour; its markets; the quality of business service support; and access to key source of innovative information.

Today, therefore, a distinction can be drawn between:

- the old industrial areas of decline in the north of the city;

- areas in the north-east that have favoured high-technology industries;

- the agricultural and residential areas of the south, which have also seen some industrial and service developments;

- the centre, increasingly dominated by advanced services.

The analysis presented in Chapter 3 is characteristic of the GREMI group of French and Italian researchers which has undertaken much detailed work into the success of Italy's distinctive regional/urban concentrations of successful small–medium manufacturing. Milan, of course, is not generally regarded as characteristic of this much-researched 'Third Italy' phenomenon. The influences on innovativeness in the city are nevertheless interpreted in terms of two types of supportive economies:

- 'urbanisation economies', related to the scale and diversity of urban economies, favouring all activities in the city. These include scale economies, accessibility to transport and service infrastructure, and diversity of knowledge sources;

- 'milieu economies', favouring specific industries clustered within the city, especially small firms. These benefit from the continuity and synergy of specialised knowledge and skills exchange among firms and public institutions.

The survey reported in Chapter 3 is employed especially to examine the distinctiveness of the high-technology north-eastern district and the influence of firm size on their need for urbanisation or milieu economies. Small firms were found to benefit more than large firms from both milieu and urbanisation economies. The benefit of milieu effects is greater in the more high-technology north-east, where the quality of expertise, labour supply, suppliers and collaborators is a significant advantage.

This analysis is used to outline the diversity of firms' experience, and relationship of their innovativeness to the wider urban environment, thus:

- the most innovative (BRITE) firms, often based in the north-east, benefit from general urbanisation economies;

- firms in the city that are 'catching up' on innovation appear to value neither milieu nor urbanisation economies, except for a high-quality labour force;

- the small, competitive, clustered firms in the north-east are the most locally oriented, and thus most value milieu-based economies;

- larger firms generally throughout the city value urbanisation, rather than milieu factors.

Thus, in Milan, milieu-based industrial clusters are limited to specific sectors, firm types and areas within the city which are not generally the most innovative. This is confirmed by a closer examination of firms in the north-east of the city. Small firms have strongly networked behaviour, but larger innovative firms in this area, while using local research centres and universities, generally value their broader location in Milan, including access to services of the city centre, supporting access to wider, non-local contact networks.

The Dutch Model: Amsterdam

Despite the country's economic success during the 1990s, economic policy in the Netherlands is preoccupied with the need to encourage innovativeness. This is reflected in the active promotion of innovation especially among small–medium firms. In comparing the role of Amsterdam with the other sample cities, it should be remembered that the whole of the Netherlands, with its dispersed pattern of small–medium cities, is much the same size as the London Metropolitan Region. Amsterdam itself has a population of 700,000, with a further half million in its defined hinterland. The city's traditional strengths lie in trade and finance, with manufacturing playing a secondary role. It has recently benefited, as elsewhere, from the rapid growth in financial and business services, public services and tourism.

By conventional measures, unlike Milan and Stuttgart, Amsterdam is not among the most industrially innovative areas of the Netherlands. These are found in surrounding areas, and in south-east Holland. The city's advantage lies in the information sector. It supports a concentration of knowledge-based activities, especially in universities and research institutes (medical, economic and management) and in the private services, including information and data processing. Other economic activities have tended to decentralise from Amsterdam. The information sector thus still favours the city, more by general urbanisation economies than any specific milieu effects. The survey evidence suggests the importance for innovative firms of access to expert labour, enabling the information resources of the city to be tapped; to adequate space (always a preoccupation in cities); and good accessibility to road and air transport. The latter especially enables contacts with clients, which are often influential in stimulating innovation, located throughout the country and abroad.

Amsterdam is an unusual hybrid – a relatively small city with relatively insignificant manufacturing and an array of internationally tradable services. Its innovative role may again best be seen within the context of the Dutch urban system as a whole, which offers complementary specialisations elsewhere, on about the same economic scale as south-east England or the Ile de France. Conventional micro-economic measurements of the innovativeness (and productivity) of urban firms generally take no account of such complementarity of functions within cities, and between them and their regional/national hinterlands. The innovativeness of other parts of the Dutch economy probably still depends on the strengths of Amsterdam, with its international labour- and information-intensive trading and

Peter Wood

financial

financial activities. Similar complementarities within national urban systems no doubt apply between different parts of the London, Paris and, as we have seen, the Milan metropolitan regions. They may be less significant in larger and more economically freestanding cities such as Stuttgart.

The French Model: Paris

Commercial center

The role of Paris within the French urban system has, of course, dominated thinking about regional, and even national economic development since the Second World War. The city has always been the prime industrial, as well as administrative and commercial centre of France, although its national share of many functions has declined in recent decades. The Ile-de-France, constituting the extended Paris metropolitan region, includes about 11 million people. Like London in the UK, key national sectors are still concentrated within it, including government and administration, wholesale financial services, business services (including consultancy, marketing, real estate and computing), major corporate headquarters and air transport. Paris is also the focus for innovative manufacturing sectors, including electrical and electronics, aerospace, power production and distribution, chemicals and pharmaceuticals, printing and publishing and vehicles. As well as production, the emphasis of activity in these sectors is generally on management, and research and development functions.

There are long-term continuities in patterns of urban development, especially between the materials-handling industrial and transport functions of the north and east of the city and the more prosperous south and west, based on large-scale manufacturing and services. The widespread decline of manufacturing has favoured the western and southern areas, within a more general pattern of urban decentralisation. Long-term strategic planning, for example, through the new towns programmes and the evolution of the transport infrastructure, has also encouraged out-movement. The devolution of government agencies and some political power to new *départements* has also had a cumulative decentralising effect.

The burgeoning outer suburbs have developed multiple poles of activity. For example, economic complexes have developed near the major airports, and around the headquarters and R&D centres of the principal vehicle, information and computer technology, and aerospace firms. Office-based business services have also focused on key poles. Some high technology clusters have emerged from these developments, primarily supported by corporate networking between major company sites within the city and outside. Their R&D function, together with design, management, business services, and higher manufacturing functions have gravitated to the southwest of the city.

Such 'clusters' nevertheless appear to be very loose, as is also the case in Milan and London. They do not depend on close local proximity to other

238

businesses, but more on general facets of the 'metropolitan milieux'. Once more, these include the availability of qualified and flexible staff capable of supporting innovation, access to international information and markets through airports and other transport networks, and the international status of major firms. Innovation is characteristically encouraged by inter-enterprise collaborative partnership and networking arrangements with a range of other large and innovative smaller firms. The dynamics of such patterns depend on widespread contact systems and networks, including large and small firms, and private and public sector agencies, allowing exchange of personnel and ideas, and the flexible development of professional technical and managerial skills.

To the extent that various stages of local 'micro-milieux' are influential, supporting innovative SMEs, these are largely based around public and private research centres, including universities, often supported by state schemes. This is exemplified by the promotion of *La Cité scientifique* on the Saclay Plateau. Large firms and national and local state research support have encouraged locally linked SME-based developments in electronics, computing and optics. Public centres for innovation and technology transfer (CRITT) are also active in wider technology transfer. More generally, however, the role of state institutions, often emphasised in commentaries on French economic experience, is perhaps less direct in Paris than elsewhere. More general support for the city's international status, for example, through major infrastructure, including especially transportation projects, and through universities and the defence industries, are more significant than any targeted area-based innovation policies, of the type favoured in other parts of France.

The British Model: London

The UK, even more than Europe as a whole, has traditional problems of transforming a high level of basic R&D and scientific excellence into practical economic benefits. A high proportion of R&D is government sponsored, especially in defence and related industries or in the universities, which generally still often focus on longer-term projects. Incentives are now being offered to encourage closer links between industry and publicly-funded, including university research (e.g. through the 'Technology Foresight Programme'). By international standards, the UK has persistently low levels of private-sector R&D, although its national share has risen since the mid-1980s mainly because of declining public sector spending and the influence of inward investment. Some sectors, such as pharmaceuticals, are more successful than others, including much engineering. A strategic approach to R&D is generally lacking in UK corporate manufacturing, although some UK service sectors are innovative, especially in the implementation of information and computer technologies. The UK lacks the collaborative public–private research institutes and common link between fundamental and applied research found, for example, in Germany (Bennett and McCoshan, 1993, Part 1).

The 1990s has seen renewed interest in stimulating UK innovativeness through support for regional clusters of small firms. The practicability of this model, and its implications for UK cities, has been one of the main questions addressed in this volume. A critical and overriding element in UK innovativeness, however, is the dominant position of the Greater South East, functionally linked in many ways to the extended London economy, and distinct from other parts of the UK (Allen, 1992). No application of any spatial economic model of innovativeness in the UK can ignore this situation. London is one of the leading global cities, characterised by a diversity of internationally orientated economic and cultural activities. Its scale also dominates the UK domestic economy, with at least 12 million residents in its functional urban region. Even more than Paris in France, its economy dominates financial and business services, communications and public services. There is also nevertheless a huge diversity of local economic experience within the London Metropolitan Region, which includes some of the poorest, as well as the wealthiest areas in the UK.

One factor in London's innovativeness, as Chapter 6 shows, is the presence of large proportions of nationally innovative firms. Although manufacturing has a relatively low representation, over a long period the metropolitan region has supported high national proportions of innovative firms, especially in the Outer Metropolitan Areas to the north, west and south of London (Castells and Hall, 1994b). These complement innovative service functions based in London itself, such as finance, the media and business services, as well as the computing and data analysis, communications, health care and transportation services that thrive across the whole South East. Innovation in London also benefits from the opportunities made available by its international connections. Access to international communications has become universal, but Heathrow appears to be as significant a node for innovative manufacturing as is the City of London for financial services. Finally, innovative firms consistently value the human and physical infrastructure of the city and its region (i.e. the 'urbanisation effect'), whether in the ability to recruit skilled labour or gain access to international airports.

In this context, the benefits to manufacturing firms gained from clustering together for mutual support appear much less significant. In fact, any such tendency seems to be overwhelmed by the richness of all forms of interaction across south-eastern Britain. To this may be added its spatially extended markets and sources of inputs arising from its international orientation, and the speed of company change and interchange. Innovation is dominated by market-driven, international, service-based demands for complex goods and services, not primarily by the producer-driven conditions favoured by traditional cluster theory. The very technical and sector-based definition of such 'localisation economies' seems anachronistic in these dynamic metropolitan conditions.

In explaining urban innovativeness, of course, we have addressed only the most positive components of London's economic performance. Any possible advantages gained from modern economic restructuring must be tempered by at least two major causes for concern. The first, as in Paris and Milan, is the continuing inequality of wealth and opportunity across the city and its region. Innovation has destroyed many jobs, as well as created them, often in different parts of London. Many inner city areas have lost most of their manufacturing and associated producer services, including the port. The 'trickle-down' of employment from new activities, especially from high technology manufacturing, has largely proved to be a myth, even within cities. Many older suburban areas are also in relative economic and social decline. Public action to support and create employment and businesses may still be required in many areas. Second, even for innovative activities, the London region faces chronic threats to the quality of life, primarily because of pressures on land for development and the chaotic framework for transport investment. Unfavourable comparisons are often made with Paris and other continental cities. In an international context, these are likely to become increasingly critical in sustaining its ability to attract innovative functions and competitiveness.

The Essence of Urban Innovativeness

At the beginning of the twenty-first century, if cities remain innovative this is because of the continuing adaptation of their historical role as centres of exchange. Chapter 1 outlined the theoretical context of the comparisons undertaken in this study. Our case studies suggest that urban innovativeness is heavily influenced by the context of both national innovation systems and national urban systems. Within national technical and institutional innovation systems, the urban system supports cities of various sizes and functional base. This offers them scope either to specialise or diversify in responding to competitive national and, increasingly, international production opportunities.

Local outcomes also seem to reflect the presence of particular types of 'urban asset', based on specific knowledge 'spill-overs' from other characteristics of urban activity. Since at least the 1940s these have been recognised as stemming either from specific local sectors (localisation economies, or milieu economies as defined in Chapter 1), or from urban activity in general (urbanisation economies, or metropolitan economies in Chapter 1). Our evidence indicates that two other stimuli of innovativeness are also important. Most obvious, especially as large firms have increasingly exerted a dominant influence, are the innovative resources of

241

inter-industries mutual exchange in EU country

companies. These, in fact, remain the main subjects of study in innovation economics and policy. Many corporate/sectoral studies of innovativeness give no credit to urban or regional influences, although the significance of inter-firm relations is increasingly recognised. Corporate strategies, however, undoubtedly have important urban–regional dimensions, most notably in recent decades by favouring investment in smaller over larger cities.

Finally, some cities may now possess knowledge assets that allow them to reach beyond the capacity of the national innovation and urban systems within which they are embedded. This arises from the development of their global role. Within our sample this condition most strikingly applies to Paris and London. As we have seen, it also supports the innovative performance of cities such as Milan and Amsterdam, while perhaps on balance threatening that of cities such as Stuttgart in spite of their traditional strengths.

The Urban System and City Size

Smaller cities evidently benefit less from the general urbanisation economies that favour larger cities. Instead, their innovativeness is more dependent on investment by key firms, and any specialised clusters of related activity that may emerge, either through historical adaptation or the encouragement of public investment. When successful, smaller cities tend to be able to develop the advantages of a localised, focused, supportive institutional/political regime, directing infrastructural investment, including educational and training policies, towards the needs of local business. There are reasons, however, to believe that, by 2000, such localised arrangements are increasingly special cases.

In particular, the traditional agglomeration advantages of large cities, based on input and market scale economies, have been reinforced in recent years by:

- the growing diversity and scale of specialised markets, no longer defined simply in terms of conventional manufacturing or service sectors;

- a growing volume and quality of information exchange supporting the clustering of knowledge-intensive service functions;

- the development of on-the-job experience of change for key knowledge-based workers;

- increasing flexibility and mobility of the labour force, adapting both within and between firms;

- the increased value of adaptive innovations arising from a wide range of available skills, not just those that are technically- or industry-specific;

- the ability to exploit a risk-taking culture in a more liberal regulatory regime;

- growth of opportunities at intersections both of traditional sectors and between large, medium and small businesses.

Compared with smaller cities, relying on one or a few key sectors, large cities thus offer multiple clusters of activity, combining various markets, technologies and types of firms.

It may be that different urban scales support different types of innovation. Long-term, technical, analytical innovation, the traditional form that is the subject of most promotional and policy effort, has in the past formed the basis of successful industrial cities such as Stuttgart and Milan. It depends on local traditions in the training and recruitment of skilled workers led by key anchor companies in close association with public authorities and other institutions. In some cases, it may also support localised 'cluster' configurations of small–medium firms. Evidence from both Milan and even Paris suggest that such configurations may survive within cities, even though in metropolitan contexts they are unlikely to be the dominant basis for innovation. They may be no more than relic features or the outcomes of conscious policies to support clustering around private or public research centres.

In contrast, much modern innovation is synthetic, and apparently more short-term, based on putting old and new technologies together in different ways to serve rapidly changing market opportunities. This is more difficult to identify and measure, but likely to have a more immediate market impact. Examples include value-added functions attached to IT networks, new product design features, and products directed to new niche markets. Many such innovations are service-based and ephemeral, but some may have more profound longer-term effects on the direction of technical innovation. They are characteristic of cities such as London, Paris and Amsterdam, with their access to global market information and wide range of input resources. They require flexible and experienced, rather than highly specialist labour, recruited from wide regional or national sources. This is directed, not to the development of particularly new technologies or products, but to taking advantage of access to national and international market awareness.

Both forms of innovation are economically important, and mutually interdependent, especially in large cities. High-risk, longer-term, technical innovation attracts theoretical and policy attention partly because it may be neglected by short-term commercial pressures. Market-led, synthetic innovation nevertheless feeds off technical novelty. Innovation policies need to recognise that the two modes of innovation, broadly 'technical' and 'global market-led', and the urban environments that foster them, may also be mutually supportive, within both national urban systems and major cities. As we have seen, this is most evident in the Dutch case, but also emerges even within Milan and, on a larger scale, in and around Paris and London. The relationships between them in supporting both economic and regional change need to be more fully understood. They are most complex in major cities, such as London and Paris, in which flexibility to global market needs is their main advantage, but there are also important sources of technical innovation scattered across the metropolitan region.

Diversification or Specialisation of Cities?

Cities filter and select elements in national innovation systems, exploiting their specific advantages not available elsewhere. Traditional models of urban innovativeness have emphasised industry-specific advantages, and especially milieu economies, which apply more to small and relatively specialised urban centres. Large cities, such as London, have benefited from the modern reinforcement of traditional urbanisation economies associated with multiple specialisation. These most directly derive from the special advantages of access and responsiveness to complex global market trends.

Our comparisons of cities thus indicates four main sources of knowledge-based support for urban innovativeness:

1 from internal company resources, especially among large firms;

2 from local industrial effects ('milieu economies'), perhaps especially favouring small firms;

3 from urbanisation benefits, available to all urban activities;

4 from globalisation benefits, especially market information availability.

The first two require 'specialised knowledge spill-overs', specific to particular sectors, and are more dominant in successful small cities. The latter two are based on diversified knowledge spill-overs, especially available within larger cities.

The balance between these may vary between sectors, firms and cities. The lessons of our case studies, especially as they relate to London, include:

1 The innovative capabilities of major companies may not be particularly concentrated in large, compared with smaller cities. Their headquarters, specialist management and commercial R&D functions, however, tend to be located in the metropolitan cores. The R&D location policies of some of the most innovative sectors have favoured outer metropolitan areas. This has stimulated associated business service and SME developments. The same might generally be said about non-commercial, including government R&D agencies.

2   Milieu economies appear to be low for manufacturing in the London Metropolitan Region, although they are significant in Stuttgart and some districts in Milan. This may reflect the nature of the UK innovation system, with its prevalence of 'serial markets', oriented to low-risk links to dominant clients in defence, health and welfare, and other businesses. A similar situation seems to prevail, however, in Paris, as we have suggested indicating that metropolitan influences reduce the force of such benefits. On the other hand, some of the most successful tradable services in London, such as finance, business and the media, appear to thrive on localised relationships. These are based much less on mutual exchange, however, than on access to national and international markets and urbanisation economies.

3   Urbanisation economies favour larger cities. As we have seen, among the most significant in London, as in Paris and Milan, are the quality of accessible professional labour, access to international airports, the information infrastructure, including the expertise of general support services, and the scale of key urban markets, for example, in consumer including cultural/tourist activities.

4   Globalisation effects add to urbanisation benefits in a relatively few large cities. In a European context, these are especially important in London. They are best demonstrated through the 'hyper-development' of financial and business services. In London compared with other UK regions, both major firms and individual entrepreneurs in these sectors are primarily orientated through network links to various types of international client, rather than other UK firms. These services not only support employment, but are also a flexible repository of commercial expertise for other business in the region. They are also successful in export markets through specialisation, again to serve international corporate needs. The South East as a whole also has access to a markedly more expert and experienced staff in these activities than other UK regions. ROSE benefits from spill-over from the London nexus, as well as a growing and accessible local market, especially in corporate headquarters and divisional offices, some decentralised from the capital.

Conclusion: On Clusters and Agglomeration in the UK

If industry-specific manufacturing clusters, based on milieu effects are less powerful in the UK than elsewhere in Europe, the reasons for this reflect wider conditions. These include a weakly entrepreneurial innovation system, dominated by large firms, including many multinational companies and public agencies. The UK also lacks the supportive, institutional–political infrastructure that can be developed in a system of relatively autonomous medium-sized cities. Just as the UK's political and institutional structure is highly centralised, so its urban–regional system is dominated by a world city. There is also a long-standing antipathy towards French-style integrated planning. At least across the greater South East, innovative activities can be relatively geographically diffused, with little obvious benefit from mutual dependence based on co-location.

On the other hand, London possesses strong 'multiple sector' innovative clusters, in and around central London, largely based on various 'service' markets, drawing in manufacturing innovations, especially in computer applications and IT. These include finance, business services, media, communications, and potentially transport and construction. This is where the London milieu supports most innovation, spurred by its unique position in relation to globalisation trends.

Perhaps this service-driven, multiple cluster configuration is the model of successful area innovation for the twenty-first century? Industrial clusters, in their much-discussed form, were 'discovered' by Alfred Weber over 100 years ago (Weber, 1929), and have been revived at various times since, by Marshall (1919), Hoover (1948), Isard (1951, 1956), and more recently by Scott (1990), Storper (1993, 1997), Porter (1990) and Krugman (1991). Silicon Valley, the Third Italy, and even the 'M4 Corridor' have revived interest in them over the past thirty years. In retrospect, these may come to be seen as only a passing, late twentieth-century phase or, at best, part of a larger picture. As a basis for innovation in a globalising world they may once more have had their day. Today, the economic position of large cities and their hinterlands, together with the Internet-driven revival of some peripheral regions, may be strengthening. They are the integrating centres for the future networks of expertise exchange that will support future innovation.

References

Allen, J. (1992) 'Services and the UK space economy: regionalism and economic dislocation', *Transactions, Institute of British Geographers*, NS 17, 292–305.

Bennett, R.J. and McCoshan, A. (1993) *Enterprise and Human Resource Development*, London, Paul Chapman Publishing.

Braczyk, H.-J., Cooke, P. and Heidenreich, M. (1998) *Regional Innovation Systems*, London, UCL Press.

Brotchie, J., Batty, M., Blakely, E., Hall, P. and Newton, P. (1995) *Cities in Competition*, Melbourne, Longman.

Castells, M. (1989) *The Informational City*, London, Blackwell.

Castells, M. and Hall, P. (1994a) *Technopoles of the World: The Making of 21st Century Complexes*, London, Routledge.

Castells, M. and Hall, P. (1994b) 'The metropolis as an innovative milieux', in M. Castells and P. Hall (eds) *Technopoles of the World*, London, Routledge, Chapter 7.

Graham, S. and Marvin, S. (1996) *Telecommunications and the City*, London, Routledge.

Isard, W. (1951) 'Location theory and trade theory: distance inputs and the space economy', *Quarterly Journal of Economics*, 65, 181–98.

Isard, W. (1956) *Location and Space Economy*, New York, Wiley.

Hoover, E.M. (1948) *The Location of Economic Activity*, New York, McGraw-Hill.

Krugman, P. (1991) *Geography and Trade*, Cambridge, MA, MIT Press.

Marshall, A. (1919) *Trade and Industry*, London, Macmillan.

Porter, M.E. (1990) *The Competitive Advantage of Nations*, London, Macmillan.

Sassen, S. (1994) *Cities in a World Economy*, Thousand Oaks, CA, Pine Forge Press.

Scott, A.J. (1990) *New Industrial Spaces*, London, Pion.

Storper, M. (1993) 'Regional "worlds" of production: learning and innovation in the technology districts of France, Italy and the USA', *Regional Studies*, 27, 5, 433–55.

Storper, M. (1997) *The Regional World: Territorial Development in a Global Economy*, New York, Guilford Press.

Weber, A. (1929) *The Theory of the Location of Industries*, trans C. Friedrich of 1909 original, Chicago, University of Chicago Press.

Index

Index

demand-pull theories 17–18, 42, 44
  Amsterdam 147–50
  London 212, 225
Dosi, G. 31
dynamic location economies *see*
  location economies
dynamic theories of growth 19–21

Economic and Social Research Council
  (ESRC) 1
Edquist, C. 56
education systems, Stuttgart 72–4, 91
embeddedness 25–6, 29, 79–84
employment
  Amsterdam 136–8
  London 200–2, 204–5
  Milan 101
  Stuttgart 62–3, 64–7, 77
  see also labour
endogenous growth theory 109
entrepreneurs
  product life-cycle theory 20
  Schumpeter I model 16–17, 41–2
ESRC *see* Econommic and Social
  Research Council
European Commission, Directorate XIII
  (Science and Technology) 1–2, 14
evolutionary theory 11–44
exogenous invention 16
exports
  Amsterdam 148–9
  London 221–2
  Paris 184–5
  Stuttgart 64–5, 67
external economies 18–19

factor analysis 20, 217–22
  Amsterdam 147–51
  Milan 116–19, 122–4
  Stuttgart 79–84
finance
  Amsterdam 150–1
  Milan 119–21
  Stuttgart 77
financial sector
  international knowledge transfers
    39–40
  London 193–4, 200, 201
  Paris 164
first industrial divide 21
flexible specialisation 12, 21–2, 23, 26,
  29
Freeman, C. 16, 17, 40–1

Galbraith, J.K. 35

Germany 56, 68, 233–5
Glaeser, E. 37
global economy, Schumpeter II model
  32
global scanners 33, 39, 43
globalisation, Stuttgart 86–7
globalisation economies 20, 97, 244–5
  London 217, 225
Gordon, I.R. 210
government *see* local government;
  national government; regional
  government
Government Office for the South East
  (GOSE) 198, 209
Granovetter, M. 25
Gregersen, B. 85
GREMI *see* Groupement Européen des
  Milieux Innovateur
Groupement Européen des Milieux
  Innovateur (GREMI) 2, 12, 23–5,
  109, 236
growth pole theory 2, 11, 20–1, 27

headquarters
  London 40
  Schumpeter II model 32
high technology sector
  absolute trading advantages 14
  Milan 98, 101, 102, 103–8, 112, 113,
    119, 122–5
  Paris 166, 167, 169–70, 171–3,
    174–85
  product development time 76–8
Hilpert, U. 55, 140, 157
Hoover, E.M. 2, 11, 19–21

incubator hypothesis 98, 145, 152
industrial districts 22–3, 109
  see also new industrial districts
Industrial Revolution 21
information
  Amsterdam 142, 150, 151–2, 237
  innovative milieux 24
  knowledge distinction 36
  London 195, 214–15, 218
  Milan 114, 115, 119–21, 122, 125
  Paris 178–9
infrastructure
  Milan 119, 121, 124
  Stuttgart 58–9, 83
  see also transport
innovation
  agglomeration theory 18–21
  Amsterdam 141
  definitions 1–2, 14–15

Index

division of labor
forms of the divisions of production

Index